SPECTACULAR

Fishing

THIS IS A CARLTON BOOK

Distributed by Andrews McMeel Publishing
4520 Main Street
Kansas City, MO 64111 - 7701
(800) 851-8923

10 9 8 7 6 5 4 3 2 1

A CIP catalogue reference for this book is available from the British Library.

ISBN 1 84222 596 0

Printed and bound in Dubai

Project Editor: Luke Friend
Project Art Direction: Darren Jordan
Production: Lisa French
Picture Editor: Debora Fioravanti
Design: Mercer Design

PICTURE ACKNOWLEDGMENTS

All pictures by Ken Schultz

SPECTACULAR

Fishing

by Ken Schultz
Fishing Editor of Field & Stream

CARLTON
BOOKS

Contents

Introduction 7

Saltwater Introduction 8
Bella Bella 10
Boca Grande/Lee Island Coast 14
Campbell River 18
Cape Cod 20
Cape Fear 21
Cape May 25
Cozumel 28
Florida Keys 30
Hampton Roads 34
Huatulco 38
Ixtapa–Zihuatanejo 40
Langara 44
Los Cabos 48
Mazatlán 50
Mississippi Delta 52
Montauk Point 56
Morehead City/Cape Lookout 60
Outer Banks 64
Rivers Inlet .65
Texas Gulf .68

Freshwater Introduction 71
Alagnak River 72
Beaverkill River 74
Big Sand Lake 76
Bow River 79
California Delta 80
Cayuga Lake 82
Columbia River 83
Coppermine River 86
Dean River (Lower) 88
Delaware River (Upper) 91
Ena Lake 94
English River/Awesome Lake 96
Ferguson Lake 98
French River 100
Georgian Bay (Upper)/
North Channel 102
Gouin Reservoir 104
Great Bear Lake 106
Great Slave Lake 110
Hudson River 113
Kawartha Lakes 116

Kennebec River 118
Kesagami Lake 120
Lac Beauchene 123
Lake Aguamilpa 125
Lake Athabasca 128
Lake Erie .129
Lake Eufaula 131
Lake Fork .134
Lake Guerrero 135
Lake Huites 137
Lake Mead 140
Lake Michigan 142
Lake Oahe 144
Lake Okeechobee 146
Lake Ontario 148
Lake Powell 151
Lake Sam Rayburn 154
Lake Simcoe 156
Lake Texoma 158
Lake of the Woods 160
Miramichi River 162
Mississippi River (Lower) 164
Moose Lake/Blackwater River 166
Niagara River 170
North Seal River 173
Nueltin Lake 174
Ottawa River 178
Pere Marquette River 180
Platte River (North & South) 182
Red River .184
Saginaw Bay 186
El Salto Lake 188
Santee Cooper 192
Scott Lake 194
Selwyn Lake 198
St. Croix River 202
St. Lawrence River/1,000 Islands . . .204
Table Rock Lake 206
Toledo Bend Reservoir 208
Tree River 210
Verendrye Reserve/
Dozois Reservoir 214
Victoria Island 216
White River 220
Wollaston Lake 222
Practical advice for the traveler 224

Introduction

When I was a young editor at *Field & Stream* one of my chores was to organize and edit the voluminous text sent in by local contributors every spring for the magazine's roundup of "fishing hotspots." Covering every state in the U.S. and every province in Canada, these lengthy reports forecasted good fishing sites for the coming season.

I came to loathe that annual project, in part because of the heavy editing, but also because the long lead times made the information somewhat stale by the time readers saw it, and there wasn't enough space to say much in detail about so many places—despite the fact that we used such a small typeface that you virtually needed a magnifying glass to read the text. And there were no photos. Those hotspot reports were canned a long time ago.

Times have changed a lot since then. Now you can get instant information about fishing spots from hundreds of sources by surfing the Internet. Some of that information is of suspect origin and value, but a lot of it is helpful, especially if you're an experienced angler who knows that water isn't the only thing you have to wade through.

To write *Spectacular Fishing* I did not need anyone to tell me how good the fishing is at these places or provide me with credible information because I've been there and know first-hand. Some of these sites I've fished many times. I took almost every one of the photos in this book. There's no fluff or anecdotes about glory days.

Although this book covers a lot, it doesn't include all of North America's great fishing spots. This continent is blessed with loads of coastal water, great numbers of rivers and lakes, and a tremendous diversity in highly desirable sportfish. No other continent can match it. Yet, many great fishing sites didn't get included, mainly for space reasons. If your favorite place is missing, I plead *mea culpa*.

The destinations featured in this book collectively provide opportunities for most of the greatest gamefish in the world. These sites not only provide good fishing today, but are also likely to continue to do so in the future, which was a factor in deciding what to include in this book.

Part of my goal with the sites selected for this book was to provide a balance between countries, saltwater and freshwater opportunities, and major species. Some of the sites are very remote and visited by few people, while some are accessible to large numbers of people. Some are noted for just one prominent gamefish while others are noted for a host of species.

Since this is a travel guidebook to some extent, there are sidebar details on traveling to these sites, information sources, prime times, guide and tackle availability at these locations (which varies considerably), and other helpful planning matters. Price information, where provided, is in U.S. funds unless otherwise noted.

Angling-related travel is greatly different than routine vacation travel, especially if you bring your own equipment, which you must, in many cases. For a detailed review of booking angling travel, selecting destinations / lodges/outfitters, trip planning, packing, gear and clothing needs, and a host of other matters related to this subject, I refer you to *Ken Schultz's Fishing Encyclopedia,* which contains the most comprehensive information available anywhere on this topic, including extensive details about selecting guides and charter boats. A practical, condensed review of this topic appears at the back of this book.

In reviewing the page proofs of *Spectacular Fishing* and seeing the layout and the photos, my motor gets cranked and my soul itches to re-visit these places.

While I hope that *Spectacular Fishing* becomes a fixture on your coffee table or end table, I also hope that it spurs you to get out to some of these places and experience the great angling first-hand.

Ken Schultz

Saltwater

It is not an exaggeration to say that nothing could be finer than to be at any one of the following saltwater fishing sites in the morning, just as dawn is breaking and before a glorious sun rises. As the boat moves away from the dock you suck in a lungful of crisp, melon-y air, feel goosebumps on your arms, and cinch up the windbreaker. You're loaded with high expectations for the day.

The following pages detail terrific saltwater fishing opportunities for an eclectic group of premier gamefish in a diverse array of coastal locales. That means casting for roosterfish along the Pacific beaches of Mexico and mooching for chinook salmon along the rocky shoreline of British Columbia. It means casting plugs to small tailing redfish in the shallow Texas Gulf marshes and fishing with bottom rigs for giant reds in the pounding Atlantic surf off North Carolina. It means drifting live eels for aggressive stripers in the turbulent Cape May rips, and pitching flies or hooked shrimp to wary bonefish in the clear shallow flats of the Florida Keys.

You can drive to the Keys, pull a kayak down from your roofrack, and paddle to some flats and backwaters, but you'll have to take a helicopter to get to Langara in the northern Queen Charlottes. You can watch people fishing one of the best striper spots in the Atlantic Ocean as you drive across the Chesapeake Bay Bridge-Tunnel, but there isn't a soul around as you fish the secluded beaches south of Zihuatanejo, Mexico. Campbell River in B.C. sometimes gets so crowded you can count fishing boats by the hundreds and, while there may be a similar number of boats on a given day in the Mississippi Delta, back in the marsh it seems like you've got the planet to yourself.

And they all have good fishing.

Bella Bella

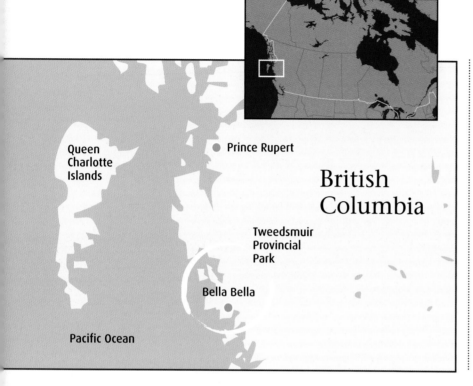

Queen
Charlotte
Islands

Prince Rupert

British Columbia

Tweedsmuir
Provincial
Park

Bella Bella

Pacific Ocean

British Columbia, Canada

Fishing around and between the islands, sounds, channels, fjords and passages that exist in the vicinity of Bella Bella is an experience close to that represented by even the most promising of tourism brochures.

Here you might have the opportunity of seeing a grizzly bear or a wolf prowling among beach driftwood at low tide. You might spot dozens of seals swimming in a bay near a creek, looking from a distance like an array of crab pot buoys. You might put fish heads in a trap that will later produce Dungeness crabs, which you will enjoy steamed and dipped in melted butter while the sun sets behind a snow-capped peak. You can walk amongst the old buildings and equipment of an abandoned cannery that once contained 600 year-round residents, and meet the intrepid family that now calls it home. You can follow

Chinook Salmon

Coho Salmon

Halibut

OPPOSITE
Sixteen pounds of coho salmon brings a lot of joy.

Details

Bella Bella, British Columbia, Canada

Location/getting there: This region is more than midway up along the main British Columbia coastline, north of Hakai Passage. Access is via a scheduled air service from the south terminal of Vancouver Airport. One of the most distinctive and first-rate operators is Westwind Tugboats, which meets its guests in Bella Bella and then cruises throughout the area, moving daily to where the fishing is best.

Info sources: Contact the Sport Fishing Institute of British Columbia, 200-1676 Duranleau St., Granville Island, Vancouver, B.C., Canada V6H 3S4; call 1-800-HELLO-BC for a free Sport Fishing Planning Guide; or visit www.sportfishing.bc.ca. For information about fishing on a Westwind tugboat, contact Westwind Tugboat Adventures, 1160 Holdom Ave., Burnaby, B.C., Canada V5B 3V6; call 888-599-8847; or visit www.tugboatcruise.com.

Prime times: Fishing is steady throughout the season, with chinooks most prominent early, and cohos most prominent later.

Gear needs: Mooching and levelwind tackle are best for larger fish, but you can use baitcasting, spinning and fly tackle if conditions are right for casting and you have both ample line capacity and a good drag.

Guide/tackle availability: Most anglers fish unguided, although there are limited guided-fishing options. Anglers receive good pre-fishing instruction, but it helps if you have handled boats and trolled/mooched before. Mooching/downrigging tackle is supplied, but bring your own casting gear.

Accommodations/dining: Area lodges have good accommodations on fixed-land or floating lodges, and good, ample food. Westwind Tugboats, which take eight to 12 passengers, have snug berths, shared baths and showers, and excellent food.

Etcetera: Lodges and tugboats provide rain gear, rubber boots and flotation jackets, and take excellent care of fish (if you keep them), which can be taken home or sent to a

cannery for smoking and canning. They clean, flash-freeze, vacuum-pack and box fish. Many visitors to this area make annual trips. Binoculars and plenty of film are a must. The cost for a seven-day/six-night Follow the Fish tugboat trip is $3,590, which includes airfare from Vancouver, but is exclusive of tips. If you stay in Vancouver for a day or two, consider visiting the Vancouver Aquarium at Stanley Park; the Museum of Anthropology at the University of British Columbia; and the Granville Island Sport Fishing Museum. For overnight travelers who have early-morning connections, the two-year-old Fairmont Vancouver Airport Hotel is easily accessible to all airlines, and has a freezer to store transported fish. For dining, try Cin-Cin for Italian food; Yoshi's on Denman for great sushi; and the Pacific Culinary Institute on Granville Island.

a pod of killer whales cruising the middle of a channel without evident concern or haste. You might wake up in the morning and see low fog and wispy clouds hanging below the rain forest, and then travel through stunning vistas where bald eagles seem to exist at every stop.

You will fish island heads and points where the current rushes by at a swift pace and be in some areas where coho or pink salmon leap or roll on the surface wherever you look. This is where you can, as weather and whim dictate, fish at almost any time for coho salmon, pink salmon, chinook salmon, halibut, lingcod, or rockfish, and choose whether your dinner will be any of these items plus crabs, prawns or clams preceded by some coho sushi or sockeye sashimi. This is the good life.

The expansive area from Hakai Passage to Milbanke Sound is certainly beautiful and remote, and there are enough hideaways to be found without having to go too far away. Cruise ships may pass through the deep, wide channels, and commercial fishing boats may head to and from Bella Bella, but although there are not many land-based sportfishing lodges in the region, it is easy to find places where you can cruise or fish in tranquility, and you can easily find protection, no matter the wind direction.

Burke Channel, Fisher Channel, Fitzhugh Sound, Queens Sound, Coltus Sound, Milbanke Sound and Seaforth Channel are the major avenues of travel, and there are so many island heads and steep, current-washed shores to fish that you cannot possibly hit them all.

Coho and chinook salmon are the main angling attractions. Chinooks, locally called spring salmon, are most abundant in late spring and early summer and fairly scarce later, while cohos are abundant from August on. Spring salmon especially are caught in areas closer to the ocean, such as the prominent northern and western island points fronting the big water of Queen Charlotte Sound, while cohos are also found in these locations, as well as in deep interior channels with lots of tidal current. Tides can be as high as 17 feet in this area, so flows are strong and fishing action is often centered around tide changes and moving water.

The best fishing results, especially for larger salmon, occur when fishing deep, so the mainstay technique here, as along much of British Columbia, is mooching with cut herring in relatively deep (30–90 foot) water. However, you will also find opportunities to skip-troll streamer flies across the surface with flycasting tackle (in creeks, and in places where many pinks and cohos gather in August), to cast spoons, spinners and flies to moving fish, as well as to hike inland on a trail (watching out for grizzly bears) and cast for rainbow and cutthroat trout in an upstream lake.

The other species, of course, are caught deep, often in 120 to over 200 feet of water, using huge jigs and heavily weighted bait. Halibut in excess of 200 pounds are possible, with some areas, like Burke Channel, especially conducive to halibut action. You may also find rockfish and lingcod over 20 pounds. In some locales, notably the area near Milbanke Sound, you can have near-constant action for assorted bottomfish, with the right drift and a good feel for the bottom. It's hard work, but fun, and the result is fine table fare.

It rains a lot here, but with all of the creatures tugging on your line, and all of the great scenery and wildlife, that does not seem to matter.

ABOVE
A traveling lodge, the Westwind *tugboat moves about the coast.*

LEFT
Photographing killer whales in Fisher Channel.

OPPOSITE
Big smile for a big halibut from Burke Channel.

Boca Grande/ Lee Island Coast

Florida, United States

Atlantic
Ocean

Florida

Gulf of
Mexico

Boca Grande • Fort Myers

Palm
Beach

Tarpon

Redfish

Snook

Seatrout

King Mackerel or Cobia

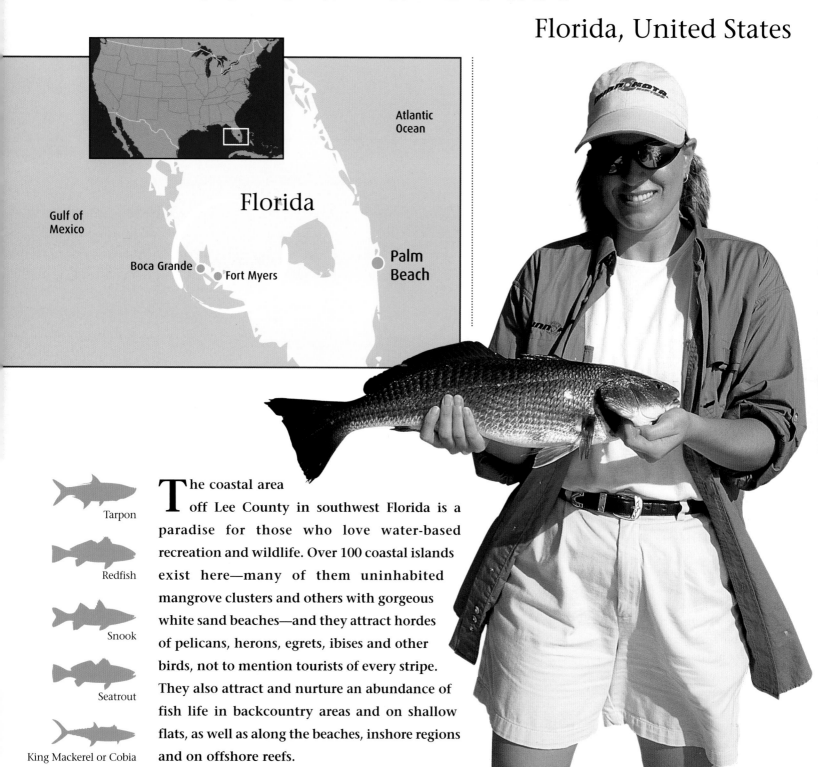

The coastal area off Lee County in southwest Florida is a paradise for those who love water-based recreation and wildlife. Over 100 coastal islands exist here—many of them uninhabited mangrove clusters and others with gorgeous white sand beaches—and they attract hordes of pelicans, herons, egrets, ibises and other birds, not to mention tourists of every stripe. They also attract and nurture an abundance of fish life in backcountry areas and on shallow flats, as well as along the beaches, inshore regions and on offshore reefs.

The best known of this region's sportfishing attractions is the phenomenal run of tarpon that occurs in spring and early summer, especially in Boca Grande Pass. A deep spot at the entrance to Charlotte Harbor and north of Pine Island Sound, Boca Grande Pass is billed as the "Tarpon Fishing Capitol of the World." For the average person using a good guide, there's nearly a 100 per cent chance to catch one of these huge silvery jumpers.

Spawning-run tarpon move into the entire Lee Island Coast area in late April and early May, depending on the severity of the winter and current water temperatures. The top fishing time is from then through the second week of July, but a good number of fish are around into September. A few stay all year, but provide spotty fishing.

In Boca Grande Pass, top guides fish two six-hour charters a day during the prime period. The traditional method involves controlled drifting with live crabs, pinfish, or other baitfish on the bottom using heavy tackle; many guides employ lighter gear and heavy breakaway jigs with a large circle hook, and often hook more fish. There's a lot of traffic here, mostly in 72-foot-deep Lighthouse Hole, and it is necessary to move away from the pack once a tarpon is hooked.

The biggest fish, all females, arrive from about the third week in May to the second week of June. Some have been caught to an estimated 260 pounds and about three dozen per year are landed in the 200-pound or better class. By mid-July tarpon leave the Pass and move into Charlotte Harbor through September, where anglers sight-fish for them, generally with live crabs or threadfin herring. In the first three weeks of May, there is an influx of large bull sharks into Boca Grande Pass, and

ABOVE
Shallow-draft boats skim anglers across the flats throughout the Lee Islands.

OPPOSITE
Redfish are a common catch on flats and near mangrove islands; this one was caught near Gasparilla Island.

ABOVE
*A snook caught in
Pine Island Sound.*

Details

Boca Grande/Lee Island Coast, Florida, United States

Location/getting there: Florida's Lee Island Coast is located on the eastern end of the Gulf of Mexico. Air access is via Fort Myers. Interstate 75 traverses the area, with southerly routes leading to Pine, Sanibel and Captiva Islands and northerly routes leading to Gasparilla Island and Boca Grande.

Info sources: For area information contact the Lee Island Coast Convention and Visitors Bureau, 2180 West First St., Fort Myers, FL 33901; call 888-231-6933; or visit www.LeeIslandCoast.com.

Prime times: April through July is prime for tarpon, with late May and early June monster time. Fall is a great time for snook, redfish, seatrout and king mackerel, with lighter fishing pressures, good weather and less boat traffic. Winter is when most people are around, but it can be windy then.

Gear needs: Assorted flycasting, spinning, baitcasting, and conventional tackle is used, depending on species and technique.

Guide/tackle availability: There are loads of guides throughout the area, some specializing on the flats and backcountry, some on tarpon and some on inshore/offshore activities. For Boca Grande fishing, contact Capt. Dave Markett, 813-962-1435 and 813-997-3474; for inshore and flats fishing in the Captiva-Sanibel area, contact Capt. Robert Reed, 941-283-4427; for inshore and offshore fishing throughout the area, contact Pro-Guides Co-op of southwest Florida, which represents numerous charter boats, at 800-945-9858 and visit www.guidescoop.com. Try to book a weekday, especially mid-week, if you can. Expect tarpon fishing to cost $500 per day and inshore fishing for snook, redfish, seatrout, etc., to be $400.

Accommodations/dining: There are numerous options suiting every budget. Many anglers stay in Sanibel and Fort Myers Beach. Contact the Lee Island CVB for info; also try 'Tween Waters Inn on Captiva Island; contact 800-223-5865 and visit www.tween-waters.com.

Etcetera: Birding, boating, sunbathing, beachcombing, shell-hunting and the like are all enormously popular here, and there are many attractions, museums and nature centers. A must-visit is the J.N. "Ding" Darling National Wildlife Refuge on Sanibel Island, which consists of 6,300 acres of mangrove forest, cordgrass marshes and West Indian hardwood hammocks; some 2,800 acres of this are federally designated as a Wilderness Area. The refuge is noted for endangered and protected species havens, has important habitat for over 170 bird species and receives over 600,000 visitors annually. It has two launch areas and both freshwater and saltwater fishing, although special fishing and boating regulations apply. Contact 941-472-1100; or visit www.iline.com/ddws/ding/htm.

many attack angler-caught tarpon at boatside in an exciting spectacle.

Tarpon are scattered throughout the southern part of this area, and while only a few over 150 pounds are landed each season, there are many in the 70- to 100-pound class. Some are caught in Pine Island Sound, at Captiva and Redfish Passes, and along the beaches, usually by stalking and sight-fishing. Some of the best tarpon action, however—including occasional hook-ups of four to six fish at a time—occurs five to ten miles offshore from Sanibel. The coastline of the area is such that the southern-facing lower end of Sanibel Island acts as a big bait trap. Anglers intercept migrating fish by chumming for them. Tarpon hang around this region throughout September, and it is quite possible to achieve a slam—catching at least one each of tarpon, snook, and redfish—in a single day.

Snook are another top attraction here. In winter, these fish move into the backcountry mangroves. From May through July they can be caught by sight-casting along beaches. Many are caught in the fall on flats, and can be sight-cast to while angling for redfish. Snook average in the mid-20-inch class here, with some up to 28 or 30 inches. Big snook are caught at night, often by bridges.

Redfish are available year-round. Fall is the time for bigger specimens, with some available from 20 to 30 pounds. They are often found in schools at this time. September through November is prime for bigger reds. Seatrout are also very popular, with the largest fish (up to ten pounds) mainly caught in late winter and early spring. They are fairly abundant in the summer and early fall on flats and grassy shallows. From fall through spring, anglers stand a good chance of catching a snook-redfish-seatrout slam in one day.

Cobia fishing is good from April through June, while king mackerel are also migrating through in spring and again from September through November. Both are caught off reefs drifting live bait. Some kings in the 40- to 50-pound range are landed.

Reefs provide the offshore attractions here; most are man-made (of rocks and rubble) on an otherwise fairly flat bottom. There are no sailfish or tuna within reasonable range, but reefs have plenty of groupers and snappers, which are popular with winter anglers. There are also permit on the reefs in summer and fall, and lots of Spanish mackerel along the coast.

BELOW
Tarpon are a premier attraction from spring through summer, especially in Boca Grande.

Campbell River

Port Hardy

Campbell River

Pacific Ocean

Vancouver Island

Vancouver

British Columbia

British Columbia, Canada

From a sheer fishing standpoint, there are many places in British Columbia that have great fishing, bigger salmon and fewer people than the Campbell River region. On the other hand, there has to be something about a place that has numerous fishing lodges, hundreds of guides employed at one time, and which for some time has billed itself as "The Salmon Capitol of the World."

Situated midway up Vancouver Island, the Campbell River area is convenient to reach and is a place where numbers of salmon have historically funneled their way through Discovery Passage between Vancouver Island and the mainland. Really large chinooks have not been caught here

Details

Campbell River, British Columbia, Canada

Location/getting there: Campbell River is located on eastcentral Vancouver Island. It is a one-hour flight from Vancouver and is accessed by floatplane (with water taxi service) or wheeled aircraft from the mainland. Anglers with boat in tow can ferry to Victoria and drive north.

Info sources: Contact the Sport Fishing Institute of British Columbia, 200-1676 Duranleau St., Granville Island, Vancouver, B.C., Canada V6H 3S4; call 1-800-HELLO-BC for a free Sport Fishing Planning Guide; or visit www.sportfishing.bc.ca.

Prime times: May and June for numbers of fish; August for larger chinook; September and October for larger coho.

Gear needs: Mooching and levelwind tackle are best for larger fish, but you can use baitcasting, spinning and fly tackle if conditions are right and you have both ample line capacity and a good drag.

Guide/tackle availability: There are hundreds of guides in the area; tackle is supplied by most lodges and is also available locally.

Accommodations/dining: A wide range of lodging and dining options exist for both guided and self-guided anglers.

Etcetera: The waters here are tricky, both from a boat handling as well as a what-to-do standpoint, and tidal movement is important. Fish caught can be taken home or sent to a cannery for smoking and canning. If you stay in Vancouver for a day or two, consider visiting the Vancouver Aquarium at Stanley Park, the Museum of Anthropology at the University of British Columbia and the Granville Island Sport Fishing Museum.

Chinook Salmon

Coho Salmon

Steelhead

BELOW
Angler with a coho salmon, caught on a trolled fly off Whilby Point.

in significant numbers lately, and in this respect the area is greatly overshadowed by Langara. But despite this, it is not as remote as Langara, and even without the monsters there are still plenty of fish. In addition, because of its protected location, the Campbell River area is fishable all season, no matter what direction the wind may be from.

The premier salmon fishing spot is the gigantic back eddy in front of the lighthouse where the Strait of Georgia and Discovery Passage meet. This is where there are often many hundreds of boats fishing, and where thousands of salmon, waiting to ambush bait, annually fall to the hook. When the run is on, boats routinely have doubles and triples.

Another extraordinary spot, though not one that is conducive to heavy traffic or to boaters with a weak heart, is Seymour Narrows. Here, when the tide is high and really moving the current can flow as fast as 16 knots, and there may be 50- to 60-foot-wide whirlpools. At ten knots it is estimated that one million gallons of water moves per second—nonetheless, this dangerous water draws salmon.

There are times when coho salmon are especially abundant, with an excellent spot being Whilby Shoal on the extreme southern tip of Quadra Island. A major kelp bed shoal there attracts fish, which feed on massive pods of tiny shrimp.

Although salmon are the main attraction in Campbell River, there is some river fishing for sea-run cutthroat trout and for steelhead. The latter enter the area in the fall and winter.

With all the activity, the nearby towns, the boat traffic and so forth, this is clearly not the wilderness fishing which one tends to associate with British Columbia. The salmon do not mind, though, and neither do legions of anglers.

Cape Cod and the Islands

Massachusetts, United States

Atlantic Ocean

Boston
Massachusetts

Provincetown
Cape Cod

Nantucket
Island

Martha's
Vineyard

Striped Bass

Bluefish

Bonito

False Albacore

There is fine sportfishing these days, particularly for striped bass, throughout eastern Massachusetts, not only at Cape Cod, but in Cape Cod Bay and Nantucket Sound, and around Martha's Vineyard and Nantucket Island.

Shallow fishing is a hallmark of the Cape's northern shore, which is especially notable for light-tackle fishing. The far eastern end of the Cape, particularly the National Seashore from Race Point to Nauset Inlet, produces huge striped bass and bluefish from June through October,

especially at night along the beach—it's a hike for surf anglers, however, since vehicular access is severely restricted. Nauset Inlet, which has strong currents, is a hotspot for big stripers.

There is good fishing around Monomoy Island south of Chatham, including great sight-casting along shallow sand flats on the western side, and excellent action around rips on the east and south.

Martha's Vineyard and Nantucket are renowned for shore- and surf-fishing for striped bass, bluefish, bonito and false albacore. Numerous saltwater ponds on the Vineyard offer protected fishing for shore and small-boat anglers. Surf casters score well on big fish along the south shore of the Vineyard, where they prowl the beach with four-wheel-drive vehicles. On the southeast, rips off Wasque Point draw all the major gamefish, making it a popular summer location.

ABOVE RIGHT
Evening and at night are prime fishing times along Cape Cod beaches.

Details

Cape Cod and the Islands, Massachusetts, United States

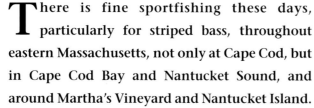

Location/getting there: Cape Cod and nearby islands are located in eastern Massachusetts. The Cape is reached by major roads; Nantucket and Martha's Vineyard have small airports, but are mainly reached by ferries.

Info sources: For area information contact: Cape Cod Chamber of Commerce, 800-332-2732 and www.capecodchamber.org; Martha's Vineyard Chamber of Commerce, 508-693-0085 and www.mvy.com; Nantucket Island Chamber of Commerce, 508-228-1700 and www.nantucketchamber.org.

Prime times: Fall is excellent for striped bass. Late summer through September is prime for bonito and false albacore.

Gear needs: Varies with species, methods and situation.

Guide/tackle availability: Charter boat captains are available for varied fishing, including light-tackle boat and shore/surf angling.

Accommodations/dining: A wide range of lodging and dining options exist, especially on Cape Cod.

Etcetera: There is summer action for yellowfin tuna and white marlin southeast of Nantucket if Gulf Stream water pushes inward. Out at the continental shelf there is a chance for blue and white marlin; bigeye, yellowfin, and albacore tuna; wahoo; and big mako sharks.

Cape Fear

North Carolina, United States

Diversity is the name of the fishing game in the Cape Fear region, which blends a little bit from more southerly fisheries and a little bit from northern fisheries with a whole lot of the best from the mid-Atlantic. Although the Cape Fear region—which encompasses the greater Wilmington area, the lower Cape Fear River, the estuary areas around assorted islands and nearby inshore and offshore environs—does not have the fall false albacore blitz that occurs up near Cape Lookout, it does have much overlooked and under-appreciated tarpon fishing in the summer (with 100-pounders caught in and around the mouth of the Cape Fear River), and also receives a good number of big striped bass (30 pounds and better) during the winter. However, those species are overshadowed by more prominent opportunities both inshore and offshore.

King Mackerel

Seatrout

Drum

Dolphin

Sailfish

LEFT
The king mackerel is a major attraction in the Cape Fear region.

Chief among the glamorous attractions is king mackerel. The Cape Fear region, thanks to numerous attractive underwater formations and a trio of shoals, including Frying Pan, which extends 22 miles offshore, may well be the kingfish capitol of the east coast. From June to October there's just about one king mackerel fishing tournament each weekend here, topped by the richest kingfish competition of them all, the Greater Wilmington King Mackerel Tournament, which advertises a first-place prize of $103,000 based on a field of 560 boats.

These events are usually won by a fish of 40 pounds or better. A 50-pounder is a sure top finisher, but bigger kingfish exist. The state record for this species, which stood at 79 pounds for 15 years, was re-established twice in 2000, first by an 80-pounder and then by an 81-pounder.

King mackerel are theoretically available all year long off the Cape Fear Coast, although the fishing season is generally from late March or early April through December. Kingfish start moving closer to the beach in April, generally in the ten- to 15-mile range, and are usually close enough by Memorial Day to get crowds of boats going through the Intracoastal Waterway and main

BELOW
The Kure Beach Pier attracts weekend crowds.

LEFT
Anglers with four-wheel drives find good fishing in the surf near Carolina Beach Inlet.

river channel after them. In December the fish start moving back well offshore, and in winter they are about 35 miles offshore, though few bother to make that journey then.

Peak fishing occurs from June through October, largely because of favorable winds and because the fish can be found from right off the inlets to 15 miles out. Many of the bigger kingfish are caught by trolling with live baits (menhaden, bluefish and cutlassfish), but anglers also troll using plugs and spoons fished off planers and downriggers. These fast-growing, voracious fish are constantly moving, and trolling helps cover a lot of territory.

Seatrout are probably more popular, though less glamorous, than mackerel, and are present in estuary and inlet areas throughout the year, with the larger specimens available late in the season and in winter. Many flounder over five pounds are caught locally, and some in the ten-pound class, especially in the Southport area. Spanish

North Carolina

South Carolina

Wilmington

Cape Fear

Myrtle Beach

Atlantic Ocean

Details

Location/getting there: The Cape Fear region in southeastern North Carolina is reached by commercial air carrier into Wilmington, and is about a 90-minute drive from Interstate 95 via I-40.

Info sources: For area information contact the Cape Fear Convention and Visitors Bureau, 24 North Third St., Wilmington, NC 28401; call 800-222-4757; or visit www.capefear.nc.us /water.htm.

Prime times: Summer for offshore fishing; June through October for king mackerel; winter for big seatrout; and fall for red drum.

Gear needs: Varies widely by species and fishing methods. Light spinning and fly tackle use is growing, especially for inshore fishing.

Guide/tackle availability: For a list of fishing guides, charters, etc., visit www.ncfishing.com; also view the seasonally informative web site www.wrightsville.com. Numerous charter captains and guides exist in the area, plus head boats and fishing piers.

Accommodations/dining: There is a full range of services throughout the area. For upscale try the Holiday Inn SunSpree Resort at Wrightsville Beach; for mid-range try the Docksider Oceanfront Inn at Kure Beach, or Carolina Temple Apartments in Wrightsville Beach. The Oceanic in Wrightsville Beach has excellent food.

Etcetera: Attractions abound along the beaches and in Wilmington. Anglers may want to visit the recently reopened and expanded North Carolina Aquarium at Fort Fisher. The centerpiece exhibit is a 200,000-gallon saltwater tank with two-story, multi-level viewing of large sharks, groupers, barracudas, and loggerhead sea turtles among the re-created rock ledges. Call 800-832-3474; or visit www.acquariums.state.nc.us /ff/index.htm.

ABOVE
Fishing for flounder and drum on the Intracoastal Waterway.

mackerel are popular as well, and are available around local inlets from May through fall.

Huge black drum—from 50 to 70 pounds—are caught each year in the lower Cape Fear River, and, in 1998, a 100-pound state record was taken there. Red drum have rebounded here in recent years and have a very significant local sportfishing catch. Smaller fish in the five- to ten-pound range are targeted in the marshes behind local islands, especially from Wrightsville Beach to Bald Head Island. Fly fishing for red drum has become increasingly popular locally. As is the case elsewhere in North Carolina, cobia are available in late spring and early summer, and they average from 20 to 50 pounds.

There is fishing offshore for sailfish, marlin, yellowfin tuna, dolphin and wahoo, most of this being from June through August in the Gulf Stream, which is within 45 miles of the beach. In recent years dolphin have been quite numerous and a larger part of the offshore catch; kingfish anglers often catch a couple while trolling. Sailfishing has also improved recently, and some better days have seen as many as eight hook-ups.

Shore anglers enjoy a number of pay-to-fish piers in the region. Notable are the 712-foot-long, handicap-accessible Kure Beach Pier, and the rebuilt Carolina Beach Pier, plus the new all-concrete Johnnie Mercer Pier in Wrightsville Beach. There is also public access along the area's 31 miles of beach. Four-wheel-drive vehicles can access the popular north end of Carolina Beach by Carolina Beach Inlet for surf fishing. Another access area for wade fishing is at the end of Rt. 421 at Fort Fisher. Shore-based anglers fish for spots, pompano, drum, seatrout and bluefish in particular.

Cape May

New Jersey, United States

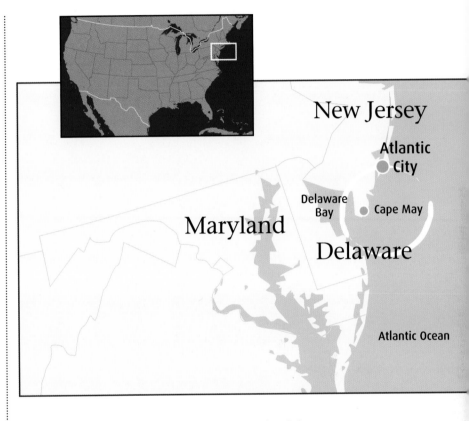

O n any given weekday in October and November you can look offshore from the Cape May Lighthouse and see a hundred or more boats scattered about shoals—locally called "The Rips"—that exist at this confluence of the Atlantic Ocean and Delaware Bay. On weekends the boats number in the multiple hundreds. If you are among them you had better get out early, as traffic tends to spook the fish, but a lot of stripers are attracted here, especially as the tide gathers steam and pulls more water over them. Drifting with bottom-bouncing eels is the main activity.

Recently the larger stripers—20- and 30-pounders—have been caught up the Bay, mainly by anchored boats that chunk in sloughs with bunker. Some stripers, mainly smaller ones, are also caught at this time along the beaches and jetties, especially if the small, "peanut" bunker are packed inshore.

Watching and following the birds is like a religious activity in fall, for both surf and boat anglers. The enormous amount of bait around, and the tendency of

schools of stripers to maraud baitfish and even herd them toward the beach, means that there is easy food to be had. When the stripers are plundering baitfish, gulls, terns, and gannets swarm. If they are dipping up and down, and diving into the water, anglers know what to do; get there as fast as they can.

There is no doubt that the striper is king here, and fall is a great time, not only for fishing but also because the weather is often excellent and most of the usual tourist crowd has gone. But Cape May's fishing opportunities extend to other seasons and species as well.

Bluefish and weakfish are historically major catches in the area, although they have not been as abundant as striped bass lately. Small blues are caught by beach and jetty anglers, but the larger ones come to those in boats. Weakfish are in the bays and along the beaches in spring and summer; one area community, Fortescue, which is along Delaware Bay in Cumberland County, bills itself as the "Weakfish Capitol of the World" and holds an annual

LEFT
Fishing in the surf, with the Cape May lighthouse in the background.

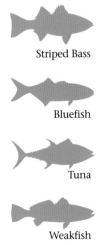

Striped Bass

Bluefish

Tuna

Weakfish

tournament for this species. Delaware Bay also holds some good-sized black drum, which are mainly a spring phenomenon.

Offshore fishing is also a hot commodity here, although big boats have to run for two hours—more or less, depending on the boat and its speed—to get far enough offshore to reach blue water or the canyons.

However, tuna—primarily yellowfin and some bigeye—are the main attraction, with occasional marlin and dolphin action, plus albacore and bonito. Each year in late August one of North America's top-purse offshore fishing tournaments, the Mid-Atlantic $500,000, is held in Cape May, and it attracts big-game anglers from up and down the Atlantic Coast.

Details

Cape May, New Jersey, United States

Location/getting there: Cape May is the southernmost tip of New Jersey at the entrance to Delaware Bay. It is about a 45-minute drive south of Atlantic City and two hours from Philadelphia.

Info sources: For general area information, contact the Cape May County Dept. of Tourism, P.O. Box 365, Cape May Court House, NJ 08210; call 800-227-2297; or visit www.thejerseycape.net. Also visit www.capemay.com. A good source of information for the Delaware Bay area is Cumberland County Tourism; call 800-319-3379; or visit www.co.cumberland.nj.us.

Prime times: June is good for weakfish and stripers along the beaches; October and November are prime for larger striped bass; August for tuna.

Gear needs: Varies widely according to species and technique.

Guide/tackle availability: Charter boats are available at several marinas. South Jersey Marina is one hub of activity and across the street from that, the party boat *Miss Chris* is a favorite with many anglers, usually having two vessels sailing early each morning. On weekends the boats fill up fast, so arrive well ahead of the scheduled departure time. For surf fishing information, tackle, or guided light-tackle angling, contact Bob Jackson's Surf Fishing Center, 719 Broadway, West Cape May, NJ 08204; call 609-898-7950; or visit www.fishcapemay.com.

Accommodations/dining: There are numerous lodging and dining options in Cape May and the surrounding villages.

Etcetera: There are many worthwhile side attractions in the area. Each spring there is a renowned migration of horseshoe crabs onto Delaware Bay beaches. Cape May is a premier east coast bird watching area, especially in the fall. The Cape May Migratory Bird Refuge is located at Cape May Point State Park, which is also the site of Cape May Lighthouse, built in 1859 and featuring a 199-stair climb to the top. While fishing at Sunset Beach on Delaware Bay you can also collect "Cape May Diamonds," which are pieces of nearly pure quartz. Nearby, deluxe ferries cross the bay to Lewes, Delaware.

Cozumel

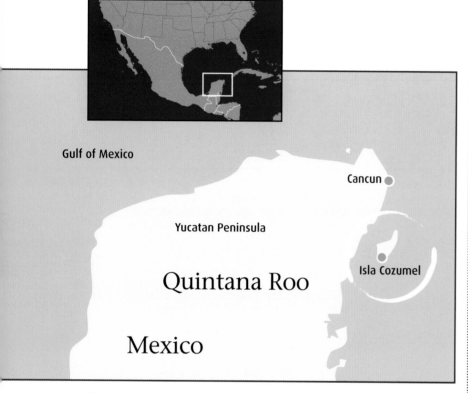

Gulf of Mexico

Cancun

Yucatan Peninsula

Quintana Roo

Isla Cozumel

Mexico

Quintana Roo, Mexico

Often the fishing is near Playa del Carmen along a sharp drop from ten to 60 fathoms of water. Sailfish migrate northerly, usually in groups (which is why multiple hook-ups are common), coming from the open waters of the Caribbean and working their way up the coast past Cozumel, passing the head of the Peninsula at Isla Mujeres and Cancun, and then moving into the Gulf of Mexico. Some Cozumel boats run north toward Isla Mujeres later in the season, when the main run of sailfish is more clustered in that area. Trolling with bait is the primary technique for sails, and some live bait fishing is also done.

White marlin are occasionally caught while fishing for sailfish. Blue marlin are usually caught further offshore and over deeper water, especially while trolling large baits or lures. Swordfish are occasionally spotted finning along the surface here, and there is a slight chance of hooking one by casting a live bait to a sighted broadbill or by fishing at night.

Although bonefish are abundant along the Yucatan flats on the mainland, they are not as abundant at Cozumel because the island has little shallow water. There are some bonefish and permit to be caught here, however, in lagoons at either end of the island. The fish are not big in either locale, but the setting is both pristine and tranquil. Southeast of Cozumel, there is excellent flats fishing for bonefish at Boca Paila and Ascension Bay.

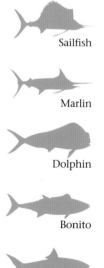

Sailfish

Marlin

Dolphin

Bonito

Bonefish

The Cozumel region is among the best places in the world to catch one, or more, sailfish, as it has a truly abundant population of this species when they are migrating through the area. Large numbers of sailfish make Cozumel an excellent place to catch this tail-walking species on light spinning, levelwind tackle or on fly gear. It is also an excellent place to be part of a multiple hook-up; several anglers playing two or three sails simultaneously is a common sight.

Sailfish are most abundant from February to June, and a slow day during this period is hooking up with three or four. Dolphin, kingfish, bonito and blackfin tuna are also in the mix, sometimes in good numbers and sizes, although they're usually an incidental catch while billfishing.

Trolling at Cozumel predominantly takes place between the island of Cozumel and the mainland of the Yucatan Peninsula, which is separated by 12 miles of deep water.

RIGHT
Cozumel anglers fight a sailfish with Playa del Carmen in the background.

Details

Cozumel, Quintana Roo, Mexico

Location/getting there: Cozumel is on the eastcentral coast of Mexico's Yucatan Peninsula and is served by many airlines.

Info sources: For area information, visit www.discovercozumel.com.

Prime times: February through June.

Gear needs: Tackle is provided by charter boats; experienced anglers wanting light tackle fishing are advised to bring their own gear.

Guide/tackle availability: Numerous charter boats are available for offshore fishing; costs for a charter boat for a day offshore range from $350 to $500.

Accommodations/dining: There is a broad array of lodging and dining options in this huge resort area.

Etcetera: Cozumel is a prime tourist destination and easily accessed from the United States. The island is 33 miles long and nine miles wide, and worth exploring if you tire of fishing and of frolicking on the beach. Some of the world's finest diving exists here. Palancar Reef, which surrounds the island, is the world's second-largest coral reef, and a diving favorite. Reef fishing produces groupers and red snapper, plus dolphin, kingfish and, on occasion, amberjack.

ABOVE
A sailfish is captured for unhooking and release.

Florida Keys

Florida, United States

ABOVE
Prospecting for tarpon at sunset near Marathon.

No saltwater fishing destination has been written about more than the Florida Keys. Consisting of 42 islands connected by bridges and stretching 110 miles, the Keys offer a bunch of destinations with a *potpourri* of inshore and offshore fishing opportunities. Such sites as Key Largo, Islamorada, Marathon and Key West are legendary for fishing, with Islamorada having long proclaimed itself as the "Sportfishing Capitol of the World."

Most anglers know the Keys for bonefish, permit, and tarpon on the flats. Many think of it mainly as a winter getaway spot, but the Florida Keys are a great year-round angling destination. Some of the best action occurs in the heat of summer and there is plenty of diversity. From bottom fishing on reefs and wrecks to sight-fishing for tarpon to tossing live bait to sailfish, there is something here to suit any interest.

Tarpon are a main quarry, and fly fishing on the flats for these bruisers is a specialty in the Keys, although it is not the only technique, nor is it necessarily the best. The tarpon are mostly in the 50- to 100-pound class, but there are plenty of them seasonally, as well as fish over 100

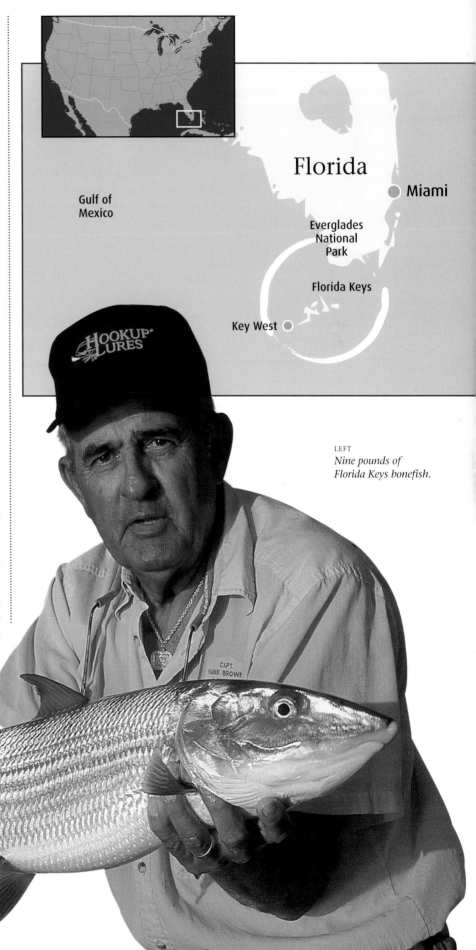

pounds and some even in the 150-pound class, virtually all of which are released.

Tarpon do not regularly appear until the water temperature hits 75 degrees or better. May and June are prime months, as northerly migratory schools become numerous. April may be very good, too, if the weather has been favorable. Tarpon are found in many locales throughout the Keys and favor the raised banks of flats, bridges (especially at night) and channels that connect bridges and harbor areas. Seven Mile Bridge and Bahia Honda Bridge, south of Marathon, are especially good for tarpon, as are the channels in the Key West Harbor area.

Primarily caught on flats, bonefish are widely available, although the upper Keys and Florida Bay have greater concentrations and somewhat larger fish. Islamorada is a bonefishing hub and well situated for running north to Key Largo flats or south to Marathon flats. These fish typically run from six to eight pounds but can top 15 pounds locally; numerous line-class world records have been set in the Keys. Bonefish may be caught year-round, but the best period is in late spring and in the fall. Cold fronts cause their temporary disappearance in the winter and early spring. In summer, the better fishing to be had is early in the morning.

Permit are the hardest of the three major flats species to catch, and the most wary. Nevertheless, the Keys has produced many line-class and fly rod tippet-class world records for this species. Permit here average 15 to 20 pounds, are occasionally caught over 40 pounds, and are found on many of the same flats as bonefish, although on a higher tide, and also in holes and channels and on rockpiles. Key West and the Content Keys are considered among the best permit spots.

Key West is a popular port for wreck fishing, exploring both Gulf and Atlantic waters. Gulf wrecks are fairly shallow, in 50 to 100 feet of water, but in the Atlantic they

LEFT
Nine pounds of Florida Keys bonefish.

Tarpon

Bonefish

Permit

Sailfish

Dolphin

Details

Location/getting there: The Florida Keys is the southernmost point in the continental United States, readily accessed by auto and by commercial flights connecting through Fort Lauderdale and Miami to Marathon and Key West airports.

Info sources: For area information, contact the Florida Keys and Key West Visitors Bureau, P.O. Box 116, Key West, FL 33041; call 800-352-5397; or visit www.fla_keys.com.

Prime times: See the main text.

Gear needs: Varies by species and fishing methods.

Guide/tackle availability: Inshore guides and offshore charter boat captains are plentiful. Tackle is readily available in local shops. Charter boats, and many guides, provide tackle. An excellent source of charters, guides, bait and tackle, and local information is Bud N' Mary's Fishing Marina, Mile Marker 79.8, P.O. Box 628, Islamorada, FL 33036; call 800-742-7945; or visit www.budnmarys.com.

Accommodations/dining: Lodging and dining options are extensive throughout the Keys, although you must arrange ahead in peak tourist and fishing seasons.

Etcetera: There is a host of things to interest people in the Keys. Visit Big Pine Key, home to the diminutive Keys deer and the National Keys Deer Wildlife Refuge, and also a gateway to Looe Key, a shallow coral formation and top diving site. In Marathon, visit the Dolphin (as in porpoise) Research Center and historical Pigeon Key. Do not overlook some late evening tarpon fishing in the channels, as well as bridge fishing at night for tarpon. You will find it a different and enjoyable experience to kayak-tour and fish the mangrove islands; kayaks can be rented at various places, and are a terrific tool for accessing the backcountry, probing the great expanses of ultra-thin water around many of the mangrove islands, and quietly approaching and observing bird and marine life.

RIGHT
Playing a small tarpon near Big Pine Key.

can be much deeper. Much of the good wreck fishing takes place throughout the winter. Popular species here include amberjack, various groupers, mutton snapper, cobia, barracuda, mackerel and permit, plus other species and the occasional pelagic fish.

In the offshore realm, the Keys have plenty of entertainment, especially for dolphin and sailfish, but also for blue marlin, blackfin tuna, wahoo, king mackerel, cobia, amberjack and other species.

Sailfishing is very popular in the upper Keys early in the year, and in the lower Keys from November through winter, with December and January prime. Fish are quite plentiful, and are a great target for light-tackle use. A lot of searching is done for sailfish in the winter, especially looking for schools of pilloried bait. Live bait is tossed to sails, and is very effective.

Dolphin may be encountered throughout the year, but are usually most prominent from April through the summer. They are usually found in schools offshore, and

are sometimes quite numerous. Most dolphin run from five to 20 pounds; larger fish, known as "slammers," are fairly common, though they are usually caught further offshore. These fish are caught on various tackle, but the smaller sizes are especially well suited to light-tackle use.

Blue marlin arrive in the lower Keys soon after the main body of dolphin, and are caught in the same locations. A prime Keys spot for blues is The Wall, which is 19 miles south of Key West; there the ocean bottom drops off sharply. Blues range from 100 to over 500 pounds.

Other common offshore catches include 15- to 40-pound blackfin tuna, especially in winter and early spring around offshore humps; king mackerel, which are especially prominent along coral reefs, and are most prominent off Key West; amberjack; and cobia. Reefs provide a lot of action for various snappers and groupers year-round; yellowtail snapper, which run up to five pounds, and mutton snapper, which can top 20 pounds, are especially favored.

ABOVE
Offshore anglers proudly display a 49-pound slammer dolphin.

Hampton Roads

Virginia, United States

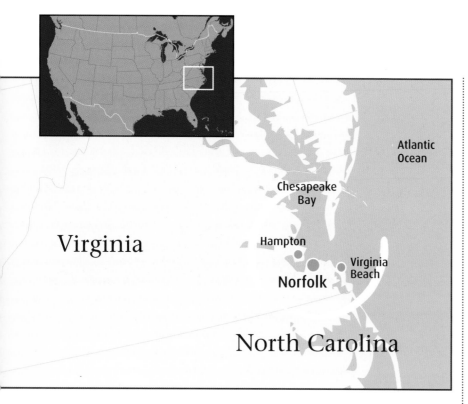

Virginia

Chesapeake
Bay

Atlantic
Ocean

Hampton

Virginia
Beach

Norfolk

North Carolina

Excellent angling for small stripers on light tackle takes place from September into mid-October. After Thanksgiving in a normal year (when the cold weather has set in) there are generally big fish in the bay until the season closes at the end of the year. Hardy anglers fish in the ocean out to the three-mile limit for monster stripers from January through March.

Among other species, cobia and spadefish become available between Memorial Day and the middle of June; both stay around all summer. Spanish mackerel show up in late June and July and are caught along tidelines in the bay and in the ocean. June is also a good time for red

Striped Bass

Seatrout

Drum

Tuna

Cobia

The southern Virginia Coast and lower Chesapeake Bay, accessed primarily from the cities of Virginia Beach and Hampton, is one of the finest fishing areas in North America. Locally called Hampton Roads, a term that encompasses a broad area, this region has a load of fisheries resources, none more prominent than striped bass, as witnessed by the fact that Virginia Beach bills itself as "The Striped Bass Capitol of the World."

Chesapeake Bay is the east coast's foremost nursery for this species, and in the fall, huge numbers of these fish move out of the Bay and also migrate down from the north, converging in the lower Bay near its confluence with the Atlantic Ocean. Top anglers can have a ball catching fish from 20 to 40 pounds, with some over 50 caught each season. The 1996 state record, 61 pounds 12 ounces, is likely to be broken soon as fish from the terrific year class of 1982 fatten up here before winter.

drum in the bay, while there are good numbers of black drum in April and May. Flounder fishing occurs all year, and these fish have been producing extremely well recently, with over one thousand six-pounders caught in each of the past two seasons, plus several dozen ten-pounders. Amberjacks are caught in the ocean in August and September, which is also when king mackerel show up, staying well into fall. Big bluefish, some in the 15- to 20-pound class, show up in late fall.

The major offshore fishery takes place up to 100 miles out in the Atlantic, beginning at 60 miles at the Norfolk Canyon. There is a good white marlin catch in late summer, especially in September. Bluefin tuna show up in June on their way north, followed by yellowfin tuna in July and August. The yellowfins slack off for a bit and then pick up again in early fall, and bluefin action is good again in late fall, especially in November when these fish move southward.

Many of the offshore fishing fleet berths can be found in Rudee Inlet in Virginia Beach, which is 14 miles closer

ABOVE
Thirty-seven pounds of night-time striped bass.

LEFT
Fishing around the pilings of the Chesapeake Bay Bridge-Tunnel.

Details

Hampton Roads, Virginia, United States

Location/getting there: Hampton Roads is located along the southern coast of Virginia, and is easily accessed by interstate highway, the Chesapeake Bay Bridge-Tunnel and airports in Norfolk and Newport News.

Info sources: For information contact the Virginia Beach Dept. of Convention and Visitor Development at 800-822-3224 or visit www.vbfun.com, and Hampton Conventions and Tourism, 2 Eaton St., Suite 106, Hampton, VA 23669, at 800-487-8778 and www.hamptoncvb.com.

Prime times: November and December for striped bass; June and November for bluefin tuna; June for red drum; late summer for king mackerel.

Gear needs: Varies widely according to species and fishing method.

Guide/tackle availability: There are numerous charter boat services for bay, coastal, and offshore fishing, with major concentrations in Rudee Inlet and Lynnhaven Inlet in Virginia Beach, and in Hampton. Try

Capt. Herb Gordon in Virginia Beach, 757-464-3974; and Capt. Paul Anderson in Hampton, 804-550-2746. Expect to pay in the neighborhood of $450–$500 for a full day in the bay, and nearly double that for offshore fishing. A good party boat, which specializes in family fishing and education, is Venture Inn Charters at the Hampton Public Piers; call 757-850-8960; or visit www.ventureinncharters.com. There are also a number of public fishing piers in Virginia Beach and in Hampton. Tackle is supplied by charter operators, and it is widely available at marinas and tackle/bait shops.

Accommodations/dining: Numerous lodging and dining options exist throughout the area. A good place to stay is the Virginia Beach Resort Hotel and Conference Center, 800-422-4747. Another good and especially convenient place to stay on the Hampton waterfront is the Radisson Hotel, 757-727-9700; the chef there is an avid angler and will gladly cook your catch.

Etcetera: A great attraction in the area is the Virginia Marine Science Museum, which is

both an aquarium and a museum dedicated to the aquatic resources and phenomena of the Chesapeake and coastal Virginia region. It includes more than 300 interactive exhibits, a 300,000-gallon Norfolk Canyon Aquarium, and a 50,000-gallon Chesapeake Bay Aquarium. For information call 757-425-3474 or visit www.va-beach.com/va-marine-science-museum. Also of note is Back Bay National Wildlife Refuge and Virginia's most heavily visited park, First Landing State Park. Hampton is the official visitor center for NASA's Langley Research facilities and for visiting Norfolk Naval Base and Langley Air Force Base. The Virginia Air and Space Center in downtown Hampton contains the Apollo 12 command module that went to the moon, and much more. For information, call 800-296-0800 or visit www.vasc.org. The Chesapeake Bay Bridge-Tunnel is a 17.6-mile-long engineering achievement linking Virginia's Eastern Shore and Hampton Roads. It costs $10 each way, with a restaurant and fishing pier three-and-a-half miles from Virginia Beach being the only place where you can idly view surroundings. For information call 757-331-2960 or visit www.cbbt.com.

to the offshore grounds than the major harbor area of Hampton. However, Hampton, situated where the James River meets Chesapeake Bay, is an area with good fishing in its own right, and is an excellent protected harbor. Good striper fishing can be had at the Hampton Roads Bridge-Tunnel, and the Hampton Bar upstream of that is noted for excellent striped bass, flounder, gray trout, sea bass and croaker fishing.

This area can be easily fished, especially by small boaters, when the lower Bay is too rough, especially as the result of a northeast wind. A 20-minute run upriver puts you into a section of the James that has largemouth bass and big catfish. There is always the chance here, incidentally, as well as elsewhere in the Bay, of seeing an aircraft carrier or submarine, as well as all manner of freighters headed to and from Baltimore.

LEFT
A freighter enters Chesapeake Bay amidst a flotilla of fishing boats in Thimble Shoals Channel.

OPPOSITE
Big lures trolled deep catch large stripers in the fall.

Huatulco

Oaxaca, Mexico

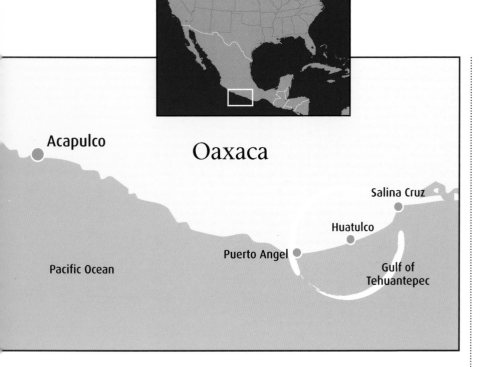

Acapulco

Oaxaca

Salina Cruz

Huatulco

Puerto Angel

Pacific Ocean

Gulf of
Tehuantepec

The southwestern coast of Mexico below Acapulco has a lot of shoreline without nearby roads and without significant access. Yet there are various small villages here, some with lightly developed sportfishing; one in particular, Huatulco, is becoming increasingly known for low-key fishing efforts, good action and reasonable costs.

A small village east of Puerto Angel and west of Salina Cruz in the state of Oaxaca, Huatulco (pronounced "*wha-tool-co*") was unheard of until a resort facility went in there in the late 1980s. Fishing then was truly unexplored, but a lot of resources are being devoted to tourist development, and, as a result, local fishing acumen, boats and equipment have improved. Not to the standards of Los Cabos or Cozumel, but better than you might expect.

Situated on the edge of the Gulf of Tehuantepec, and not far from the Middle America Trench, with associated drop-offs and several seamounts, Huatulco is nicely positioned to receive the warm northerly flowing current. This brings with it a bounty of bait as well as lots of sailfish, plus

RIGHT
Fishing out of a cramped Huatulco tourist panga, a fisherman enjoys the aerobatic maneuvers of a sailfish.

marlin, yellowfin tuna, dolphin and wahoo. While the inshore opportunities are lightly explored, the sailfishing is often so good that poorly equipped anglers, even first-timers, have been able to go a few miles offshore in modest pangas and hook up with a number of Pacific sails.

Sailfish are present to some degree all year, although the prime period is from June through September. Midsummer is also a time for blue and black marlin; a 750-pound black was caught here in August of 1996. There are nine bays around Huatulco and they are noted for numerous beautiful, soft, sandy beaches. Some sailfish are caught at the outskirts of the bays and within two miles of the beach, and many more within a few miles further out. The period from November through March is usually excellent for yellowfin tuna and dorado (dolphin).

Strong winds occasionally whip up the wide Gulf waters, and make it very rough on the Pacific side. September is the wet end of the rainy season and also hurricane season.

LEFT
This fine sailfish was caught within a few miles of Huatulco.

Details

Huatulco, Oaxaca, Mexico

Location/getting there: Located along the Pacific in southwestern Mexico, Huatulco is about 300 miles south of Acapulco and 450 miles from Mexico City. It is accessed via Huatulco International Airport, primarily with connections through Mexico City.

Info sources: For general tourism info call Mexico Tourism at 800-446-3942; or visit www.visitmexico.com. For area info visit the Huatulco area tourism web site at www.baysofhuatulco.com; also visit www.oaxaca-travel.com.

Prime times: See main text.

Gear needs: Offshore captains on the few larger boats here have good big-game gear. Bring your own light tackle, especially spinning and flycasting gear. For inshore fishing, bring your own spinning, baitcasting and fly outfits, as well as lures.

Guide/tackle availability: Local boats are available, and vary in both luxury and pricing, but if you have your own gear (and preferably speak Spanish), you can find knowledgeable skippers with pangas who can provide good fishing at a modest price. Some of the

captains have decent tackle and boats and speak some English. Do not count on finding tackle to purchase locally.

Accommodations/dining: Varied accommodations and dining options exist. Local restaurants will cook your catch at a nominal charge.

Etcetera: The state of Oaxaca is known for archeological sites, deep caverns, tall mountains (some over 3,000 meters tall) and lush jungle areas with tropical birdlife, and is well worth touring.

Sailfish

Marlin

Dolphin

Tuna

Wahoo

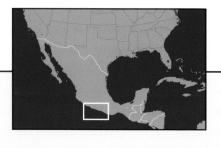

Ixtapa-Zihuatanejo

Guerrero, Mexico

Guerrero

Ixtapa/
Zihuatanejo

Acapulco

Pacific Ocean

Ixtapa-Zihuatanejo seems to have it all for anglers: superb offshore and inshore fishing; capable local captains with good equipment who speak English; a beautiful location nestled between calm blue Pacific waters and Sierra Madre peaks that rise to 7,500 feet; a relative lack of crowds; good accommodations and food; and comparably low prices.

Ixtapa (pronounced "*eeks-tah-pa*") and Zihuatanejo (pronounced "*zee-watt-a-nay-ho*") are located on the Pacific mainland coast of southern Mexico. Zihuatanejo is a relatively small old fishing village with cobblestone streets at the doorstep of small, but picturesque,

Zihuatanejo Bay. A more modern resort city, Ixtapa is smaller than Zihuatanejo and just four miles away; it was developed by the Mexican government as a tourist destination.

Sportfishing boats have been plying the waters off Ixtapa-Zihuatanejo since the late 1980s, but there are relatively few boats fishing here on a daily basis, and offshore fishing commands the most attention. In terms of billfish catch per effort, Ixtapa-Zihuatanejo compares very favorably with Cancun and Los Cabos, which are more developed, have many more charter boats, many times the tourist room capacity, and often rougher waters.

Sailfish are available all year off Ixtapa, although March and April are generally slower months. They average 75 to 90 pounds, but 100- to 120-pounders are not uncommon, with an occasional specimen over 120.

OPPOSITE
This is the offshore fishing thrill that many visitors to Ixtapa enjoy.

LEFT
Dolphin like this are a common catch off Ixtapa.

Sailfish

Tuna

Dolphin

Marlin

Roosterfish

Details

Location/getting there: Ixtapa and Zihuatanejo are southwest of Mexico City in the state of Guerrero and 156 miles north of Acapulco. The Zihuatanejo airport is served by several airlines, most notably AeroMexico, which has daily flights.

Info sources: To book a trip or obtain more information, contact Stan Lushinsky at Ixtapa Sportfishing Charters, 19 Depue Lane, Stroudsburg, PA 18360, USA; phone 570-688-9466; or visit www.ixtapasportfishing.com. For general information about this area, visit www.ixtapa-zihuatanejo.com and www.zihuatanejo.net. For general tourism info call Mexico Tourism at 800-446-3942; or visit www.visitmexico.com.

Prime times: December through early April is the prime tourist season, and also good for most species; boats get reserved early. Late April through July is off-peak and pre-rainy season, and a great time to visit; fishing for sailfish, tuna, dorado and roosterfish is usually good then. September has high winds and daily afternoon rain.

Gear needs: Offshore captains provide good, well-maintained, big-game gear, lures and terminal tackle. Bring your own light tackle, especially spinning and flycasting gear. For inshore fishing, bring your own spinning, baitcasting and fly outfits, as well as lures.

Guide/tackle availability: Inshore and offshore captains are available through Ixtapa Sportfishing Charters. The better captains all have good tackle and well-maintained boats. Many are personable and know what to do for proper inshore and offshore sportfishing success. A few tag and release billfish, although some sailfish that are deeply hooked are killed and taken ashore for food. Tackle is not available locally.

Accommodations/dining: There are luxury hotels with ocean frontage, plus less expensive bungalows and villas. Peak season is December 15 through the week after Easter. The Riviera Beach Resort in Ixtapa (call 800-710-9346 or visit www.rivieraixtapa.com) is highly recommended and caters to anglers.

There are many restaurants; Bucanero's and El Faro are top spots, and a great idea is to take your catch to a sunset dinner on the Las Gatas beach in Zihuatanejo Bay at Arnoldo's, which can be arranged by panga captains and is only accessible by boat. Any of the local restaurants will prepare your catch as dinner and/or sashimi/ceviche at a nominal charge.

Etcetera: Most people fish out of super pangas (about $190 and $250 respectively for eight- and ten-hour days), which are very seaworthy 25-foot-long vessels with a permanent canopy (best for two anglers, although you can do three); *La Hawaiiana* and *Dos Hermanos* are two of the best. Larger boats range from fairly basic 30-footers to more deluxe boats such as the *El Soltar*, a 35-foot Cabo; these cost more (about $650 per eight-hour day), but have a greater offshore range. Ixtapa has restaurants, boutiques, grocery stores and other shops and services.

BELOW LEFT
An angler poses with her sailfish, caught from a super panga, before releasing it.

BELOW RIGHT
A hooked Ixtapan sailfish displays its aerial ability.

December through February is best for consistent action, when some boats average six sails landed a day. Some sails are caught just a few miles from the beach, although the fishing is generally from five to 12 miles offshore. Captains here troll almost exclusively, using rigged bigeye scad (goggleyes) on flatlines, offshore trolling lures on flatlines, and lures and baits on Z-Wing diving planers.

Blue and black marlin action is best from February through May, with some fish caught from October through January and also in June. They average 250 to 350 pounds, with some in the 350- to 450-pound class and a few (about ten a year) over 500 pounds. A 1,000-pound black marlin was caught in 1993, and two more granders have been hooked and lost since. The marlin are

ABOVE
*This large
roosterfish took a
popper cast toward
a beach south of
Zihuatanejo.*

often caught further offshore than other species. The 1,000-fathom curve is about 17 to 19 miles offshore, depending on where you start from; boats sometimes fish out to 30 miles offshore.

Prime time for yellowfin tuna is usually December through May. They are commonly caught in the ten- to 50-pound class; 70- to 150-pounders are taken fairly often, and specimens over 150 are usually seen in March and April. Huge yellowfins (over 300 pounds) are also caught from time to time.

Dorado (dolphin) are usually available all year, with November through February and June through September being prime, although numbers have been down in recent years. They average ten to 30 pounds, but some 50- and 60-pounders are caught each winter.

Among inshore species, roosterfish are a top draw for good casters. These highly prized fish can be caught up to 70 pounds, and many are landed in the 20- to 40-pound class. The prime period for roosterfish is from June through September. Yellowtail jacks are also plentiful with the roosters, and they run to over 20 pounds.

Roosterfish and jacks inhabit the surfline, primarily along deserted beaches south of Zihuatanejo. The way these species are caught, and the conditions under which they are pursued and fought along the coast south of Zihuatanejo, make this fishery truly one of the world's most impressive. Basically, the only access is by boat, and a skilled boat-handling captain positions his panga about 85 yards from the beach, bucking the swells, while anglers cast with large popping plugs as close as possible to the beach, then reel rapidly, which draws big jacks from the surf wash out for explosive surface strikes and hard-fought battles.

In summer, the better surfline fishing usually occurs before noon, because afternoon winds make the inshore water too rough for getting the pangas close enough to the surf, and make for a tough ride back home. A favored spot is about 17 miles south of Zihuatanejo, along miles of deserted beach and surf from Rocas Poloci to Bahia de Tequepa.

Inshore waters also have numerous rock outcroppings to fish for a variety of snappers and groupers, plus barracuda and needlefish. Many anglers have gotten their line busted by nasty red snappers and some cuberas.

Langara, Q.C.I.

British Columbia, Canada

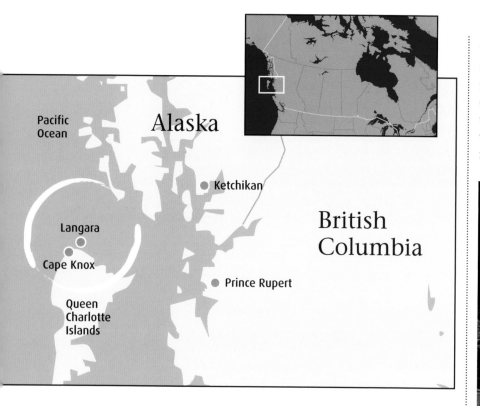

Pacific Ocean

Alaska

Ketchikan

Langara

Cape Knox

British Columbia

Queen Charlotte Islands

Prince Rupert

Chinook Salmon

Coho Salmon

Halibut

The salmon compete with others for their meals, including killer whales, seals and sea lions, and it is not unknown for a seal or sea lion to rob an angler of a prize catch that is played too close to the kelp. Nor is it unknown for a monster salmon to frustrate an angler by wrapping the line in thick kelp during its fight. That does not happen when boaters can maneuver their boat away

While some may dispute it, Langara is generally considered the finest place in the Pacific Northwest for catching large coastal salmon. At the head of the Queen Charlotte Islands—known to natives as Haida Gwaii—which sit out in the northern Pacific west of mainland B.C., the tip of Langara is just 50 miles from Alaska. Chinook salmon from 20 to over 70 pounds, plus hordes of coho and pink salmon, first meet land at Langara on their southerly migration from the northern Pacific. Here, especially off McPherson, Andrews and Coho Points, the salmon feed on massive bait balls of herring, which find the deep nearshore waters, swift tidal flows and the abundance of nutrients to their liking.

from the kelp once a fish is hooked, but such maneuvering is not possible when two or three salmon are on at once. Often the salmon come in waves, and multiple hook-ups in a boat, whether of coho or chinook, are a regular occurrence.

It is quite likely that Langara will maintain its position as the prime place for big chinooks because commercial fishing has been reduced in recent years, and the numbers and size of fish throughout B.C. have been improving lately. The 2001 season at Langara produced more monster chinooks—at least a dozen from 60 to 70 pounds—than any year in the previous decade.

What particularly distinguishes Langara, and the Queen Charlotte Islands in general, from other coastal salmon destinations is that there is a strong chinook

ABOVE
Huge chinooks, like this one about to be released, are the main draw at Langara.

LEFT
A 69-pound chinook caught off the head of Langara Island.

The view from the main lounge at Langara Fishing Lodge.

BELOW
Early morning off Langara and two fish are already on.

fishery from May through September, whereas others have a prime chinook period that lasts four to six weeks and a modest "shoulder" season the rest of the time. That means you stand a chance of catching a monster on any visit.

The predominant method of catching these salmon is by mooching with long, limber rods, using four- to eight-ounce weights to get cut herring baits down in the swiftly moving current. With frozen bait supplies low in recent years due to provider problems, packaged herring baits have been scarce, so at Langara, guides have taken to using Sabiki rigs (multi-hook bait rigs) to catch their own when they locate tight schools of herring on sonar. This results in larger, fresher and more effective baits.

It is possible to fish with lighter tackle here when the fish are very thick. Some people tie up to the nearshore kelp and cast outward with spoons and flies, although this is unlikely to produce the bigger specimens of either coho or chinook. Some lodges can arrange for a fly-in by helicopter to fish streams on other Queen Charlotte islands.

The waters around Langara also provide good bottom fishing for those willing to take time off from salmon when sea conditions are favorable. Halibut are the main deep interest, and some monsters exist within a mile of Langara Point Lighthouse, albeit in 250 to 300 feet of water. The Langara Fishing Lodge halibut record is 273 pounds. Plenty of rockfish and lingcod are also available.

The conditions under which this fishing takes place are as captivating as the fishing itself. Rugged rocky cliff shorelines, tall cedar trees and tidal fluctuation up to 13 feet provide exceptional scenery. Fishing is done close to much of it because the water is deep near shore; in some places 90 or more feet deep within casting distance of the rocks and 200 feet deep a few hundred yards away. Currents and tidal flow make it productive to fish near the shore—from 50 to 300 feet—for salmon. Often you are fishing under the watchful eyes of bald eagles, which populate every point. There is also a year-round manned lighthouse at Langara Point, and a native Haida village inland.

Details

Langara, Q.C.I., British Columbia, Canada

Location/getting there: Langara Island is the top-most area of the Queen Charlotte Islands. It can only be reached via a two-hour plane ride from Vancouver to Masset, and then a 25-minute floatplane or helicopter flight.

Info sources: Contact the Sport Fishing Institute of British Columbia, 200-1676 Duranleau St., Granville Island, Vancouver, B.C., Canada V6H 3S4; call 1-800-HELLO-BC for a free Sport Fishing Planning Guide; or visit www.sportfishing.bc.ca. For information about fishing at Langara Island, contact Langara Fishing Adventures, South Terminal Bldg., 201-4440 Cowley Crescent, Richmond, B.C., Canada V7B 1B8; call 800-668-7544; or visit www.langara.com.

Prime times: Big chinook salmon are available from May through September. Early in the season, the catch is primarily chinooks; later in the season it is primarily cohos. The period from early June through early July has the most hours of daylight, and therefore the longest fishing days.

Gear needs: Mooching and levelwind tackle are best, but you can use baitcasting, spinning and fly tackle if conditions are right for casting and you have ample line capacity and a very good drag. Regulars fish with 17- to 25-pound line and long rods.

Guide/tackle availability: Many anglers fish unguided out of tiller-steered, and occasionally console-steered, boats. Guides are available at some lodges (though not all) and are recommended if you are completely unfamiliar with boat handling, or the tackle and rigging methods. Guide boats at Langara Fishing Lodge are fiberglass 20-foot center console models. Lodges provide tackle, which consists of single-action mooching reels, ten-and-a-half foot mooching rods, weights, herring bait and leadered hooks.

Accommodations/dining: Langara Fishing Lodge, which is the leading operator, has excellent accommodations via a deluxe barge-hulled lodge. Private baths and showers are in every room, and there is a lounge, bar, sauna, and several hot tubs, plus a drying room for wet rain gear and clothes. Food is very good and is available throughout the day.

Etcetera: Lodges also provide rain gear, rubber boots and floatation jackets, and take excellent care of fish (if you keep them), which can be taken home or sent to a cannery for smoking and canning. They clean, flash-freeze, vacuum-pack and box fish. Many visitors to this area make annual trips. Binoculars and plenty of film are a must. Cost for an unguided four-day visit at Langara Fishing Lodge is $2,250, all inclusive from Vancouver except for fishing license and tips.

If you stay in Vancouver for a day or two, consider visiting the Vancouver Aquarium at Stanley Park, the Museum of Anthropology at the University of British Columbia and the Granville Island Sport Fishing Museum. For overnight travelers who have early-morning connections, the two-year-old Fairmont Vancouver Airport Hotel is easily accessible to all airlines and has a freezer to store transported fish. For dining, try Cin-Cin for Italian food; Yoshi's on Denman for great sushi; and the Pacific Culinary Institute on Granville Island.

There are several lodges, some fixed and some either mobile or anchored, around the island, so fishing is not done in a vacuum or in solitude. Sometimes the lodge boats get a little cluttered on certain points when the fishing is hot, or in the same protected areas when the wind is bad. Early-in-the-day efforts are often productive, as is fishing before and after high tide, yet new arrivals come at any time, often in waves, and fishing action sometimes runs in streaks. When this happens you can look around and see people hooked up in the majority of boats.

Being on the water when one of those blitzes occurs, and when two or three of the rods on your boat suddenly start bowing down into the water, is the best of fun.

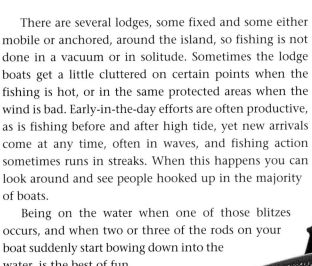

LEFT
Big coho are available later in the season.

Los Cabos

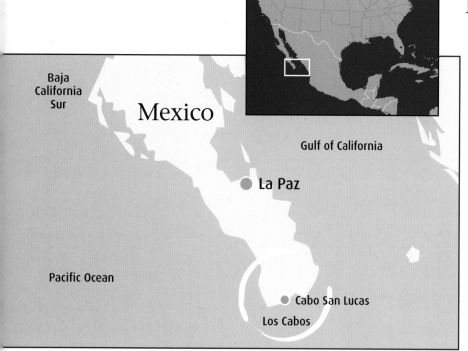

Baja California Sur
Mexico
Gulf of California
La Paz
Pacific Ocean
Cabo San Lucas
Los Cabos

Marlin

Sailfish

Dolphin

Tuna

Roosterfish

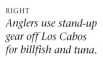

Baja California Sur, Mexico

Nearly every bit of tourism information that you can find mentions fishing in the Los Cabos area of Mexico's Baja Peninsula. The deep waters off the tip of this peninsula, where the bountiful Sea of Cortez merges with the Pacific, teems with baitfish and has strong currents, attracting a variety of inshore and offshore species and causing this area to be considered one of the best billfishing locations in the world. Striped marlin are the major attraction, available virtually year-round and sometimes in numbers that permit multiple hook-ups. Most range from 90 to 170 pounds.

The foremost billfishing area in this region is located in the deep waters off Cabo San Lucas, especially at Jaime and Goldengate Banks. Marlin feed here on extensive schools of mackerel. Striped marlin are receptive to trolled offshore lures and are especially fond of live bait. Live mackerel are the most commonly used bait, but small green jacks, or *caballito*, are very effective. Large yellowfin tuna also cruise here, and a few people each year catch 200- to 275-pounders.

Fishing for the larger blue and black marlin gets better in summer and peaks in the fall. This is when major tournaments are held. The larger marlin are hooked on trolled jigs and large live baits such as skipjack, small dorado and football-size yellowfin tuna. Though marlin are the main target, wahoo, dorado, roosterfish and school yellowfin fishing can also be very good inshore. Roosters to 50 pounds are caught.

Northeast of Cabo San Lucas, toward the Sea of Cortez, is the town of San José del Cabo. This former small fishing town has grown rapidly, with new hotels and golf courses springing up along the landscape. The fishing is also very good here, with anglers fishing the nearby Gordo Banks for billfish, and also enjoying some good reef fishing for grouper and pargo. The spring and summer months see

good numbers of wahoo on the Gordo Banks. Large cruisers from Cabo San Lucas will fish this area, along with numerous 20- to 25-foot local center-console pangas, which take the seas well.

There is also good fishing in the East Cape, which is the area northeast of Cabo San Lucas from Punta Frailles to the southern end of Cerralvo Island near La Paz. Several fishing resorts serve this area, with well-equipped fishing fleets. Striped, blue and black marlin are caught here during spring and summer months, and there are also swordfish, yellowfin tuna, dorado, wahoo and sailfish. Roosterfish, jack crevalle, and ladyfish are caught along the beaches and on the edges of rock formations, and there are various species to be found on nearby reefs.

Details

Los Cabos, Baja California Sur, Mexico

Location/getting there: Los Cabos is located at the tip of Mexico's Baja Peninsula, and is served by many airlines.

Info sources: For area information, contact the Los Cabos Tourism Board; call 866-567-2226; or visit www.visitcabo.com. For fishing information, contact PanAngling, 5348 W. Vermont, Suite 300A, Indianapolis, IN 46224; call 800-533-4353; or visit www.panangling.com.

Prime times: Striped marlin action is usually best from the beginning of the year into early spring.

Gear needs: Tackle is provided by charter boats; experienced anglers wanting light-tackle fishing should bring their own gear.

Guide/tackle availability: Numerous charter boats are available for offshore fishing; costs for a charter boat for a day offshore range from $400 to $500, but prices are less

for fishing from pangas and super pangas. Surf fishing guides are also available.

Accommodations/dining: There is a broad array of lodging and dining options.

Etcetera: Although the fishing is good in Los Cabos, there are a lot of boats out and it is not as unknown or undeveloped a fishery as it was as recently as the mid-1980s. Well developed now as a resort area, Los Cabos offers many other attractions as well.

Mazatlán

Sinaloa, Mexico

Gulf of California

Sinaloa

Culiacán

La Paz

Mazatlán

Cabo San Lucas

Pacific Ocean

Sailfish

Marlin

Dolphin

Tuna

Snook

Just below the Tropic of Cancer and at the southern end of the Sea of Cortez where it meets the Pacific, Mazatlán has scores of well-equipped charter boats, and although some light-tackle inshore fishing is possible, the focus is primarily offshore, where deep canyons begin about 30 miles from shore. Three species of marlin, plus sailfish, swordfish, mako shark, yellowfin tuna and dolphin (dorado), are on the agenda, although not all the time and not always together.

Striped marlin are the primary marlin species, and are sometimes available in the winter, with February through April being the optimum time. April is often the best month. Striped marlin average 110 to 120 pounds, and the local record here is 246.

Although Mazatlán captains troll to locate finning marlin, they primarily catch them by using live bait that is either slow-trolled once a fish is located on the surface, or cast to them. In the absence of live bait, which occurs

RIGHT
Angler displays two large snook at the Mazatlán dock.

ABOVE
*Sportfishing boats
leave the Mazatlán
harbor.*

here occasionally in winter due to unseasonably cool water, they will troll with whole dead bait, which is often not as effective.

Blue and black marlin are available from May through November when the water is warmer, and although they are seldom really large here, there are often lots of fish from 200 to 250 pounds. Sailfish are an especially popular catch, and are found from May through December, although the warmer summer months are best. There are lots of dorado around from July through October. Swordfish are also caught occasionally, when two fins are spotted poking through the surface. March through June is the season; the fish are small, averaging 110 to 120 pounds, but some larger ones are occasionally encountered.

Yellowfin tuna are caught throughout the year. Recent years have produced many tuna, from fish in the 15- to 20-pound range to those in the 150-pound class. Also available all year are mako shark, which are usually seen basking on the surface and intercepted with trolled dead bait. Most are in the 100-pound range.

An inshore fishing lodge, about an hour's drive north of Mazatlán, was recently opened by Anglers Inn; it hosts a small number of anglers for light-tackle saltwater action. Roosterfish and snook will be the main targets, and dorado, grouper, snapper, jacks and corvina will also be available. Peak fishing should be in May and June.

Details

Mazatlán, Sinaloa, Mexico

Location/getting there: Mazatlán is on Mexico's northern Pacific Coast; a major tourist destination, it is serviced by numerous airlines.

Info sources: Contact Anglers Inn, PMB 358, 2626 N. Mesa, El Paso, TX 79902; call their headquarters office in Mazatlán at 011-52-69-807474 or 800-468-2347; or visit www.anglersinn.com.

Prime times: This varies by species. Although many Mazatlán vacationers try a day of fishing in the winter, this can often be more of a boat ride than heavy action; consider later in the spring when the water is warmer.

Gear needs: Tackle is provided by charter boats, which use 80-pound outfits when trolling and 30 when pitching live bait. This is partly because most customers have little or no offshore fishing experience. If you prefer lighter gear, bring your own.

Guide/tackle availability: Numerous charter boats with experienced captains exist here, especially at the El Cid Marina where the Aries fleet is berthed.

Accommodations/dining: There is a wide range of lodging and dining options in Mazatlán.

Etcetera: A charter boat costs about $400 plus tips; plan to bring your own food and beverages. Some captains speak English, and some mates understand a little English. They will release fish if you want, and more do now than ever before, but you have to tell the captain upfront and make sure they follow this. Chances are good you will see a dead billfish or shark at the dock. You can have your dolphin or tuna catch cooked at local restaurants.

Mississippi Delta

Louisiana, United States

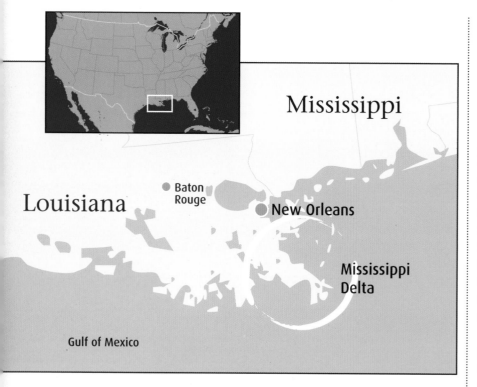

Mississippi

Louisiana

Baton Rouge

New Orleans

Mississippi Delta

Gulf of Mexico

The Mississippi Delta is a huge, extraordinary place and North America's greatest delta, befitting its namesake river, which flows from the third largest drainage basin in the world. The floodplain of the lower Mississippi covers an area from 40 to 70 miles wide, where rich sediments, freshwater current and saltwater tidal flows combine to constantly change the landscape and add to the rich aquatic resources. New Orleans is at the head of this region, and the triangular area from Venice to Lafitte to Grand Isle provides some of the best fishing in the United States.

RIGHT
Navigating through the vast Mississippi Delta marsh.

OPPOSITE
A big redfish caught from the marsh near Hackberry Bay.

Since the commercial industry was banned from netting seatrout and redfish, the populations of these fish have boomed, and the fishing lately has been superb. Excellent

action for redfish and seatrout, as well as black drum and flounder, draws anglers not only from the nearby region, but from the likes of Dallas, Little Rock, Memphis, Tallahassee and Birmingham—all seven to ten hours-drive time away. It is also increasingly drawing day-fishing tourists from New Orleans.

Looking at this region on nearly any map does not give you a full sense of its magnitude. In addition to the large expanse of open, shallow saltwater areas here that are called lakes and bays, there is a phenomenal expanse of marsh that is constantly changing and which gets somewhat lightly explored because of its size, the fact that it is a good run from major boat-access areas, and because it is so shallow that many boaters cannot really traverse it. The marshes are actually islands, and there are thousands here, intertwined with a patchwork of canals, some no wider than a boat. The interior portions have many small open areas that the locals call ponds.

These marshes are the lifeblood of the region, providing critical habitat for crabs and juvenile redfish, and they are also a great place to fish if you are a capable caster. Loads of redfish call the marshes home for much of the year—until it gets cool back in the shallows—and they can be stalked here, often sight-fished and hooked on jigs, topwater plugs, weedless spoons and flies.

Redfish and seatrout (which are locally called speckled trout or specks) are around all season cruising for shrimp, small crabs and minnows, but the main period for redfish in the marshes is from late summer through November.

Bigger reds are caught in the deeper water of passes and lake edges, with April into June best for them. Spring is also the time for big seatrout, which like the warming water in the bays and along the beaches, and the presence of abundant shrimp. September through November sees huge schools of seatrout available in bays, and anglers can catch these in great numbers, often finding them by following schools of working gulls. Black drum are also abundant in the fall in the bays. Weather at these periods is also favorable for anglers (it gets damp-cold in winter and humid-hot in summer). Seatrout spawn in the summer near oyster reefs and islands, and they are so abundant that they are often caught two at a time.

There is some fine black bass fishing in this region, too, although this takes place in the areas with brackish water or a primarily freshwater influence. There is a possibility that bass fishing will become very good in the Lafitte area in the future, once the Davis Pond Project, which will divert some of the freshwater flow of the

Mississippi into the westerly Delta region, has its impact.

Offshore, the various flow levels of the big river affect the presence of baitfish and pelagic gamefish like yellowfin tuna, blue marlin and wahoo. Low river levels bring blue water close to shore, while high levels push it up to 60 miles out, with most departures for these grounds originating from Venice, Empire or Grand Isle. A lot of fishing occurs around thousands of oil rigs as well. The rigs hold cobia, king mackerel, amberjack, barracuda and other species, plus tuna, wahoo, and, on occasion, marlin.

Tarpon are a main attraction out of ports like Venice and Grand Isle, where anglers mainly find them 40 to 100 feet deep, and landing them entails lots of deep-water muscling. They occasionally feed on the surface, where casting is possible, but you can seldom count on this, which is why this is not a fly fishing destination. These fish arrive here in May, and are numerous until September. Many are in the 100-pound range and fish from 150 to 200 pounds have been caught here.

Details

Location/getting there: The Mississippi Delta is east, south, and west of New Orleans. From the Big Easy it takes two hours to drive to Grand Isle, about 90 minutes to Venice, and about 30 minutes to the shrimp, crab and oyster fishing community of Lafitte, which is a hotbed for redfish and seatrout angling.

Info sources: For information about fishing in the Lafitte area, contact Raymond or Belinda Griffin at Griffin Fishing Charters, 800-741-1340; or visit www.griffinfishing.com. For information about the Venice area, contact Plaquemines Parish Tourism, P.O. Box 937, Belle Chasse, LA 70037; call 888-745-0642; or visit www.plaque-minesparish.com. For information about the Grand Isle area, contact Grand Isle Tourist Commission, P.O. Box 817, Grand Isle, LA 70358; call 504-787-2997; or visit www.sportsmans_paradise.com/grandisle.html.

Prime times: Spring is best for big redfish and seatrout, and fall for lots of fish and comfortable weather; summer is prime for tarpon and offshore.

Gear needs: Assorted gear is used depending on species and method. Anglers use topwater plugs, plastic-bodied jigs and weedless spoons for big redfish, and live shrimp or minnows, and sometimes surface lures and flies, for big seatrout.

Guide/tackle availability: Guides and charter boats can be booked at marinas and fish camps throughout the area. Most supply the necessary tackle, including bait, although fly anglers should bring their own gear.

Accommodations/dining: There are lots of housing and dining options throughout the Delta.

Etcetera: Fish on a weekday during prime periods to avoid crowds, and be out early and late on clear days for superb sunrises and sunsets. Bring binoculars for the prodigious amount of bird life here. Use a fishing guide for best results, although a good self-guided angler can do well. Wind direction has a big impact on where to fish, and changing tides are also a strong influence; moving water is especially important inshore. Costs for an inshore guide range from $250 to $450 for one to three anglers per day, and include bait, tackle and fish cleaning.

Redfish

Seatrout

Cobia

King Mackerel

Tarpon

Montauk Point

New York, United States

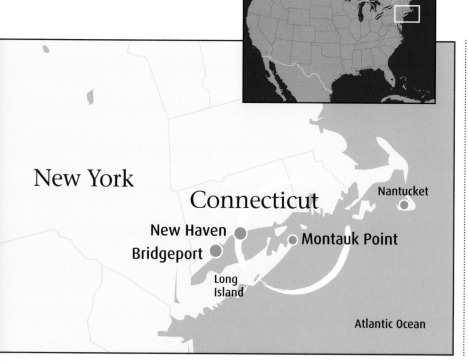

New York

Connecticut

Nantucket

New Haven
Bridgeport

Montauk Point

Long
Island

Atlantic Ocean

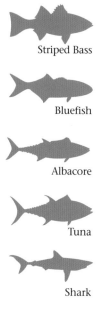

Striped Bass

Bluefish

Albacore

Tuna

Shark

The sign outside Montauk Harbor says "Fishing Capitol of the World," a boast that only a few other saltwater fishing destinations in North America can dispute. There are times in the fall at Montauk that this claim can be made in the biggest and boldest letters.

To the uninitiated it is hard to imagine that there could be fishing within 100 miles of New York City that ranks with exotic and far-away waters. But the fishing, both inshore and offshore, is truly exceptional. There is hardly a time in the season when an angler cannot be satisfied here with some manner of angling, from surf casting to rip jigging to tuna chunking to billfish trolling.

Jutting into the Atlantic at the eastern tip of New York's heavily populated Long Island, Montauk and its environs are like a magnet for migrating gamefish, which

RIGHT
Warm weather surf fishing on Montauk's south shore.

LEFT
*Thirty-five pounds
of striped bass,
caught by trolling a
tube in the rips.*

find the many rips, reefs and banks in the area conducive to foraging. The availability of some species is as dependent on currents and water temperatures as much as on fish stocks and bait. Area anglers are easily able to head offshore to the deep-water canyons, or to north or south attractions, as well as find productive fishing inshore and in close proximity to the Point, which, incidentally, was the site of the first lighthouse ever built in the United States.

Montauk has striped bass, bluefish and bottom fishing throughout the season from spring through fall. Resident stripers, which exist in Long Island Sound and move throughout the area following bait, are available all summer and are joined in the fall by migratory stripers, which come from up north, stay in the area for a while from September into November and then head south.

In recent years there has been a plenitude of bass but a dearth of specimens over 40 pounds, which were a regular fall highlight in years past. There are still a lot of fish to catch in the 25- to 35-pound class, however, with an emphasis on fishing at night around the full moon period. Surf casters and boaters all score well here, the latter trolling, jigging, casting and fishing with live bunkers (menhaden).

In 1976, a 76-pound striper was taken off the heavily fished Shagwong Reef, located within minutes of the Montauk Marine Basin. Shagwong is still a striper hotspot, but so are Pollock Reef, Jones Reef and a number

of other shoals that confuse bait when the tide is running. The rocky rips here concentrate baitfish, the surface is confused and sometimes turbulent, and both resident and migratory fish find easy foraging. Some people anchor and use live or dead bait, and some drift and cast flies or lures, but most, especially the charter boats, troll, carefully working through and around the perimeter of the rips. Everyone catches fish when they are plentiful, which makes casting more practical in the fall, but it is mostly the trollers who take the larger specimens.

Bluefish are usually available here in good numbers until the middle of October, and are another prominent catch. Although often found in schools of similar-sized individuals, occasionally the fish are mixed, with some 12- to 15-pounders showing up with fish half that size. From the Point to Block Island is especially notable, and many rips and ledges regularly produce. Jigging and trolling are popular, and cut bait is also widely used. Some

casting is done when bluefish are working a school on the surface, or when they roam the shallows and become the target of surf pluggers.

Speaking of casting, false albacore are a favorite with flycasters each fall, generally in September and October, when they are plundering schools of menhaden near shore and are observed by schools of diving birds. On the other side of the coin, sea bass fishing, which is a deep weight-and-bait proposition, is generally good through the season, with recent years yielding above-average-size fish. In-the-know anglers target this delicious species, as well as other bottomfish. Also doing very well here lately has been summer flounder, locally called fluke. Three- to seven-pounders have been common.

Offshore from Montauk, in blue water, there is also fishing for bluefin tuna, yellowfin tuna and longfin albacore. These fish are all reachable on day trips, although occasionally there is some tuna fishing close to

Details

Montauk Point, New York, United States

Location/getting there: Montauk Point is the easternmost part of Long Island in New York State. The nearest commercial airport is at Islip.

Info sources: For area information, including accommodations, dining, parks, access, marinas, Montauk Lighthouse, etc., visit www.onmontauk.com. For surf fishing from April through November contact guide Tom Melton, Surf Fishing Made Easy, 631-878-8146; tackle is provided, except waders, and guiding costs $225 per six-hour session. For inshore and offshore charters, contact Capt. Fritz Hubner, *The Mistress Too*, 516-668-2938,

and the *Rainbow Runner*, 631-277-4426. The boat takes up to six anglers; rates vary by time and type of fishing; an eight-hour inshore day costs about $750.

Prime times: Mid-September through mid-November is usually prime for both bass and bluefish; summer is best for offshore.

Gear needs: Varies widely with species and angling methods.

Guide/tackle availability: Guides and charter boats are widely available; tackle is provided on boats, and gear is available in

local shops and marinas.

Accommodations/dining: Lodging and dining options are ample in Montauk.

Etcetera: Surf anglers with four-wheel-drive vehicles can obtain permits to gain vehicular access to portions of the beach at Montauk. If it is too rough for boat fishing and the surf does not appeal to you, try fishing for largemouth bass at Montauk's Fort Pond. A visit to the Montauk Point Lighthouse is also worthwhile.

shore where even smaller boats can get to them. Usually, the bluefin fishery is from mid-September through mid-October. However, yellowfins are caught from early July to mid-September, and sometimes later.

Montauk is also known for shark fishing, having produced one of the biggest great white sharks of all time, a 3,427-pounder in 1989, and a former all-tackle world record mako, a 1,080-pounder in 1979. The most abundant species is blue shark, but the main targets are makos and threshers. Some great whites and

hammerheads are caught, and occasionally a tiger shark. Shark fishing occurs within 15 miles of Montauk Point from mid-June into October.

Other species in the offshore mix include bigeye tuna, bonito, dolphin, swordfish and marlin. A number of blue marlin in the 800- to 1,000-pound range have been caught, plus a 1,174-pounder. These monsters have come from waters in the 65 to 80 fathom curve, which is well offshore but still inside of the deep shelf that canyon tuna anglers work.

BELOW
A school bluefin tuna taken offshore.

Morehead City/ Cape Lookout

North Carolina, United States

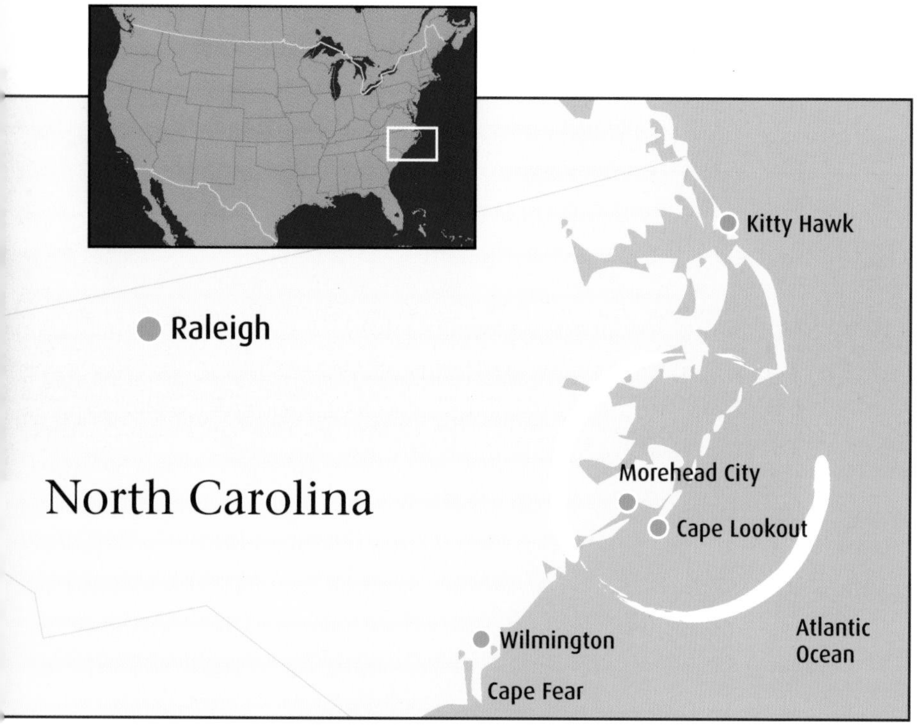
Kitty Hawk
Raleigh
North Carolina
Morehead City
Cape Lookout
Wilmington
Atlantic Ocean
Cape Fear

Great beaches and the Cape Lookout National Seashore draw many visitors to Carteret County in North Carolina. But the existence of Beaufort and Bogue Inlets, the protruding curve of Cape Lookout and its nearby banks, the relative proximity to the warm Gulf Stream and the usually prodigious presence of baitfish, all combine to create sportfishing opportunity galore.

Perhaps one of the most exciting things that happens locally is the fall false albacore blitz. False albacore appear in numbers in this area from October through December, with November usually prime. The first ones to appear range from six to ten pounds, but by mid-fall, 12- to 15-

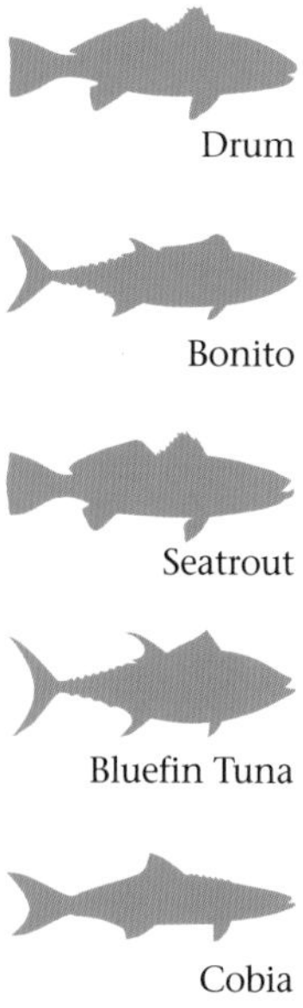
Drum
Bonito
Seatrout
Bluefin Tuna
Cobia

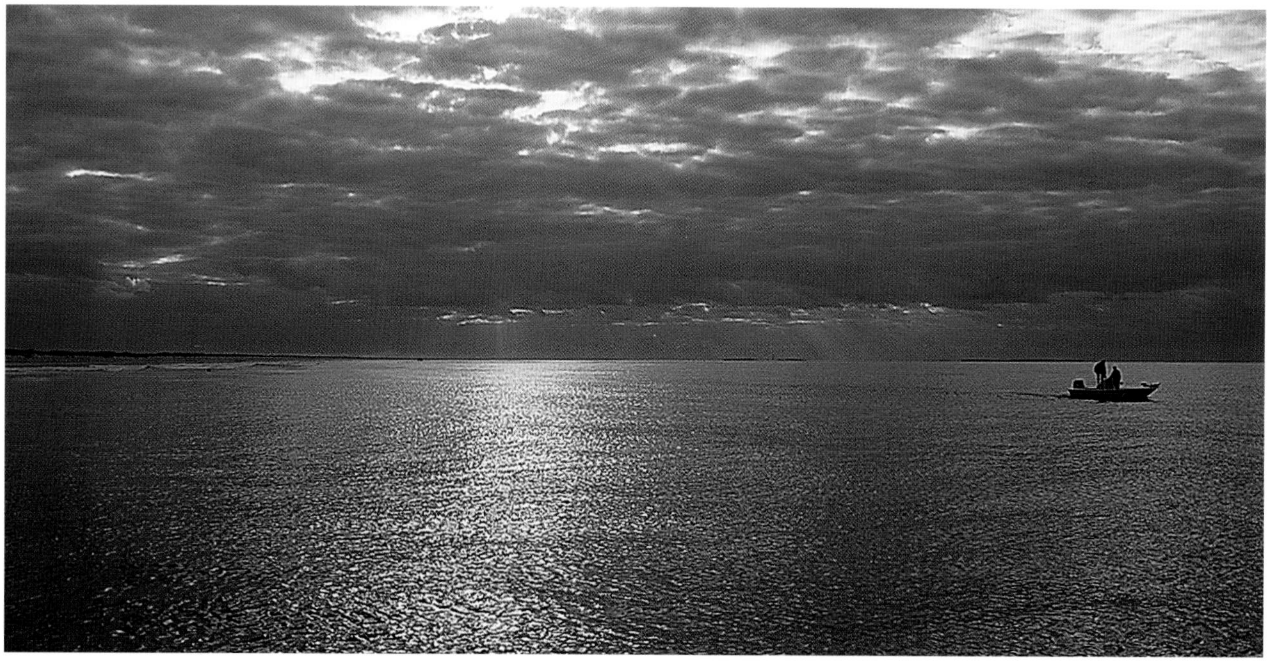

pounders are common, with some to 18 pounds likely later. By the end of October, these fish draw people from all over, especially fly anglers, because Beaufort Inlet has the reputation of being the best place on the east coast for false albacore fly fishing, and because the air temperature and sea conditions are usually quite favorable as well.

False albacore primarily feed on small pelagic fish near the surface. The idea is to look for a surface feeding disturbance, or a flock of birds in the distance, rush over within casting range without cruising over the top of the school, then cast into the fray and hook a fish. It is exciting at the peak of this activity, and beats endless blind casting, which seldom pays off.

Rivaling false albacore, and increasing annually in popularity, is red drum, also known as channel bass or redfish. Conditions permitting, sight-fishing for drum in the marshes and occasionally along the beaches is very good in October and November, which makes this especially attractive to casters using jigs, plugs and especially flies. In late October, the water becomes gin clear, even in the marshes, and you can pole a shallow-draft boat and cast to fish. Red drum are sometimes visible, especially in the winter.

Details

Morehead City / Cape Lookout, North Carolina

Location/getting there: Located on the central Carolina coast, Morehead City is reached by driving from Interstate 95 via state routes 64, 17 and 70. The Cape Lookout National Seashore, which is open year-round, is surrounded by water and can only be visited via private or commercial boat. Ferries depart from several communities to transport vehicles and people over, and anglers with beach buggies and campers make the trip to camp on the islands and fish for multiple days or the week in the surf.

Info sources: For information about the region, contact the Carteret County Tourism Development Bureau, P.O. Box 1406, Morehead City, NC 28557; call 800-786-6962; or visit www.sunnync.com. For the Cape Lookout National Seashore, contact 252-728-2250; or visit www.nps.gov/calo/.

Prime times: Fall is prime for drum, false albacore and seatrout; summer is best for offshore species; and summer through early fall for king mackerel.

Gear needs: Tackle needs vary widely depending on species and fishing methods. If you are trying albacore, you will need

spinning tackle with 12- to 15-pound line and lead spoons, and/or ten-weight fly tackle incorporating a reel with good drag, 200 yards of 20- to 30-pound backing and a weight-forward intermediate line (sometimes a 300- to 400-grain sink tip line or full-sink line is necessary for getting really deep).

Guide/tackle availability: There are numerous guide and charter boat services in the area. For an overview of marinas, guides, charter boats and piers, visit the fishing section of www.sunnync.com. Capt. Joe Shute, who is widely known and specializes in light-tackle and fly fishing charters, has a bait and tackle shop near the Atlantic Beach Causeway, as well as the Cape Lookout Fly Shop next door. Contact: Capt. Joe Shute's Bait and Tackle, 800-868-0941; also visit www.captjoes.com.

Accommodations/dining: There are many accommodation options. Recommended is the full-service Sheraton Oceanfront in Atlantic Beach (800-624-8875), which also provides free access for its guests to its own fishing pier. Most anglers stay in Morehead City or Atlantic Beach because of its convenience to marinas and tackle shops. Food options are

extensive; recommended are the Beaufort Grocery Company in Beaufort, and Amos Mosquito's Swampside Café in Morehead City.

Etcetera: As a general guideline, expect a half-day of inshore fishing to run from $250 to $275, and a full day to be from $450 to $475; an offshore charter is from $850 to $1,100, with a bluefin tuna charter costing $1,000 to $1,100 per day. Two attractions to consider are the North Carolina Maritime Museum in Beaufort, contact 252-728-7317 or visit www.ah.dcr.state.nc.us/sections/maritime; and the North Carolina Aquarium at Pine Knoll Shores; contact 252-247-4003; or visit web site address. History buffs take note that Blackbeard's house in Beaufort still stands; it dates back to the early 1700s.
Not to be overlooked is the Cape Lookout National Seashore, a 56-mile-long section of the Outer Banks running from Ocracoke Inlet on the northeast to Beaufort Inlet on the southeast. The seashore is comprised of three undeveloped barrier islands: North Core Banks, South Core Banks and Shackleford Banks, the latter of which has over 100 wild-roaming horses. The Cape Lookout Lighthouse, built in 1859, is a main attraction as well.

ABOVE
A brilliant sunset blankets the offshore fleet in Morehead City.

OPPPSITE
Early-morning anglers look for surface-feeding albacore near Shackleford Banks.

Fishing with bait in the marshes and along the beaches is good all summer and fall, and in the inlet and along the surf it often yields fish over 15 pounds, and sometimes up to and over 50 pounds. Big red drum are often caught on the ocean-facing beaches of the Core Banks on the National Seashore. The red drum population has been getting better here in recent years due to new regulations, particularly those affecting commercial fishermen. Recent years have yielded a good number of 60- and 70-pounders.

Seatrout angling in the fall is also usually excellent, especially off the rock jetties at Cape Lookout National Seashore, and along the beaches and jetty at Fort Macon State Park. Seatrout are available all year here. The largest, from five to ten pounds, are usually caught in winter, often on plugs.

King mackerel are another favorite quarry, and may be caught from Beaufort Inlet out to 15 to 20 miles offshore. While sizes vary, king mackerel from 20 to over 40 pounds are locally available, with some coming in even heftier.

In 2001, a 45-pounder was caught off the ship wall by the turning basin inside Beaufort Inlet. Live bait trolling is preferred by many anglers, although some troll with lures.

Cobia come inside the inlet to spawn in May and June, and specimens ranging from 40 to 80 pounds are caught annually in the vicinity of Shackleford Banks. Recent years have been good for cobia, with a few landed in the 80- to 90-pound class, although most average 40 to 50 pounds. Dead and live menhaden are favored baits.

Offshore there is a lot of billfishing through the summer months. White and blue marlin, sailfish, dolphin and wahoo are the attraction in the Gulf Stream, which is 40 to 45 miles out, although it occasionally sweeps closer to land. Dolphin are sometimes caught only a few miles from the beach; 25- to 30-pounders are possible.

An exciting winter bluefin tuna fishery only developed a few years ago, and has been somewhat inconsistent, but it does happen to some degree each December and January. Numerous fish can be available in the 400- to 600-plus-pound range, and they are caught with standup

tackle, usually by trolling and often fairly shallow. Most of this activity occurs within a few miles of the beach, sometimes within 400 or 500 yards, and occasionally in as little as 25 feet of water.

In addition to all of this, there are very big striped bass here during the winter just off the shoals, plus lots of bluefish, as well as sizable flounder.

Shore-based anglers have five or six piers to visit, including three—Sportsmans, Oceanana and Triple S— near Morehead City in Atlantic Beach. There is public beach access in many locations, with Fort Macon State Park, whose 1.5 million annual visitors make it the most popular state park in North Carolina, being the most favored. It fronts on Beaufort Inlet, the Atlantic Ocean and Bogue Sound. The 345-acre park has a popularly visited Civil War fort and museum, an interpretive nature trail and a fishable rock jetty.

Outer Banks

North Carolina, United States

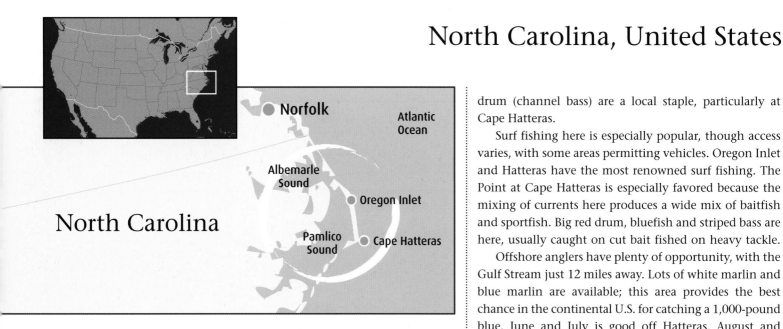

Norfolk

Atlantic Ocean

Albemarle Sound

North Carolina

Oregon Inlet

Pamlico Sound

Cape Hatteras

The Outer Banks is a 140-mile-long narrow strip of barrier islands in eastern North Carolina with excellent fishing in offshore, coastal, surf and bay environs. About half of this is included in Cape Hatteras National Seashore.

The barrier islands here are especially noted for bluefish and drum. Most of North America's biggest blues have come from coastal North Carolina. November through January is best for giant specimens, which are seldom caught in the surf, although smaller bluefish are available all season long to surf anglers and inshore boaters. Red

drum (channel bass) are a local staple, particularly at Cape Hatteras.

Surf fishing here is especially popular, though access varies, with some areas permitting vehicles. Oregon Inlet and Hatteras have the most renowned surf fishing. The Point at Cape Hatteras is especially favored because the mixing of currents here produces a wide mix of baitfish and sportfish. Big red drum, bluefish and striped bass are here, usually caught on cut bait fished on heavy tackle.

Offshore anglers have plenty of opportunity, with the Gulf Stream just 12 miles away. Lots of white marlin and blue marlin are available; this area provides the best chance in the continental U.S. for catching a 1,000-pound blue. June and July is good off Hatteras, August and September off Oregon Inlet. Whites are caught all summer.

The edge of the Gulf Stream also produces yellowfin,

blackfin and bluefin tuna, plus dolphin and wahoo. Yellowfins, dolphin and wahoo may be caught beginning in April. The best bluefin action occurs in winter, when giants make an extraordinary appearance that draws anglers from afar.

Bluefish

Red Drum

Marlin

Tuna

King Mackerel

Details

Outer Banks, North Carolina, United States

Location/getting there: The Outer Banks are located along the northeastern North Carolina coast. The northern area is reached via road, while the southern area is reached by road and ferry.

Info sources: For comprehensive area information, contact The Outer Banks Visitors Bureau, 704 S. Hwy 64/264, Manteo, NC 27954; call 800-446-6262; or visit www.outer_banks.com. Also visit

www.hatteras_nc.com and www.outerbanks.com. For information about Cape Hatteras National Seashore, call 252-473-2111; or visit www.nps.gov/caha.

Prime times: See main text.

Gear needs: Varies depending on species and methods.

Guide/tackle availability: Charter fleets exist at Manteo Island (north of Oregon Inlet) and at Hatteras. Tackle is available locally.

Accommodations/dining: Lodging and dining options are both numerous and varied.

Etcetera: Check out the Cape Hatteras Lighthouse, which is the tallest on the east coast, and the North Carolina Aquarium on Roanoke Island.

Rivers Inlet

British Columbia, Canada

LEFT
A typical summer sunrise over fjord-like Rivers Inlet.

Chinook Salmon

Coho Salmon

Halibut

Forty miles long and seven miles wide at its entrance, Rivers Inlet is situated at the southeast corner of Queen Charlotte Sound, just north of Cape Caution. It is part of the Inside Passage, a 1,600-kilometer waterway extending along the Pacific Northwest from Seattle to Skagway.

A spectacular part of the British Columbia mainland coast, Rivers Inlet is known for its scenery—the opportunity to sight bald eagles, humpback and killer whales, sea lions, and the occasional grizzly bear—and for salmon fishing. Migrating salmon land right at the doorstep of Rivers Inlet. Some are passing through, while others are returning to spawn in one of the four major rivers that empty into this fjord-like inlet.

Queen Charlotte Sound

Calvert Island

Rivers Inlet

Port Hardy

British Columbia

Vancouver Island

Pacific Ocean

ABOVE
*Seventeen pounds
of Rivers Inlet
coho salmon.*

Details

Rivers Inlet, British Columbia, Canada

Location/getting there: Inaccessible by road, Rivers Inlet is about 300 miles northwest of Vancouver, and is reached by floatplane or by private boats, which are usually trailered to Port Hardy on Vancouver Island and launched from there, with a two- to three-hour boat ride from that point.

Info sources: For area fishing information, contact Rivers Inlet Sportsman's Club at 800-663-2644; or visit www.riversinletsportsmans-club.com. For general information, contact the Sport Fishing Institute of British Columbia, 200-1676 Duranleau St., Granville Island, Vancouver, B.C., Canada V6H 3S4; call 1-800-HELLO-BC for a free Sport Fishing Planning Guide; or visit www.sportfishing.bc.ca.

Prime times: Fishing is steady throughout the season, with chinooks most prominent early, and cohos most prominent later.

Gear needs: Mooching and levelwind tackle are best for larger fish, but you can use baitcasting, spinning and fly tackle if conditions are right for casting and you have ample line capacity and a good drag.

Guide/tackle availability: Most anglers fish unguided, although there are limited guided-fishing options. Anglers receive good pre-fishing instruction, but it helps if you have handled boats and trolled/mooched before. Mooching/downrigging tackle is supplied, but bring your own casting gear.

Accommodations/dining: There are a number of lodges in the area, many of them like floating motels, with good accommodations and excellent food.

Etcetera: Lodges provide rain gear, rubber boots, and floatation jackets, and take excellent care of fish (if you keep them), which can be taken home or sent to a cannery for smoking and canning. They clean, flash-freeze, vacuum-pack and box fish. Binoculars and plenty of film are a must. Costs are about $1,800 and $2,000 respectively for four- and five-day trips, all-inclusive except licenses and tips from Vancouver.

King, or chinook, salmon are the main attraction. An 82½-pound chinook caught in 1951 at Rivers Inlet stood as the all-tackle world record for three decades until surpassed by an Alaskan fish, and that was eclipsed locally by an 84-pound fish caught at Rivers Inlet in 1986. Two more 80-pounders were reported in 1987.

While the monsters have not occurred here lately, fish in the 30- to 40-pound class are often caught, and some in the 50- to 60-pound class. Fishing here has been aided by a hatchery at the head of Rivers Inlet that was started in 1985 and is operated by the lodges in the area. Action starts in mid-June at Rivers Inlet, when there is an early run of big kings, and this species is available from the beginning of the season through the end of August.

Coho salmon get larger as the season progresses, with the biggest fish, locally called "northern coho," being available in late August and September. These fish are active, leaping, tenacious fighters. Pink and chum salmon show up in mid- to late July. When anglers tire of salmon, they can go bottom fishing for halibut, which are common to 50 pounds, plus rockfish and lingcod.

One of the best locations for all salmon species at Rivers Inlet, especially for large chinook, is a spot known locally as "The Wall," west of Goose Bay along the southern shore. Here, the water drops sharply by a cliff into 90 feet, and is 180 feet deep a short distance offshore, then drops to 400 feet 100 yards offshore. Fish congregate in this spot, allowing for mooching with cut herring as bait.

Early morning and late in the afternoon are preferred times for catching fish here, and also beautiful times to be on the water. Many a large salmon is hooked before the sun pokes over the mountains and filters through the fog that wafts up the valleys. It is cool then without the sun, but salmon that have come into the inlet during the night are more agreeable before there is a lot of boat traffic and before the brighter light sends them deeper.

BELOW
A big king salmon draws smiles all around.

Texas Gulf

Texas, United States

Redfish

Seatrout

Tarpon

Snook

There are literally hundreds of miles of clear shallow water, and loads of opportunity for wade fishing and shallow-draft boat fishing, with frequent sight-casting. Port O'Connor, Rockport, Aransas Pass, Corpus Christi, Port Mansfield and Port Isabel are among the prime jump-off spots for this area, which encompasses a lot of territory.

Wade fishing is especially good and popular in the Port O'Connor region, where there is a huge area of relatively uncrowded clear shallow water to fish, as well as nearby Matagorda Island. The 38-mile island and state park is undeveloped and reached only by boat. Pristine beaches here offer surf and small-boat opportunities for trout, redfish, ladyfish and Spanish mackerel, especially in summer.

Down the coast, Rockport is easily accessed and very popular with anglers, especially with out-of-area visitors. Summer and fall, which generally have good weather, provide prime fishing in the various bay shallows, although there is plenty of action here all season if salinity levels are good.

Further south, Corpus Christi is at the upper end of Laguna Madre, part of the Intracoastal Waterway between the mainland and barrier islands that extends for 150 miles to Port Isabel and almost to the Mexican border. Most of this is remote, though it is accessible from various

The middle and lower Texas Gulf Coast between Port O'Connor and Port Isabel has some of the finest inshore saltwater fishing in North America. The main attraction is shallow-water action for redfish and speckled trout (seatrout), although there are other species to be had.

RIGHT
Exploring the weedy shallows for redfish near Rockport.

Details

Location/getting there: The lower and middle Texas Gulf coast is in south Texas, both south and north-northeast of Corpus Christi. Road access is good in some parts and poor in others, and certain areas can only be reached by boat.

Info sources:
http://www.travelmanitoba.com/, http://www.anglersinn.com/ For general information, contact South Padre Island Convention & Visitiors Bureau on 800-657-2373 or visit www.sopadre.com. To contact The National Park Service; call 361-949-8068; or visit www.nps.gov/pais.

Prime times: See main text.

Gear needs: Varies with species and methods, although baitcasting, spinning and flycasting tackle are used for redfish and trout. Jigs with soft plastic bodies, soft jerkbaits, gold spoons, topwater plugs, streamer flies and fly-rod poppers are prime lures, while live shrimp is a mainstay.

Guide/tackle availability: Inshore guides are available throughout the area; some specialize in fly fishing. Charter boats and party (head) boats exist in larger ports. Tackle is available in local shops.

Accommodations/dining: Lodging and dining options vary widely throughout the area.

Etcetera: In the Corpus Christi area, make a visit to the Texas State Aquarium, which has over 250 species in 350,000 gallons of exhibit area.

BELOW
A typical redfish from the Texas Gulf.

ports and beaches, although parts of it can only be reached by boat.

The water is clear and the bottom has lush greenery and white sand holes, often producing large fish that lie in wait to ambush bait. Much fishing is done by stalking, using boat and foot to look for individuals or schools that are pushing mullet. Since virtually all of this angling is done in very thin water, and mostly by wading (even if a boat is used for transport), there can be great light-tackle excitement.

Padre Island National Seashore protects much of the remote Laguna Madre flats. The Seashore encompasses Padre Island, the longest barrier island in North America, where anglers can use four-wheel-drive vehicles to visit over 40 miles of waterfront. There's good fishing along the surf for a potpourri of species, with September being a good time to find a lot of action thanks to abundant, and close, baitfish schools.

West of Padre Island, remote Baffin Bay is a hotspot for big speckled trout. Ten-pounders are possible here in the spring, although there is often a lot of wind then. Shallow vegetation from Baffin Bay south to Boca Chica provides excellent sight-fishing for trout and redfish, akin to the angling experience of the Florida Keys.

Snook and tarpon are also on the target list in this region. Port Isabel is tops along the Texas Gulf for tarpon. Snook numbers have improved in this region, with the edges of the Brownsville Ship Channel producing fish in the summer and fall, while some are also caught on nearby flats. Some offshore fishing occurs in the Gulf out of Corpus Christi and Port Isabel, with a chance in summer for blue marlin, white marlin or sailfish. Sharks are also possible; a record 770-pound mako was caught by a Port Aransas boat in January 2002.

Freshwater

The front cover of this book says a lot about great freshwater fishing sites in North America, particularly with regard to many of them being in beautiful places. But it doesn't say anything about the incomparable variety of esteemed freshwater gamefish that exist, and the exceptional amount of water that this continent has.

All of the species in North America, and all of the rivers and lakes, made it tough to produce this selection from the much-larger cast of viable candidates. You want monster walleyes, try Lake Erie. Monster lake trout? Try Great Bear Lake. Trophy largemouth bass? Try El Salto. Schooling striped bass frenzy? Visit Lake Texoma.

Steelhead, brown trout, rainbow trout, smallmouth bass, muskies, northern pike, chinook and coho salmon, Arctic charr, grayling—they are all represented here as well. And not only are these North American sites great, they are among the best in the world, if not *the* best, for some of these species.

Most of the locations that follow are big bodies of water. This does not mean that small waters do not provide good, or great, fishing. They do, but they can seldom withstand a lot of pressure and, generally speaking, big waters produce big gamefish as well as good numbers of fish. Thus, many of the biggest waters in the United States, Canada and Mexico produce some of the most notable fishing. Keep in mind that, because these sites are big, there is so much angling water to cover and a lot more for you to learn about when and where to fish.

Whether you want to cast a fly to stream trout, drift an egg sac for steelhead, troll a big plug for muskies, cast a surface popper for bass, or try your hand at all of these activities and more, you will find terrific places to do so among the following sites.

Alagnak River

Alaska, United States

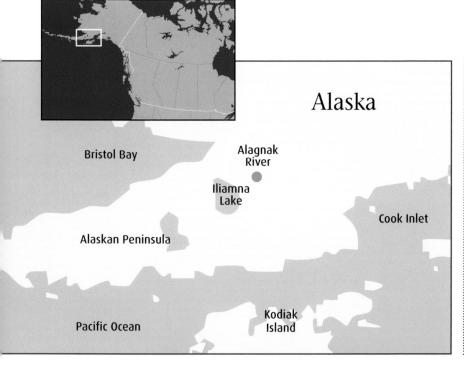

Alaska

Bristol Bay

Alagnak River

Iliamna Lake

Cook Inlet

Alaskan Peninsula

Kodiak Island

Pacific Ocean

While Alaska has a lot of good fishing, it is hard to beat the renowned fisheries and wilderness experience of the Alagnak River on the Alaskan Peninsula. Draining out of Katmai National Park and Nonvianuk and Kukaklek Lakes, the Alagnak covers 67 miles across a rolling tundra before eventually joining up with the Kvichak River (the outlet of Lake Iliamna), some four or five miles upstream from where the combined flow empties into Bristol Bay.

A federally designated Wild and Scenic River without road access, and reached only by floatplane, the Alagnak is replete with bears, eagles, and moose. It gets exceptional runs of salmon, has excellent fishing for rainbow trout

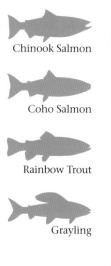

Chinook Salmon

Coho Salmon

Rainbow Trout

Grayling

RIGHT
Chinook salmon are a major attraction on the Alagnak.

and grayling, and is good for diverse fishing methods.

The lower region of the Alagnak is generally preferred for strictly salmon, because of deeper, more channelized water. King (chinook) salmon fishing is especially good here because it is close to the salt and gets power-charged fresh fish, and because kings prefer deeper pools, which are more abundant in the lower river. Deeper water means that it is hard to get down with fly or lure casting presentations, although experienced river anglers are able to do so. Backtrolling and bottom-bouncing with plugs, however, produces the best results.

Chinook are also caught further upriver, and they are more colorful here because they have been in the river longer and are undergoing physical changes prior to spawning. It is generally shallower in the upper river. Twenty-five to 30-pound kings are common, with some taken to 50 pounds, mainly during July.

Lots of action with acrobatic silver (coho) salmon follows in August and September, with the average size being eight to 12 pounds, and some specimens up to 20. They are caught throughout the river. Rainbow trout fishing is also especially good at this time. The Alagnak produces lots of rainbows in the three- to six-pound class, some from six to 12 pounds, and a few up to 15, which are a handful on fly or light-spinning tackle.

Other fish to catch include sockeye, chum, and pink salmon, plus three- to ten-pound northern pike. A myriad of brilliantly colored sockeyes arrive from June through early July. Large and strong chum salmon are available from July through mid-August, and often found on the edge of sandbars. In even-numbered years, pink, or humpbacked, salmon are in the river in late July and early August, providing light-tackle action.

The Alagnak braids, which is a wild and varied 25-mile-long, mid-section stretch of broken and ribboned water, is especially good for fly anglers and wade-fishing. Hundreds of smaller channels, excellent gravel spawning beds and remarkably clear water make it good for salmon and trout. Grayling are also caught here in June.

TOP LEFT
Floatplanes provide access to the remote Alagnak as well as to various more-remote fishing spots.

ABOVE
A fly-caught rainbow trout.

Details

Alagnak River, Alaska, United States

Location/getting there: The Alagnak River is southwest of Anchorage on the Alaskan Peninsula, and reached via a daily scheduled service from Anchorage to King Salmon. Floatplanes fly anglers from King Salmon to the lodge.

Info sources: For fishing information, contact Alagnak Lodge; call 800-877-9903; or visit www.alagnaklodge.com; and Katmai Lodge; call 800-330-0326; or visit www.katmai.com. For general information, contact the Alaska Travel Industry Association; call 907-929-2200; or visit www.dced.state.ak.us/tourism.

Prime times: King salmon arrive in mid- to late June, but July is prime. August is prime for cohos, and there is generally only a little overlap in these species. Rainbow trout are available all season, though June, and from mid-August through September, are best.

Gear needs: Varies with fishing methods, but includes flycasting, baitcasting and spinning tackle; fly anglers need ten- to 12-weight outfits for king salmon, and seven- to nine-weights for other salmon and trout. Bring waders.

Guide/tackle availability: Guides are part of the lodge package; a limited amount of tackle (mostly as backup) is available at the lodges, but bring your own.

Accommodations/dining: There are just two lodges here, Alagnak Lodge on the lower river and Katmai Lodge on the upper (see info section). Both have full amenities, good service and food, and move up and down the river as circumstances and individual desires warrant.

Etcetera: Week-long fishing trips range from $3,600 to $6,000, all-inclusive from King Salmon except for fishing licenses and tags, plus tips. Float trips are priced less. Fly-out fishing excursions are common and are included in some packages. A new one of recent note for Alagnak Lodge is the Nushagak River, which has a huge run of salmon. Many people take a fly-out to Brooks Falls in Katmai Park to see sockeye salmon trying to leap the falls while bears fish for a meal.

Beaverkill River

New York, United States

There is probably no other trout river in North America that is both as widely known within the continent and outside of it as New York's Beaverkill. No other river has been written about as widely, or has been so detailed in contemporary trout and fly fishing literature, as this body of water.

Situated in the Catskill Mountains, the Beaverkill flows for 45 miles to its confluence with the East Branch of the Delaware River. The upper portion, which spans about 27 miles and is known as the Upper Beaverkill, is almost entirely private. Its uppermost section is narrow and well shaded, with small pools. The lower region widens and contains larger pools, and it becomes wider as it flows from Lew Beach to Roscoe. A notable fishing and viewing spot here is the Covered Bridge Pool at the state camping area.

From Roscoe, which is billed as "Trout Town USA," the Beaverkill is joined by the Willowemoc River at fabled Junction Pool, becoming a larger freestone river with a lot of classic water. Junction Pool was immortalized in angling literature by the writer Red Smith, who claimed that it contained two-headed trout that lay deep facing both flowages. Fished hard and often, this is the ceremonial promotional spot for celebrating the opening of the trout season in the Catskills each year on April 1; unfortunately, though, weather and water conditions are often miserable at that time.

Referred to as the "Big River" by veterans, the remaining lower 18 miles of the Beaverkill is open to public fishing. This includes some renowned no-kill water, which produces excellent catch-and-release fishing with artificial lures only all season long, and especially when major fly hatches occur. The two stretches with special regulations often provide the best angling, although the frequently released trout are no dummies.

Included in the upper no-kill area, which is about two-and-a-half miles long, are two of the better and more well-known short sites, Horse Brook Run and Cairns Pool, the latter being long, deep and visible from the highway overpass. Much of the river's classic dry fly fishing is done here, with the river widening to 100 feet or more over a sand, gravel and boulder bottom. The lower no-kill area, which is about one-and-three-quarter miles in length, has long shallow riffles and pools.

Brown trout are the primary Beaverkill catch, brook trout are a secondary catch (especially in the cool upper flows) and rainbows are also occasionally caught. Dry flies are the preference of most anglers, especially as the many well-known pools of the Beaverkill are hallowed surface fishing water. There is barely a time when the major pools do not have some anglers giving them a fling.

There is over 1,500 miles of trout flowage in the Catskills. Numerous cold, clean Catskill trout rivers and streams are noteworthy in their own right, and not far geographically from the Beaverkill. The closest of these mountain waters is Willowemoc Creek, which is easy to wade, not very wide and has more public access than the Beaverkill River. Good angling portions can be accessed from Livingston Manor downstream to Roscoe; here, the Willowemoc snakes along the highway and includes a year-round, no-kill, artificial lures portion.

OPPOSITE PAGE
Anglers fish near the town of Horton on the lower Beaverkill.

BELOW
Emerging insects fill the air on a late-summer evening on the lower Beaverkill River.

Details

Beaverkill River, New York, United States

Location/getting there: The Beaverkill River is located in southwestern New York and is accessed by driving Route 17 (to become Interstate 86) to Roscoe.

Info sources: For area information, contact the Sullivan County Visitor's Association, 100 North Street, Monticello, NY 12701; call 800-882-2287; or visit www.scva.net. Also visit www.flyfishingconnection.com/beaverkill.html.

Prime times: The general trout season is from April 1 through September 30, although there are exceptions, including the no-kill sections, which are open year-round. May is the prime time because of insect hatches,

relatively good flows and cool water, although summer fishing, especially in the evening, is also good.

Gear needs: Five- to seven-weight flycasting outfits are standard; a range of dry flies and nymphs are fished, often according to well-identified insect hatches. Light spinning gear can be used as well.

Guide/tackle availability: A few guides in the region work the Beaverkill, seldom exclusively; most anglers fish unguided. Tackle is available at area shops, especially in Livingston Manor and Roscoe.

Accommodations/dining: A modest number of lodging and dining options exist locally, including motels and campgrounds.

Etcetera: An excellent side trip can be made to the Catskill Fly Fishing Center and Museum, located in Livingston Manor along Willowemoc Creek. The Center has heritage and educational programs and exhibits and displays flycasting equipment, art and artifacts pertinent to the region. Contact them at 845-439-4810; or visit www.cffcm.org.

Brown Trout

Brook Trout

Big Sand Lake

Manitoba, Canada

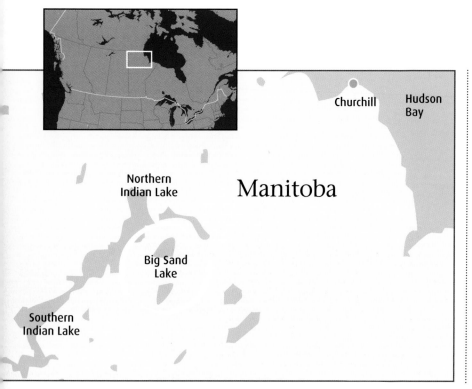

Churchill

Hudson Bay

Northern Indian Lake

Manitoba

Big Sand Lake

Southern Indian Lake

Big Sand Lake is a sub-Arctic jewel in northern Manitoba that gets its name from great sand deposits created by glaciers tens of thousands of years ago. Unlike many lakes in the far north, Big Sand has long areas of sandy shoreline; a favorite pastime of anglers here, who are stretching their legs during lunch, is to walk along the shoreline as if it were an ocean beach, looking for the tracks of wolves, bears and moose. On a half-mile jaunt you might also watch a bald eagle fly overhead and spot a pod of loons offshore (they do group here) diving for food and calling raucously to one another. It is almost enough to make you forget about fishing.

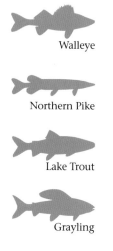

Walleye

Northern Pike

Lake Trout

Grayling

RIGHT
Sand beaches along eskers typify parts of Big Sand Lake.

ABOVE
Landing a large pike in a Big Sand Lake bay.

Saying that, though, the fishing here can be hard to forget. Walleye and northern pike are the main attractions, but there are also lake trout and grayling, so it is possible to do a northern Canada "slam" on a visit here.

Walleyes are the main attraction and are extremely plentiful. Big Sand walleyes average three to four pounds and are readily caught on crankbaits and jigs. Sometimes you can catch them by the bushelful. There are bigger fish, however, including some that meet the Manitoba minimum size (28 inches) for Master Angler recognition. There is only one lodge at the lake, and it practices catch-

Details

Big Sand Lake, Manitoba, Canada

Location/getting there: Big Sand Lake is located in a roadless area of northcentral Manitoba, about 525 miles north of Winnipeg. Visitors arrive via chartered plane from Winnipeg to a private airstrip at the lodge.

Info sources: For information about the lake, contact Big Sand Lake Lodge, Room 1, 1808 Wellington Ave., Winnipeg, Manitoba, Canada R3H 0G3; call 800-348-5824 (US) and 204-774-6666; or visit www.bigsandlakelodge.com. For Manitoba information, contact Travel Manitoba, 7-155 Carlton St., Winnipeg,

Manitoba R3C 3H8, Canada; call 800-665-0040; or visit www.travelmanitoba.com.

Prime times: Early in the season for lots of pike and walleye action; summer for lake trout and grayling.

Gear needs: Varies according to species and methods. See the information on Selwyn Lake (see page 198) for guidance. Walleye gear includes medium and medium-light spinning and baitcasting tackle.

Guide/tackle availability: Guides are provided for those staying at the main lodge.

Accommodations/dining: Big Sand Lake Lodge is a deluxe facility with excellent log cabin accommodations, good food and various amenities.

Etcetera: The lake is fished from early June through the end of August. An overnight stay, generally coming in, but sometimes also going out, is usually needed in Winnipeg. Package costs range from $2,400 to $2,900 for four to eight days, all inclusive from Winnipeg except for tips and overnight lodging. There are outpost camps as well, plus daily fly-outs to remote waters.

BELOW
Walleyes like this are plentiful.

and-release, except for shore lunches, so the only thing that harms the walleye is other fish.

A 20-pound northern pike, however, could chow down on a big walleye, and there are some big northerns in this lake. Some have been caught in the 30-pound class, and a good number each year are landed in the 18- to 22-pound range, which likewise qualifies for Manitoba trophy recognition. There is excellent fishing for numbers of pike early in the season, when the fish are shallow. Cabbage weeds abound in bays and along points and deep shorelines, making a great habitat for these sulking predators later in the season.

Big Sand Lake is roughly 70 miles long and covers about 60,000 acres, so there is a lot to explore for a limited number of people. Some areas of the lake have deep water containing lake trout; this species is caught early in the season in relatively shallow water as the lake warms, but more (and larger ones) are caught by deep trolling with heavy weights in the summer, when trout are more concentrated.

To catch grayling you have to make a jaunt to the South Seal River, which is a pleasant two-hour boat ride from the lodge. Some grayling in the three-pound class are caught, as well as numbers of smaller grayling.

A great number of water birds find Big Sand to their liking, and it is common to sight all manner of waterfowl, plus terns and herring gulls, which are larger and cleaner than any gull you have ever seen by the seashore, and which somehow always manage to find anglers parked for shore lunch. And freshly caught walleye or pike never tasted better, nor were they ever eaten in a prettier place.

Bow River

Alberta, Canada

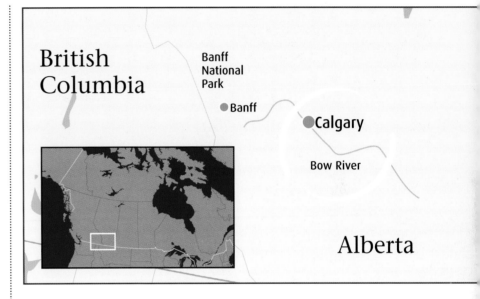

Originating in Bow Lake in Banff National Park, the Bow River tumbles southeasterly among stupendous Rocky Mountain scenery to and through Calgary. Bull trout, brook trout and Rocky Mountain whitefish inhabit the higher reaches, while the nutrient-rich lower stretches have rainbow trout and brown trout, the latter being the fish that made the Bow famous.

The best stretch of river is between Calgary and the Carseland Dam, some 40 miles downstream, which is designated catch-and-release for trout over 40 centimeters (15½ inches). Twenty-inch fish can be expected on most floats—made in a MacKenzie drift boat—through this section, which is renowned for having an oft-quoted population of 2,500 trout per mile.

The river is best known for dry fly fishing due to excellent caddis, blue winged olive and pale morning dun hatches, but anglers must also be prepared to fish nymphs and streamers for best results. The lower stretch can be drifted effectively in two days; access points allow for one-day floats as well.

The lower Bow River offers fine opportunities for large brown and rainbow trout between Carseland and Bassano Dam, though much of this stretch is inaccessible to angling where it passes through an Indian Reserve. Fly anglers enjoy tremendous success here using streamers, nymphs or dry flies, depending largely upon the season, water conditions and weather.

The predominant hatches are plenty and varied, so a wide selection of dry files is required. August on the Bow is tough and unpredictable, but can offer some outstanding hopper fishing.

Details

Bow River, Alberta, Canada

Location/getting there: The Bow River is situated in southcentral Alberta and can be accessed at numerous places; many drift boat trips originate in Calgary.

Info sources: For area information contact Travel Alberta, 319 Innovation Business Center, 9797 Jasper Ave., Edmonton, Alberta, Canada, T5J 1N9; call 800-661-8888; or visit www.travelalberta.com. Also contact Calgary Visitors Bureau, 200-238 11th Ave. S.E., Calgary, Alberta, Canada T2G 0X8; call 800-661-1678; or visit www.tourismcalgary.com.

Prime times: May to October.

Gear needs: See main text.

Guide/tackle availability: Drift boat guides are plentiful; for a list of outfitters and services visit www.discovercalgary.com.

Accommodations/dining: Lodging and dining options are extensive throughout the area.

Etcetera: Expect an all-inclusive, full-day float trip to cost about $450. For some diverse fishing, the nearby South Saskatchewan River has pike, walleye, sauger and goldeye through most of its length, as well as lake sturgeon.

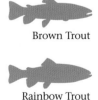

Brown Trout

Rainbow Trout

California Delta

California, United States

Pacific
Ocean

California

Sacramento

California
Delta

Stockton

San Francisco

The complex waterway known as the California Delta in northern California is an outstanding resource for largemouth bass and striped bass, and perhaps the most significant recreational playground on the West Coast.

Formed primarily by the flows of the Sacramento and San Joaquin Rivers, the Delta encompasses 738,000 acres of land and water in six counties and carries 47 per cent of California's run-off water emptying into San Francisco Bay. Hundreds of thousands of acres of farmland exist on 55 Delta islands, most of them reclaimed from swamp land in the 19th century. At one time, over 300 paddlewheel steamboats plied the Delta waters, but today there is not only traffic from thousands of fishing boats, but freighters, barges, huge yachts, pontoon boats, houseboats, ski boats and a myriad of others. Scores of marinas exist throughout the region.

Over 1,000 miles of navigable waterway, with countless sloughs, make the Delta prime for largemouth bass, although there is also good fishing for striped bass, catfish and crappie, while salmon, steelhead, shad and sturgeon also migrate through. Bass are especially popular here, however, and fishing tournaments are plentiful.

It usually takes a good catch to win a competitive event, which is indicative of an overall excellent fishery. There are lots of five-pound largemouths here, a good number of bass over eight pounds, and some over ten pounds. Bass in the mid-teens have also been caught here.

RIGHT
Tules are one of the abundant aquatic plants that Delta bass anglers key on.

Many parts of the Delta are very shallow, and the area is loaded with tules. Hyacinths have been coming on lately, and some places are thick with hydrilla. This abundance of cover, and the generally shallow nature of the water, results in great conditions both for bass and for bass fishing. If anything, there is so much good-looking water in the summer that the problem is narrowing it all down.

Tides and current are important elements of Delta fishing. The speed of current has a lot to do with where bass will be located in or near sloughs, eddies, tules, sandbars, and other backwaters, and the better activity often occurs after a tide change. Working irregular spots (points, openings, outcroppings, etc.) along the bank is a successful strategy.

Anglers can fish the Delta all year long. In the winter, water temperatures dip to the mid-40s, which makes largemouths sluggish in protected areas. However, striper fishing picks up as the water temperature decreases, with good fishing from September through winter. There are loads of school stripers in the Delta, and some over 20 or 30 pounds. Bigger stripers can be caught on surface plugs in winter.

Shad migrate through the Delta in spring, and are mainly caught up in the Sacramento River (and further up in the Feather and American Rivers), as opposed to the main lower regions of the Delta. The same is true for chinook salmon and steelhead, although the occasional steelhead and salmon are caught while fishing for bass or stripers.

ABOVE LEFT
Good-sized largemouth bass are plentiful in the Delta.

ABOVE RIGHT
This Delta bass was caught near the Sugar Barge on Bethel Island.

Details

California Delta, California, United States

Location/getting there: The California Delta is east-northeast of San Francisco, extending from Pittsburg on the west to Stockton on the east and north to Sacramento; it is readily accessed from major roads.

Info sources: For general information about the California Delta, contact the California Delta Chambers and Visitors Bureau, P.O. Box 6, Isleton, CA 95641; call 916-707-5007; or visit www.californiadelta.org.

Prime times: February and March is when many of the monster bass have been caught,

because it is the pre-spawn period. Winter can produce some good action for striped bass, including surface fishing, as there is little non-fishing boat traffic at this time.

Gear needs: Varies with fishing methods and species, although standard baitcasting and spinning tackle is used for bass and stripers. Dropping worms and jigs along the endless tule banks requires flipping tackle.

Guide/tackle availability: Many guides and charter boats are available in the area. Fishing tackle is widely available at shops and marinas.

Accommodations/dining: The Delta is loaded with diverse lodging and dining options.

Etcetera: If you are a newcomer to this area, get some good navigational charts and brush up on your navigational skills. Note that some portions of this vast area can get very rough when it is windy. Houseboat rentals are ample and popular throughout the region, and a good thing to consider for a family vacation; you can tow a fishing boat behind.

Largemouth Bass

Striped Bass

Crappie

Catfish

Cayuga Lake

New York, United States

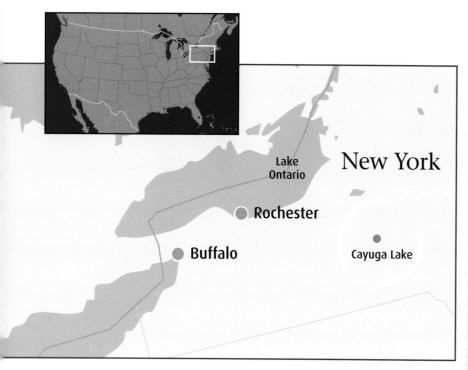

Lake Ontario

New York

Rochester

Buffalo

Cayuga Lake

Brown Trout

Atlantic Salmon

Lake Trout

Rainbow Trout

Largemouth Bass

Some people call Cayuga Lake New York's best-kept secret. Located in central New York, it is the longest and second-deepest Finger Lake, and has the best fishery in terms of size, numbers of fish and diversity.

The plump and aggressive landlocked Atlantic salmon here average three to four pounds, with an occasional fish up to ten. Brown trout are abundant, too. Though regulars here aspire to break the lake's 18.38-pound record, set in 1997, it is more likely that the catch will be football-shaped three- to five-pounders, and possibly an eight- to 12-pound drag-tester.

Rainbow trout, which have been caught to nine pounds, and lake trout, are also prominent. A 17½-pound laker was caught in the spring of 1999, and most of the better action for this species occurs in deep water after a thermocline has established and this species settles in a deeper zone. Historically, larger lake trout existed in Cayuga, and that may occur again in the future.

Most Cayuga Lake anglers start out in early April, and fishing is great once the surface temperature hits 52 to 54 late in the month. The upper six feet is all you need to target at that time, using mostly bright, shallow-running plugs fished on flatlines or off sideplaners. Switch to spoons around mid-May. The extreme southern end of the lake is tops early on. Cayuga Inlet, the major tributary, enters here via Fall Creek, and this is a rainbow trout hotspot for both waders and shore anglers.

This lake, which is 40 miles long, is relatively narrow and much like a ravine, with steep sides in many places and depths up to 435 feet. That makes for some good deep trolling in summer, once you find the appropriate depth and area to fish. There are no reefs or shoals, but there are bars off the points, and these are productive.

Cayuga also has a good warmwater fishery. The far northern end features a lot of vegetation and is noted for bass and panfish. Largemouth bass, smallmouth bass and yellow perch are the prime species.

Details

Cayuga Lake, New York, United States

Location/getting there: Cayuga Lake is in central New York near the city of Ithaca.

Info sources: For area information contact the Ithaca/Tompkins County Convention and Visitors Bureau at 800-284-8422; or visit www.visitithaca.com.

Prime times: Spring for lake and river fishing.

Gear needs: Assorted depending on species and fishing method.

Guide/tackle availability: There are a few charter captains on Cayuga; tackle is available locally. For fishing information contact Capt. Gus Freeman at G.F. Charters, 607-273-2861.

Accommodations/dining: There is a full range of lodging and dining options locally, especially in and near Ithaca; be aware of crowding if there are events at the two local colleges.

Etcetera: This region is a popular tourist destination. Several state parks and historical sites are worth visiting in the area, including Taughannock Falls. Consider a trip to Finger Lakes wineries.

Columbia River

Oregon/Washington, United States

For more than 200 miles from its mouth upriver, the Columbia is both the boundary between Oregon and Washington and a jointly managed fishery that provides the most, and largest, fish in both states. All that water provides plenty of angling opportunity for a wide range of freshwater and anadromous species.

Among the former, the most highly sought species are smallmouth bass and walleyes. Smallmouths love the rocky shorelines and are plentiful. The best fishing is in the Hanford Reach, which is the last free-flowing section of river; in Lake Celilo; in Lake Wallula; and in Lake Umatilla in the Boardman reach. Some trophy specimens, including fish over eight pounds, have been landed. Summer and fall, as well as early spring before snow melt, are good times.

Good walleye numbers exist in Lake Roosevelt (the pool behind Grand Coulee Dam), nearby Banks Lake, Rufus Woods Lake (behind Chief Joseph Dam), all three lower river reservoirs, and the free-flowing portion of the Columbia below Bonneville Dam. Walleyes up to 17 pounds have been produced in the Columbia, and fish of ten to 12 pounds are caught annually, with trolling being the main activity. The better fishing is in the cooler weather of late winter and early spring when the fish are spawning.

The Columbia and its tributaries were once the world's top Pacific salmon producer, and even though hydroelectric dams, careless agricultural practices, overfishing and other abuses have taken their toll, there are still times and places where salmon fishing can range from good to excellent.

Spring-run chinook salmon return to hatcheries on several lower Columbia tributaries from April to June, and these "springers" are a favorite of Washington anglers.

BELOW
Launching ramp scene on the Columbia River.

Landing a Columbia River smallmouth bass.

The Cowlitz River from Longview upstream to the salmon hatchery near Salkum has long been a top spring chinook spot, and the North Fork Lewis River is another good bet. Farther up the Columbia, good springer fishing may also be found around the mouths of the Wind, Little White Salmon, Big White Salmon and Klickitat Rivers. Anglers troll diving plugs and spinners or bounce large roe clusters along the bottom.

Fall-run chinooks are also available in the Columbia, with good action in dozens of places along the lower 250 miles of the Columbia from its mouth to Kennewick, especially around the mouths of major tributary streams. One of the best fisheries occurs some 300 miles from the ocean in the Hanford Reach. Anglers here commonly catch fall kings of 30 to 50 pounds.

Steelhead are another sea-run favorite of Columbia River anglers; there is steelhead angling somewhere on the main river, or on several of its tributaries, throughout the year. Boaters find good summer and early fall steelheading on the lower Columbia around Camas and Washougal, in McNary Pool, and in some of the reservoirs behind main-stem dams. Bank anglers do well casting in the Ringold

Walleye

Smallmouth Bass

Chinook Salmon

American Shad

Sturgeon

Details

Columbia River, Oregon/Washington, United States

Location/getting there: Readily accessed by parallel roads, the Columbia River borders Washington and Oregon for much of its length, with the upper reaches entirely in Washington.

Info sources: For general information, contact the Southwest Washington Convention and Visitors Bureau at 877-600-0800; or visit www.southwestwashington.com. Also contact the Dalles Chamber of Commerce at 800-255-3385; or visit www.thedalleschamber.com. Also contact Washington State Tourism at 360-725-5052; or visit www.tourism.wa.gov and the Oregon Tourism Commission at 800-547-7842; or visit www.traveloregon.com.

Prime times: See main text.

Gear needs: Varies with species and methods.

Guide/tackle availability: Guides and charter captains are available. Tackle can be found in (widely scattered) local shops.

Accommodations/dining: A range of lodging and dining options exist.

Etcetera: Regulations along the Columbia are the same in both Oregon and Washington, despite different rules in other parts of both states, to prevent angling confusion. Incidentally, this is a big river that gets mighty rough, especially when a big wind goes against the current. Hood River is regarded as the sailboarding capital of North America, so you know it gets windy in this area.

area upstream from Richland. As for the tributaries, the Elochoman, Cowlitz, Lewis, Washougal, Klickitat, Wenatchee and Methow are all well-known steelhead producers.

The lower Columbia's estimated one million white sturgeon come and go at will from their birthplace in this stretch of river to numerous other coastal bays. Sturgeon fishing is good most of the year out of Astoria, but it is best from Longview to Portland in February and March, as sturgeon follow the smelt run to the mouth of Washington's Cowlitz River. After March, they begin moving upriver to below Bonneville, where large fish spawn in the heavy spring run-off current below the dam. Anglers catch and release seven- to ten-footers, with some even larger. When the shad are in, whole shad make good sturgeon bait; at other times, sand shrimp, smelt and herring are popular.

American shad enter the Columbia in May, with fish moving well into Washington's reaches of the upper Columbia and through Portland up to Willamette Falls near Oregon City. Several million shad run up the Columbia every year, with most action in late spring, and especially good fishing immediately downstream of Bonneville Dam in June.

The Snake River, which is the largest tributary to the Columbia, provides excellent fishing for smallmouth bass, steelhead, channel catfish and white sturgeon. Another major tributary, the Yakima River, has blue-ribbon trout fishing between Ellensburg and Yakima, plus channel catfish and crappies in the lower reaches, as well as good smallmouth bass angling.

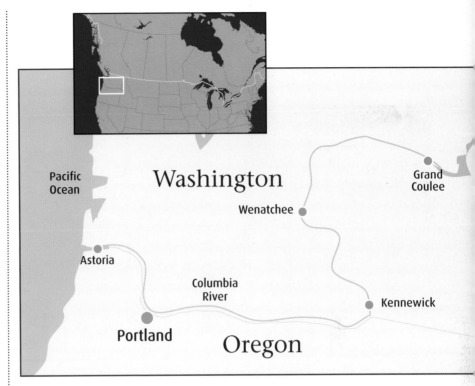

LEFT
A fine steelhead caught from the North Fork Lewis River, a tributary to the lower Columbia.

Coppermine River

Nunavut Territory, Canada

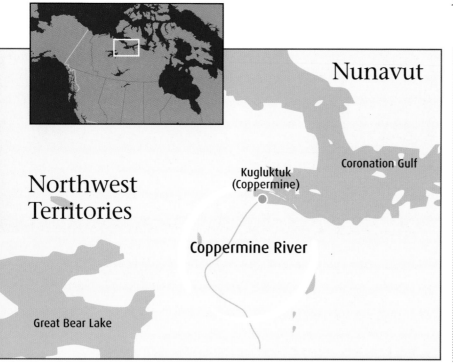

Nunavut

Northwest Territories

Kugluktuk (Coppermine)

Coronation Gulf

Coppermine River

Great Bear Lake

Arctic Charr

Named after the Copper Inuit people of the region, the Coppermine River of Nunavut is a major flow that courses northerly for 525 miles from a small body of water near Great Slave Lake to Coronation Gulf, an arm of the Arctic Ocean. It enters the gulf near the village of Coppermine, an Inuit community that is now known as Kugluktuk, which means "place of rapids."

The Coppermine River is unnavigable to larger craft due to numerous rapids and falls, beginning near the mouth with Bloody Falls. Arctic charr, however, are able to ascend Bloody Falls and migrate for hundreds of miles upriver, and canoeing adventurers are able to portage around this, and other, impediments on their voyages downriver to the Arctic Ocean.

RIGHT
Landing a charr on the Kendall River.

The Coppermine is well-known for its Arctic charr fishing, although not for producing the size of fish that migrate into the Tree River to the east and into rivers on Victoria Island to the north. However, there are many charr here, and anglers are often able to catch good numbers in a day on the river proper.

Larger and more colorful specimens tend to be most available in late August or early September, a time when the weather tends to become rough and unpredictable.

Some of the tributaries to the Coppermine also produce good fishing if the water level is high enough in a given summer to provide floatplane access. The Kendall River is one of these, and fish up to 12 pounds are easy pickings for anglers along the deep banks of the Kendall where it merges with the Coppermine and runs through a redrock gorge.

This area, and the upper portions of the Coppermine, have low brush and trees, which distinguishes the terrain from downriver near Kugluktuk, which is rocky and barren and above the treeline. The junction of the Kendall and Coppermine Rivers is just one hour by floatplane from the eastern Dease Arm of Great Bear Lake.

Details

Coppermine River, Nunavut Territory, Canada

Location/getting there: Anglers from Plummer's Arctic Lodges are flown by floatplane from the lodge to one of two base camps, separated by many miles from each other, along the Coppermine River. Anglers at the lower camp can go downriver to Bloody Falls. The only other access to this river is by traveling to the village of Coppermine (now Kugluktuk, population 1,200) on the coast. Adventure travelers are flown upriver by floatplane and make four- to seven-day floats with canoes, kayaks or inflatables, ending at a camping area in the village. One can also make arrangements through a local outfitter for a guided day trip from the village upriver to Bloody Falls.

Info sources: Contact Plummer's Arctic Lodges, 950 Bradford St., Winnipeg, MB R3H 0N5; call 800-665-0240; or visit www.plummerslodges.com. For Nunavut information, contact Nunavut Tourism, P.O. Box 1450, Iqaluit, Nunavut, Canada X0A 0H0; call 800-491-7910; or visit www.nunatour.nt.ca.

Prime times: Mid-July to mid-August. Before that you could find the water too high and rough if it has been a late winter, and after that there may be bad weather. However, the more colorful charr appear later in the season.

Gear needs: See the gear needs listed for the Tree River (see page 210).

Guide/tackle availability: Guides are provided unless you are doing a self-float trip. Plummer's lodges have terminal tackle; those using other services must bring their own tackle. Waders are necessary, and are available for Plummer's fly-out anglers.

Accommodations/dining: Plummer's anglers are well fed and housed in basic framed-tent camp structures. There is a hotel with a restaurant in the village of Coppermine.

Etcetera: Good footwear, and/or chest waders with good boots, will be extremely useful for this journey. Try some freshly caught charr sashimi for lunch.

Dean River (lower)

British Columbia, Canada

The lower Dean River, situated in a spectacular part of the Chilcotin Coast beneath the snow-capped Coast Mountains, is a British Columbia gem that is revered for its steelhead and salmon fishing. Believed by many to hold the strongest run (or strain) of steelhead in the world, the most popularly fished salmon and steelhead portion of the lower Dean is only two miles long, ranging from the tidal water of the Dean Channel to the lower canyon. There are 12 to 15 miles of river to fish above the canyon, although this is done by fewer people.

RIGHT
A typical Dean River chinook salmon, fresh from the salt.

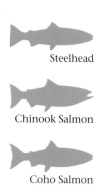

Steelhead

Chinook Salmon

Coho Salmon

The Dean River actually begins far inland, coursing through Anahim Lake and Tweedsmuir Provincial Park. But the section that is so well-known for angling, and so coveted, is the near-coast lower region, where steelhead to 25 pounds (12 pounds is average), chinook (king) salmon to 50 pounds (20 pounds is average) and coho salmon to 20 pounds can be caught or hooked. Many are not caught because they are extremely strong, the result, perhaps, of evolution because of the falls that they must pass to get

LEFT
Cabin at Dean River Lodge, with a floatplane moored in Dean Channel and a high waterfall in the background.

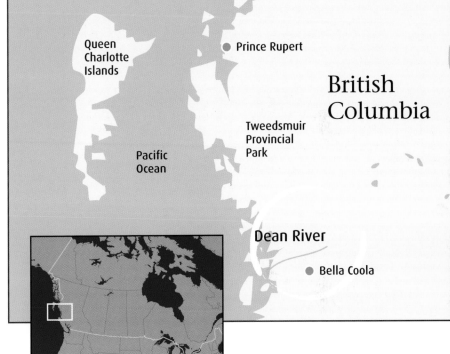

Details

Dean River (lower), British Columbia, Canada

Location/getting there: The lower Dean River is in westcentral British Columbia, north of Bella Coola. It is accessed primarily via auto or commercial plane to Bella Coola, then by boat or floatplane from there to Kimsquit at the mouth of the river, or by floatplane from Anahim Lake or Williams Lake.

Info sources: Several outfitters operate here. Contact Moose Lake Lodge (which operates Dean River Lodge), Box 3310, Anahim Lake, B.C. V0L 1C0, Canada; call 250-742-3535; or visit www.mooselakelodge.ca. Contact the Sport Fishing Institute of British Columbia, 200-1676 Duranleau St., Granville Island, Vancouver, B.C., V6H 3S4, Canada; call 1-800-HELLO-BC for a free Sport Fishing Planning

Guide; or visit www.sportfishing.bc.ca.

Prime times: July and August for steelhead; June for king salmon.

Gear needs: Flycasting, spinning and baitcasting in appropriate areas. Large-capacity reels are necessary, with good drag systems. Fly fishing is mainly with wet flies and sinking lines, and with a nine-weight outfit. Top wet flies include Purple Peril, General Practitioner, Black Woolly Bugger, Purple-Orange-Red Popsicle and Egg-sucking Leech. Chest waders are necessary.

Guide/tackle availability: Guides are available at lodges and jet boat transport can

be arranged for those not staying at lodges. Bring whatever tackle you need. Under Class 1 designation, there is a 40–60 split between guided and unguided anglers.

Accommodations/dining: Lodge accommodations and dining are excellent; Dean River Lodge is new and overlooks Dean Channel, with a high-peak waterfall adding background color.

Etcetera: Bring your insect repellent, since the Dean River could be the world's horsefly capitol; swatting flies is known here as the "Dean River handshake."

upriver, or because of the fact that they migrate, chrome-bright, into the river a short distance from saltwater, very fresh and full of vigor.

The best fishing takes place from June to October, although not all the fish are available at the same time. In general, chinook salmon are in the river from mid-June through mid-July, while cohos are later arrivals, appearing from mid-July to mid-September. Pink, chum, and sockeye salmon are also available from mid-July, and there are also some rainbows and sea-run cutthroat in this section of river. Pinks can be so numerous in August that they interfere with other fishing.

Steelhead migrate up the Dean in two different stages. One stage is a late-spring run of fish that are headed to the Takia River, a tributary to the Dean well upriver. The second stage is the main run of Dean River fish, which

migrate upriver a few weeks after the first stage, providing the best fishing from early July into early September. These summer-run steelhead attract anglers from afar. Many of the fish hooked then are only a few hours out of saltwater, bright-silver in color, aggressive in attitude and strong on the line.

The Dean River is closely regulated and designated as a "classified water." Special license classes and costs apply. Angling is only with single barbless hooks, bait is prohibited and fishing above the canyon is fly fishing only. Access to the river above the canyon by non-Canadians is restricted to an annual March lottery draw. These regulations exist in part because the lower Dean gets a lot of fishing pressure, especially the first two miles, which is not an intimate experience since it is accessible to the public, and has numerous campsites.

Delaware River (upper)

New York/Pennsylvania, United States

The upper Delaware River, which splits New York and Pennsylvania between the Catskill and Pocono Mountains, is one of the finest wild trout rivers in the northeastern U.S.. It is also a prime fishery for American shad, a terrific smallmouth bass river, and one of the most popular canoeing and rafting flowages in the east. Seventy-five miles long, the upper Delaware was designated as a National Wild and Scenic

River in 1978. Also notable are its major tributaries, which include the East and West Branches of the Delaware, and the Lackawaxen, Mongaup and Neversink Rivers.

Historically, perhaps no species is more abundant in the Delaware, nor more energetically pursued, than American shad, which migrate up the entire river and into upper tributaries to spawn, primarily from late April through mid-June. These fish are frequently caught in four- to six-

BELOW
Anglers fish the upper Delaware River near Hancock during a stonefly hatch.

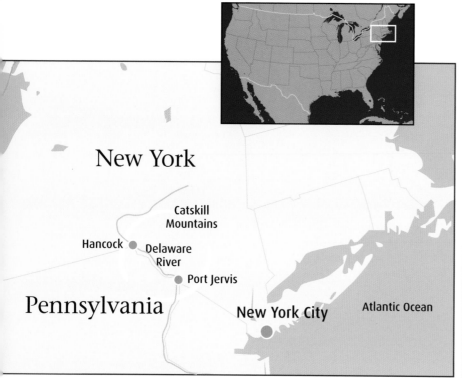

New York

Catskill
Mountains

Hancock ● ● Delaware
River

● Port Jervis

Pennsylvania

New York City

Atlantic Ocean

Fly fishing is the preferred method, although other artificials and bait are used where regulations permit. Various mayfly hatches are strong from late May on, stonefly hatches occur from June into August and caddisflies are common in June and July.

The quality of these fisheries, as in all tailwaters where trout are found, is dependent upon continuous water releases (in this case from upstream New York City reservoirs) that are ample in volume and appropriate in temperature. Drought conditions cause cutbacks in releases, which produce thermal stress and have a negative impact on the coldwater species. Maintaining necessary release levels for fisheries purposes has been a constant problem in the upper Delaware, and even more of a problem in the Neversink River, which enters the Delaware below Port Jervis.

pound sizes and are pursued by both boat and wading anglers, garnering most attention around Port Jervis, Sparrowbush, Barryville, Lackawaxen and Narrowsburg. Pools and runs below riffles are the primary spots, with the best action early and late in the day. Most anglers use shad darts, but fly fishing has also increased in popularity. Cyclical abundance of shad makes some years better than others.

The prime trout water is the 27-mile section from Hancock to Callicoon, and the two upper stems, which are essentially tailwater fisheries. There is 32 miles of the East Branch of the Delaware from Pepacton Dam in Downsville to Hancock, and 18 miles of the West Branch of the Delaware from Cannonsville Dam in Deposit to Hancock. The West Branch is the most intensely fished section, and has both the most consistently cold water and a less diverse fish population. ·

These waters have a good population of brown trout and rainbow trout. Browns predominate in the East and West Branches; rainbows are abundant in the East Branch from the village of East Branch to the confluence with the main river at Hancock, and southward on the main river. These are primarily wild fish, particularly the rainbows, and there is a good chance of getting some in the 16- to 20-inch range, which is exceptional in the northeast.

RIGHT
*A typical Delaware
River shad, caught
near Port Jervis.*

Good smallmouth bass fishing exists from Callicoon south in the Upper Delaware; here the water temperatures become more favorable. Few smallmouths over 14 inches long are caught, but there are plenty of bass to be had on light spinners, flies, jigs and small plugs. Bigger fish haunt the deeper pools.

Walleyes inhabit the upper river, too, although they are not intensely pursued; some large walleyes, eight to ten pounds, are taken annually by local residents, with most angling occurring in spring and fall. Striped bass have had an increasing presence recently, and some over 20 pounds have been caught, usually in the main river below tributaries.

ABOVE
Landing a smallmouth bass below the Ten Mile River access.

Details

Delaware River (Upper) , New York/Pennsylvania, United States

Location/getting there: The Upper Delaware River borders New York and Pennsylvania for 75 miles from Port Jervis to Hancock. The main access is via Route 97 in New York.

Info sources: For area information, contact the Pike County Chamber of Commerce, P.O. Box 883, Milford, PA 18337; call 570-296-8700; or visit www.pikechamber.com. Also contact the Sullivan County Visitor's Association, 100 North Street, Monticello, NY 12701; call 800-882-2287; or visit www.scva.net. Also contact the National Park Service office of the Upper Delaware Scenic and Recreational River, RR2, Box 2428, Beach Lake, PA 18405; call 570-728-8251; or visit www.nps.gov/upde.

Prime times: Spring for shad; spring through early summer for trout.

Gear needs: Varies depending on species and methods, but is primarily light flycasting and spinning tackle.

Guide/tackle availability: Guides are available in both states, many using drift boats to float miles of productive water. Contact Upper Delaware Outfitters, HC 1, Box 1025, Starlight, PA 18461; call 570-635-5900; or visit www.riveressentials.com. Tackle is available in local shops.

Accommodations/dining: Lodging and dining options are varied, but limited, along the river, and include motels and

campgrounds. More extensive options exist further from the river.

Etcetera: Access is limited along the Upper Delaware, and fishing is hampered from Callicoon to Port Jervis during the day on summer weekends by heavy canoe and raft traffic. The Upper Delaware River is one of the top places in the northeast to view bald eagles. Of special local interest is The Zane Grey Museum in Lackawaxen, Pennsylvania, administered by the National Park Service; the famous author lived and wrote here a century ago, and fished locally for smallmouths. Near the museum is the restored Roebling Bridge, first built as a coal-boat canal aqueduct in 1848 and now the oldest wire suspension bridge in the United States.

Brown Trout

Rainbow Trout

American Shad

Smallmouth Bass

Ena Lake

Saskatchewan, Canada

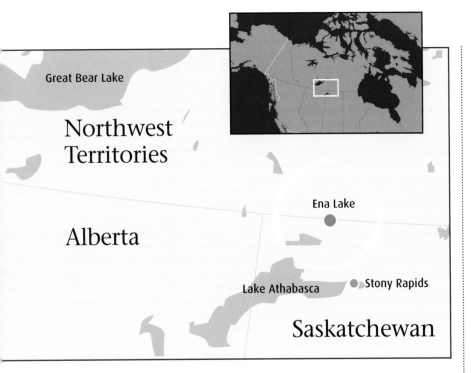

south) and Reindeer Lake, it has never received commercial fishing (a factor that impacts resources in many northern lakes) and is visited annually by comparatively few anglers.

A well-sheltered, scenic, wilderness lake that sports many bays and islands, Ena is blessed with plenty of deep troughs that keep the water cool all season long. The best angling for lake trout occurs in June, following ice-out, and in September when the fish are spawning on reefs. At these times the fish are predominantly in shallow water or are fairly close to the surface near deep water. Ena's late-season is later than most far-northern locales, and those few who visit then, wearing pac boots and a snowmobile suit, can get into some monster fish.

When the fish move deep in summer, they prove harder to catch because they are no longer as accessible. The situation at Ena is analogous to that of Scott Lake (see page 194), except that more attention is given at Ena to northern pike than trout in the summer, since pike are abundant and readily caught.

There is a summer lake trout gold mine to be tapped here, however, by those who come properly equipped, especially for those bringing their own deep-fishing tackle and portable sonar. There are a lot of 25- to 30-pound trout here; some in the 40-pound class have been caught and a 53-pounder holds the lake record, although that was caught a few years before there was a lodge.

Ena Lake also provides good fishing for northern pike. They, too, are frequently caught in trophy proportions, from 18 to 26 pounds. Bays and islands provide suitable cover, and casting all the standard pike lures is sure to produce.

For variety, anglers can try near-to-camp Bulmer Lake, where a boat and motor is stored. The lake is reached via a short hike and is popular because its pike are always agreeable. Some trophy-size pike can be had here as well.

With the exception of a few small fish that are kept for a shore lunch, all pike and trout are quickly returned to the water. Angling is done only with lures and they must have barbless hooks to aid removal and help prevent damage to the fish.

Ena Lake is one of the premier, though little-known, lake trout waters in Saskatchewan. A 15-mile-long, glacial-carved body of water that straddles the 60th parallel northeast of Tazin Lake, Ena is smaller than such huge places as Lake Athabasca (which is a short distance to the

BELOW
Anglers can only reach the lake via floatplane.

LEFT
A typical lake trout from Ena Lake; this one is destined for shore lunch.

Details

Ena Lake, Saskatchewan, Canada

Location/getting there: Ena Lake in northern Saskatchewan is only reached via floatplane from Stony Rapids.

Info sources: Contact Ena Lake Island Lodge at 888-307-9232; or visit www.insportsman.com/enalake/enalake.html. For Saskatchewan information, contact Tourism Saskatchewan, 1922 Park St., Regina, Saskatchewan, S4P 3V7, Canada; call 877-237-2273; or visit www.sasktourism.com.

Prime times: Early summer and late summer for lake trout; all season for pike.

Gear needs: Lake trout: medium to heavy levelwind trolling tackle for deep fishing; lighter baitcasting, spinning and flycasting early in the season; heavy jigs, large trolling spoons and plugs. Pike: Medium to medium-heavy spinning and baitcasting, with 12- to 20-pound line and nine- or ten-weight flycasting outfits; spoons, bucktail spinners, soft jerkbaits and shallow-running plugs. All hooks must be barbless.

Guide/tackle availability: Ena Lake Island Lodge is the only facility on the lake. Fishing is self-guided. Bring your own tackle; some lures and terminal gear are available at the lodge.

Accommodations/dining: The lodge is rustic, comfortable and pleasantly situated on a mid-lake island with a sandy beach. Cedar-sided cabins have full plumbing and hold four guests apiece.

Etcetera: The season at Ena runs from early June until late September, although late-season anglers must be a hardy bunch. Costs are about $2,895 for a week, all-inclusive from Stony Rapids.

Lake Trout

Northern Pike

English River/ Awesome Lake

Labrador, Canada

Brook Trout

RIGHT
An enormous brook trout caught on a large surface fly on the English River.

Almost due east of the city of Goose Bay, Labrador, and nestled in high mountain country in one of this province's most beautiful locales, the English River is virtually unknown to most traveling anglers and even to many Labradorians. The English rivals better-known waters in Labrador with its untapped bounty of speckled trout (brook trout), some of which are in the five- to eight-pound class.

The most popular method of fishing is with floating lines and large surface flies. This technique is beloved by all anglers because it produces exciting visual strikes and outstanding battles. Using big flies, especially deer hair mice, is a Labrador phenomenon that one has to experience to believe. Large surface flies, drifted freely or skittered or riffled across the surface, work well because they imitate waterborne lemmings, which are part of the trout's diet.

Visitors here are amazed to catch big trout with one or more of these creatures sticking out of their stomachs. And it is equally amazing to skitter a two-inch-long deer hair mouse across the current so it produces a light vee-shaped wake, then have a speckled trout viciously smash it. If the fish misses the mouse, you may be so excited that you flop the fly line around your ears in haste to cast again. Fortunately, these still-unsophisticated trout are likely to strike again when you make another presentation.

Most of this angling is done in the English River below Awesome Lake, and at five inlet flowages. The lake, which is relatively small, is fed by mountain streams, some with falls near the inlets. It is ringed on the west by the Mealy Mountains, which include peaks of 3,500 and 3,800 feet, making for an inspiring angling backdrop and interesting floatplane access. A trace of snow remains on the slopes throughout the season.

Wading is necessary for most of the angling, and you have to walk across slippery rocks and shorelines,

although a canoe is used to reach fishing spots from camp. There are 20 miles of lightly fished river below the lake.

Awesome Lake does have some depth and is very clear, unlike most of the other speckled trout waters in this province. There is an 80-foot-deep hole in one section, and some big trout have been spotted along the sand bar near there, but few anglers have concentrated on the stillwater.

There are many trout to be had in the river at certain times, especially when the season starts in mid- to late June and through July, and they could undoubtedly be caught readily with hardware, but the camp policy is to use only barbless hooks, to fish by flycasting and to release all fish except an occasional small trout for supper. Several speckled trout over eight pounds have been caught, including a mammoth 28-incher, estimated as weighing at least nine pounds, that was released. Bigger fish, including one estimated at over 30 inches long, have been seen but unhooked.

ABOVE
Fishing for trout on a tributary to Awesome Lake.

Details

English River / Awesome Lake, Labrador, Canada

Location/getting there: The English River and Awesome Lake are located in eastcentral Labrador. Goose Bay is the jump-off point for visitors. Floatplanes make the 90-mile trip from Goose Bay to the camp.

Info sources: Awesome Lake Lodge is the only facility here. Contact them at P.O. Box 358, Station C, Happy Valley, Goose Bay, Labrador A0P 1C0, Canada; call 877-677-3363; or visit www.awesomelake.com. For information about Labrador, contact Tourism Newfoundland and Labrador, P.O. Box 8730, St. John's, Newfoundland A1B 4K2, Canada; call 800-563-6353; or visit www.gov.nf.ca/tourism.

Prime times: All summer, although weather can be difficult in late August and September.

Gear needs: A seven- to nine-weight rod is useful, the larger size helping to cast bulky flies better, with a floating fly line and eight- to nine-foot leader, but anglers have had success going much lighter. A full-sinking or sink-tip line may be needed if the fish are not rising. Large deer hair flies, especially those that imitate mice, plus such patterns as a Woolly Worm, Bomber, Muddler Minnow or even a Royal Wulff, will raise fish, but even smaller flies, on No. 18 and 20 hooks, have caught five-pound fish. Bring waders with grippers on the soles.

Guide/tackle availability: Guides are supplied; tackle is not.

Accommodations/dining: An incoming overnight stay is required in Goose Bay; country-style meals are good and hearty at the main lodge, and guests stay in heated cabins with shared bathrooms in the main lodge.

Etcetera: The fishing season is from mid-July through early September. The cost for a week is $2,450, which is all-inclusive except for beverages from Goose Bay.

Ferguson Lake

Nunavut, Canada

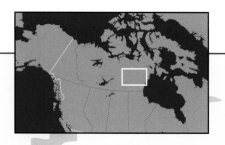

Baker
Lake

Ferguson
Lake

Nunavut

Hudson
Bay

Arviat/Eskimo Point

There are no trees here, which not only means no shade, but also no protection from the wind.

So, on a midsummer afternoon, as you stand on a gritty island-top runway at Ferguson Lake, after 32 hours and four planes worth of travel, climatic shock sets in. The southern heat and humidity that you left have been replaced by northern cool and a brisk wind. It really is not that cold, but you get goose bumps anyway because the wind blows across an endless horizon of shin-high bush and spongy undergrowth, bump-like rock croppings and 20 miles of cold, rippling rich-blue water loaded with lake trout.

Though more likely to be known for its copper and nickel reserves, Ferguson Lake has been yielding good angling to a few anglers annually since a dilapidated mining camp was converted into a lodge in the late 1980s. Many of those anglers also experience excellent action in parts of nearby Yathkyed and Kaminuriak Lakes, which hold 35- and 125-mile-length water respectively. Undisturbed by commercial fishing, domestic netters, and hardly any other anglers, these huge lakes have become a place for multi-faceted trout fishing, where trollers and casters each enjoy success, sometimes with trout that

To find shade in the flat, stark Arctic tundra you must locate a caribou, a musk ox, a person, or a building, of which there are respectively plenty, some, few, and hardly any.

Details

Ferguson Lake, Nunavut, Canada

Location/getting there: Ferguson Lake is in the Keewatin region of Nunavut Territory. It is accessed by flying from Winnipeg to Iqaluit (formerly Rankin Inlet), then by wheeled plane to a landing strip at the lodge.

Info sources: For fishing information, contact Ferguson Lake Lodge, Box 370, Iqaluit, Nunavut, Canada X0C 0G0; call 867-645-2197. For Nunavut information contact Nunavut Tourism, P.O. Box 1450, Iqaluit, Nunavut X0A 0H0, Canada; call 800-491-7910; or visit www.nunatour.nt.ca.

Prime times: Immediately after ice-out.

Gear needs: See the info in Great Bear Lake (see page 106) and Selwyn Lake (see page 110).

Guide/tackle availability: Guided fishing is part of the lodge fishing package. Bring your own tackle.

Accommodations/dining: Ferguson Lake Lodge is the only facility in the area and provides good lodging and food. Outpost camps and fly-out trips are available.

Etcetera: You can literally fish all night here most of the summer, especially in early July when the sun is on the horizon at midnight and you can read a book outside all "night" long. Some of the best fishing occurs when the angle of the sun is low or the night is darkened and the fish move shallow. Bring bug repellent and/or a head net; black flies may be present, and mosquitoes are around all summer. Some locales are accessed on foot; bring warm waterproof boots and perhaps hip waders, as you will get in and out of boats often.

Lake Trout

Grayling

exceed 30 pounds, and all of which are handsome and richly patterned.

They are hardly bothered here, as the season is short; ice usually leaves by early July, but after severe winters it may not fully melt until midsummer. That makes shallow fishing productive, and opens up opportunities for casting with light spinning and baitcasting tackle, as well as with flycasting gear. In addition to fishing in the lake, there is excellent angling to be had in area rivers, especially the Ferguson River, which exits Kaminuriak in a heavy flow with back eddies that are magnets for lake trout.

Lots of action is possible in tributary flows, always with fish that fight with the gusto that a lifetime of living in water surrounded by permafrost can provide. Grayling are also caught in these flows, and are undoubtedly among the forage that lakers depend on.

You may well encounter a small herd of musk ox or caribou while fishing in this area. The Kaminuriak herd of caribou is among Canada's largest, and their pathways are clearly visible from the air. Those who have seen thousands of these animals know what an extraordinary sight it is.

LEFT
Ferguson Lake produces big lake trout that are distinctively marked.

French River

Ontario, Canada

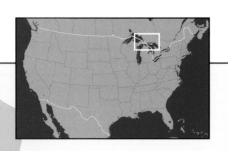

Ontario

Lake Nipissing

French River

Sudbury ●

Georgian Bay

Lake Huron

Michigan

Walleye

Smallmouth Bass

Muskellunge

Northern Pike

Crappie

The French River is situated in southern Ontario, north of Toronto and south of Sudbury. Flowing out of Lake Nipissing and into Georgian Bay on Lake Huron, and traversing a distance of some 110 kilometers, the French River is rich in many ways. Historically, it conveyed French missionaries and explorers, and later pioneers and tradesmen; geologically it exhibits pre-glacial land of the· Canadian Shield formations; recreationally it supplies countless hours of high-quality boating and fishing experiences in one of the most aesthetically satisfying areas of southern Canada.

RIGHT
A French River muskie is held for a photo before release.

The French is a different river in its upper and lower sections, and its reaches include a series of falls and

rapids, some narrow granite-walled sections, bays that have modest flowage and look more like a lake, and a delta with a course of channels leading to the big water.

Walleye, called pickerel in most of Ontario, are the most popularly sought fish of the French and its tributaries. These fish evidently migrate to and from Georgian Bay, with late May, June, July and August being particularly good for angling below the rapids of the lower river out in the delta area, and July night fishing being best for big walleye. The fall months are best for walleye in the river proper. These fish have the potential to grow to ten-pound proportions, and there are a number of such monsters reported each season. Smallmouths are taken throughout the same period, with fish over four pounds possible, and July is also a time to find lots of fish.

Muskies are the river's most fickle fish, but they, too, exist in impressive sizes. A 59-pound seven-ounce muskellunge was caught in 1989 in the Hartley Bay area, making it the largest muskie ever from this waterway on rod and reel. A number of muskies in the 30- and near 40-pound class have come from here over the past 20 years.

This region of Ontario, encompassing waters that flow into Georgian Bay and including the Moon River to the south, have yielded some of North America's biggest muskies over the past few decades. The muskie angling here is almost exclusively trolling. October is generally considered prime, but the aforementioned 59-pounder was caught in the summer. There are plenty of northern pike to be caught as well. Crappies have become more numerous in recent years and are also caught in good sizes.

ABOVE
Navigating a swift, narrow passage between islands on the French River.

Details

French River, Ontario, Canada

Location/getting there: The French River is in central Ontario, about 220 miles north of Toronto, and flows into the northeastern region of Lake Huron's Georgian Bay. Vehicular access is via Route 69. Commercial flights service Sudbury, connecting primarily through Toronto.

Info sources: For fishing and lodging information, contact Bear's Den Lodge; call 705-857-2757 and 814-839-2443; or visit www.bearsdenlodge.com. For area information contact Rainbow Country Travel Association; call 800-465-6655; or visit www.rainbowcountry.com.

Prime times: Spring, early summer and fall for walleye; summer and fall for smallmouth bass; fall for muskies.

Gear needs: Assorted depending on species and methods. Bring your own sonar if you plan to use a lodge boat.

Guide/tackle availability: Guides are available at most lodges/camps, although the majority of fishing is unguided.

Accommodations/dining: There are various lodges in the area with different package plans. Bears Den has a nice main lodge with family-style meals, plus housekeeping cottages.

Etcetera: A small boat or a canoe will suffice in many locales in this region, but a larger and more seaworthy boat is necessary if you want to venture into the big league waters of Georgian Bay. The American plan package, which includes meals, lodging, boat, gas, etc., costs about $1,500 per week for two anglers.

Georgian Bay (upper) / North Channel

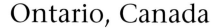
Ontario, Canada

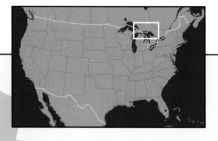

Ontario

Sudbury ●

North Channel

Manitoulin Island

Georgian Bay

Lake Huron

Michigan

Smallmouth Bass

Walleye

Northern Pike

Muskellunge

Chinook Salmon

RIGHT
A fisherman works the rocky shoreline near Baie Fine.

There is a lot of fishing opportunity to be found in the heavily wooded, craggy-bluffed region of northern Lake Huron that is encompassed by upper Georgian Bay and its connected North Channel. This is an area with thousands of islands (30,000 according to some estimates), miles upon miles of limestone cliffs and beaches, better scenery around every bend, frequent floatplane sightings, and housing that ranges from tent-camping in provincial parks to luxuriating in five-star lodges. If there is a draw-back to any type of fishing in this particular area of Lake Huron, it is that there are months if not years worth of water to cover throughout upper Georgian Bay, the North Channel, Manitoulin Island and numerous tributaries.

Details

Georgian Bay (Upper) / North Channel, Ontario, Canada

Location/getting there: The upper Georgian Bay/North Channel region is located in the northernmost area of Lake Huron in central Ontario. Routes 69 and 17 provide access to secondary roads, with prominent access being through Espanola on Route 6 to Whitefish Falls, which in turn provides road access to Manitoulin Island. Commercial flights service Sudbury, connecting primarily through Toronto.

Info sources: For area information contact Rainbow Country Travel Association; call 800-465-6655; or visit www.rainbowcountry.com. Another source of information is www.georgianbay.com.

Prime times: Mid-May through June for walleyes; summer and fall for smallmouth bass; fall for pike and muskies.

Gear needs: Assorted depending on species and fishing methods.

Guide/tackle availability: Although there is some guided fishing and some tackle availability in the area, most people fish without guides and bring their own gear.

Accommodations/dining: Assorted lodging and dining options exist throughout the area.

Etcetera: There are several museums and ten provincial parks in this area. The North Channel and upper Georgian Bay near Killarney is considered to be one of the world's top sailing grounds, and many sailboats (as well as motor yachts) ply these waters each summer. Because of its boating popularity, the region has numerous full-service marinas, and is popular for canoeing and sea kayaking. If you travel through Sudbury, experience the Science North museum (call 800-461-4898 or visit www.sciencenorth.on.ca). The most popular tourist attraction in northern Canada, it contains extraordinary exhibits pertaining to the history and geology of the area, as well as general-interest science exhibits. It is appealing to both young and old, with special hands-on displays as well as an IMAX amphitheater.

Not all of this provides good fishing at any given time. Depending on where you are and who you talk to, the angling is not what it used to be but is getting much better, or pretty darn good for the right angler. Most experienced anglers find good success, especially for smallmouth bass, perhaps the premier sportfish of the area.

The season for smallmouth bass locally opens on the last Saturday in June, and in some parts of this region the cold water still finds bass at that time on spawning nests; they may remain relatively shallow all summer. The problem, if you can call it that, is simply that there are so many rocky islands and shoals and points to fish that you have to be focused and figure out which places are best and why, rather than simply fishing every good-looking spot.

Muskies are a prime catch in and around the northeastern Georgian Bay shores, islands, bays, and tributaries, and some monsters have come out of there. Northern pike are ample in places, especially in the North Channel and in the bays and rivers of northwestern Lake Huron.

Walleyes and yellow perch are also prime catches in the lake and in the rivers. The Spanish River, which flows southwesterly from Espanola to the North Channel, is a top walleye spawning river and a prominent place for this species from mid-May through September. Fairly wide and relatively shallow, the Spanish produces lots of walleyes.

The North Channel has some deep water that produces chinook salmon, lake trout and rainbows to people who both jig (for the latter two species) and troll. Notable is the area around the western end of Manitoulin Island, from Meldrum Bay facing North Channel and around Mississagi Strait to the open water of Lake Huron.

There are numerous small lakes and rivers on the mainland and on Manitoulin Island to fish for bass, walleye, pike and perch. Manitoulin contains Manitou Lake, which is the world's largest lake within an island (30 miles long by up to ten miles wide) and has fishing for bass, perch, pike and lake trout.

Wherever you fish in this region, it is guaranteed to be scenic. Some areas are stunning. Baie Fine near Killarney is one such place. Said to be the longest freshwater fjord in North America, it is flanked by rugged, high and roadless limestone ridges. It can only be reached by boat, and is full of small islands and shoals, plus an alluring calm anchorage known as "The Pool."

LEFT
A typical upper Georgian Bay smallmouth bass, caught on a jig.

Gouin Reservoir

Quebec, Canada

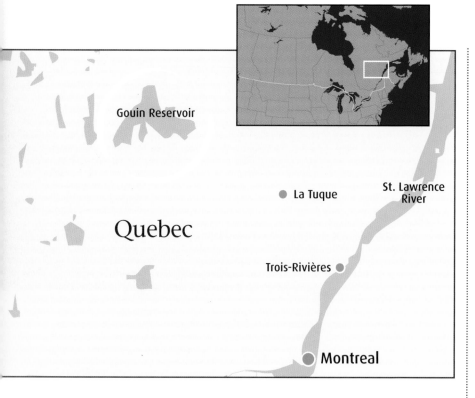

Gouin Reservoir

Quebec

La Tuque

St. Lawrence River

Trois-Rivières

Montreal

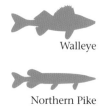
Walleye

Northern Pike

drive over washboard-rutted roads. Traveling to the *barrage* (dam) at Gouin is a mini-adventure in itself.

For the self-guided angler, navigation on this expansive water can also be an adventure, because it is an easy lake to get disoriented on. There are countless islands, bays, inlets, fingers and peninsulas, which can cause the inattentive boater to get lost in a hurry. Fortunately, that is why there are GPS navigational devices as well as maps and compasses. All of these lake features, however, mean

One of North America's least-heralded but most interesting places to fish for both walleyes and northern pike is Gouin Reservoir in Quebec. Gouin (which rhymes with "coin") is a gigantic Canadian-shield lake deep in the wilderness; however, it can be reached by auto, and, with fishing boat in tow, making it an especially desirable location to boat-owning anglers and do-it-yourselfers. Yet, despite its accessibility and excellent fishing potential, Gouin Reservoir is known only to a relative handful of North Americans.

Gouin is a hydroelectric impoundment that stretches about 65 miles from east to west and 43 miles from north to south. It sprawls across the unpaved interior of southcentral Quebec. Some anglers access lodges here directly by floatplane, others by vehicle after a four-hour

an enormous amount of shoreline, loads of places to hide if the wind kicks up and lots of habitat for both walleye and northern pike.

The walleye run to good average sizes, two to four pounds, when the spring run is on. By concentrating on some of the major tributaries in late May and early June (such as the Wapous River near Deziel Bay), you can catch plenty such specimens. Bigger fish, up to ten pounds, are caught as well, and on the lake proper. There is no end to rocky shoals, points and other desirable walleye locales.

The situation is similar with northern pike, although larger sizes are encountered. Reportedly, fish over 20 pounds are taken, and a 31-pounder was landed some years back, but it is more likely that you will find them from seven to 15 pounds, especially when you focus on the shallow portions of many bays. There are also whitefish and sauger here, and a few small nearby lakes that contain brook trout.

ABOVE
An angler gears up for fishing on Gouin Reservoir.
OPPOSITE
A dinner catch of Gouin walleyes.

Details

Gouin Reservoir, Quebec, Canada

Location/getting there: Gouin Reservoir is located in southcentral Quebec, midway between Val-d'Or and Roberval and south of Chibougamou. It is reached by driving Route 155 from Trois Rivières to LaTuque and then heading 125 miles inland to the dam via Routes 10 or 25. Floatplane access is from St. Veronique.

Info sources: For fishing information, contact Oasis du Gouin, 40 Rue de Courcelle, Repentigny, Quebec, Canada, J5Y 3X4; call 800-959-7453 and 819-974-8825; or visit www.fishing-quebec.com. Also contact Club Marmette, C.P. 129., Maniwaki, Quebec, Canada J9E 3B4; call 800-567-1265 or 819-449-3386.

Prime times: Late spring can provide excellent fishing for ice-out pike and for walleyes. Larger fish are more likely late in the summer.

Gear needs: Light- to medium-action spinning and baitcasting gear; assorted crankbaits from shallow runners to deep divers; light- to medium-weight jigs; and a selection of spoons and spinners.

Guide/tackle availability: Most anglers fish unguided, but there is limited guide availability at some camps. Bring your own tackle. When using a lodge boat without a guide, bring portable sonar and a handheld GPS.

Accommodations/dining: Lodging and dining options vary depending on whether you are at a full-service (American plan) lodge, an outpost cabin, or an efficiency-type camp.

Etcetera: Some facilities here offer houseboats, which give you the chance to move your lodging around the lake, explore at will, and bring a fishing boat at the same time; just be sure that you have the ability to navigate this big lake.

Great Bear Lake

Northwest Territories, Canada

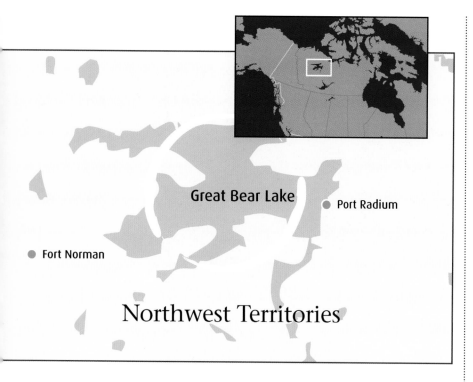

Great Bear Lake

Port Radium

Fort Norman

Northwest Territories

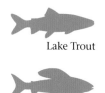

Lake Trout

Grayling

Northern Pike

Only a couple of thousand anglers—spread widely across the five arms of the lake at different camps—fish in this land of low brush and small trees. They cannot cover all of the places where fish roam, the result being that there are creatures in Great Bear that have never seen a fishhook, and probably will never see one.

The majority of visiting anglers come to catch a giant lake trout. Officially a trophy NWT laker is one that exceeds 20 pounds; the majority of people who come to one of the different camps, all now part of Plummer's Arctic Lodges, achieve this plateau. Many strike gold with trout that surpass 30 and 40 pounds, and a select few hit the 50-pound or better mark. All are released alive.

It was not always this way, as many big trout were killed in earlier decades, and, despite the enormity of Great Bear, an earlier lack of conservation took a toll on huge lakers. These fish are fairly long-lived, although recent evidence suggests they are not as aged (100) as was once widely believed. Some specimens (the red-finned, insect-eating variety) have been aged to 44 years.

It is unarguably the greatest lake trout water of all time. Together with its tributaries, it is arguably the greatest grayling water, too. Yet even the biggest grayling in Great Bear Lake is not a full meal for many of the giant lakers that swim there. Although the largest recorded lake trout known was netted elsewhere (in the 1960s in Lake Athabasca), the record books are loaded with giant *namaycush* from this body of water.

Although it is the fourth-largest lake in North America, Great Bear is more like a sea. Spanning the Arctic Circle and within the confines of the recently reconfigured Northwest Territories (NWT), the lake encompasses more than 12,000 square miles, yet is 250 miles from the nearest road. The only boat traffic it sees is by anglers in 18-foot aluminum boats propelled by 30-horsepower motors and that during just eight weeks of the year.

RIGHT
Great Bear Lake Lodge, viewed from the water.

This 74-pound lake trout, caught and released in Great Bear Lake in June 2001, became an unofficial world record.

Catch-and-release, concerted efforts by guides to carefully handle and revive big fish, the employment of barbless hooks and an increased use of sonar and GPS have contributed to a revival in big-trout catches. In 1991, a 66$^1/_2$-pound lake trout was landed, replacing a 65-pound record that had stood since 1970. In 1995, a 72-pounder established a new official mark. In 2000, an estimated 78-pounder was caught on a newly found reef; there was no scale in the boat large enough to weigh the fish, so its size was estimated from length and girth measurements, establishing an unofficial world record. And, on June 27, 2001, a 74-pounder was caught and weighed in the boat before being released.

The same day that the 74-pounder was caught, the people who did so were part of a two-boat crew that landed 11 trout over 40 pounds, surely one of the greatest lake trout feats of all time. The 74-pounder, unfortunately, did not qualify for record status because it was weighed in the boat and not on firm footing ashore.

Add to these established catches the fact that a few 60-pound-plus fish have been caught each year in recent

RIGHT
*Anglers board a
floatplane to visit
a remote area of
Great Bear Lake.*

Details

Great Bear Lake, Northwest Territories, Canada

Location/getting there: Great Bear Lake straddles the Arctic Circle in the Northwest Territories. Access is via chartered jet from Winnipeg, Edmonton, or Yellowknife. For week-long visits, a stayover in one of these cities is usually required both going and coming.

Info sources: Contact Plummer's Arctic Lodges, 950 Bradford St., Winnipeg, MB R3H 0N5; call 204-774-5775 or 800-665-0240; and visit www.plummerslodges.com. For Northwest Territories information, contact Northwest Territories Tourism, Box 610, Yellowknife, NWT, Canada X1A 2N5; call 800-661-0788; and visit www.nwttravel.nt.ca.

Prime times: The season is about eight weeks, from the beginning of July to late August. Many anglers prefer the first two weeks, which are booked well in advance, although late ice can hamper movement around the lake; big trout are more concentrated and shallow then. For grayling, the last half of the season is best.

Gear needs: Lake trout: medium to heavy levelwind trolling tackle for big fish; lighter baitcasting, spinning and flycasting for smaller specimens; large trolling spoons (Eppinger, Thompson, and Lucky Lures) and plugs (mainly the T-60 model Flatfish). Grayling: light spinning and five-weight flycasting; small jigs, spinners, dry flies, nymphs, and wet flies. Pike: medium to medium-heavy spinning and baitcasting, with 12- to 20-pound line and nine- or ten-weight flycasting outfits; spoons, bucktail spinners, soft jerkbaits, and shallow-running plugs. Hooks should be barbless.

Guide/tackle availability: Guides are part of the package cost. The lodges are well equipped with appropriate lures, flies, swivels, insect repellent, batteries and other incidentals, and can lend rubber chest waders to those going on river fly-out trips. Some loaner rods and reels may be available, but it is best to bring your own.

Accommodations/dining: There is good, ample food for breakfast and dinner at the lodges and a cash bar. The entire day is spent on the water, and shore lunch of freshly caught lake trout is part of the daily regime if you want. Accommodations are motel-style, with private baths, heaters and daily housekeeping. There is electricity at the camp and standard outlets for electrical devices, as well as a limited (and very costly) emergency satellite telephone service. Trout are occasionally smoked for appetizers; ask for some to take in the boat.

Etcetera: Many of the largest fish are caught at locations accessed by day-long fly-outs (ranging from $200 to $400 per person) from one of the lodges. Big fish are caught all season but are less concentrated and more scattered after the first few weeks. Without a fly-out, it may be necessary to run from 45 to 90 minutes to get to less pressured fishing ground. This huge lake can get very rough at times. Warm footwear, a good rain/wind suit, fishing gloves and insect repellent are musts. Costs for a week (Saturday to Saturday) are $3,995, which includes transportation from Edmonton/Winnipeg/Yellowknife, but excludes beverages, licenses and tips.

times as well as a number over 50 pounds, plus the fact that eight out of ten current world record line-class categories come from Great Bear Lake, and you can see that no other body of water comes close even in the mega-trophy department.

The tried-and-true method of lake trout fishing here—trolling with the biggest spoons and plugs—works day after day, week after week and season after season. The big lakers come at all times of the summer. Some regulars—there is a very high percentage of returnees to Great Bear—prefer early in the season, which means the first days of July, to get the shallow, concentrated ice-out advantage, while others prefer late in the summer when the fish are heavier and ready to spawn, albeit more widely scattered.

Many visitors here enjoy a diversion with lighter tackle for Arctic grayling, which are so abundant that specialists can easily catch dozens a day (one fly rod angler managed 200 in a single day at the Horton River in August 2001). Seven of eight line-class world records, plus the all-tackle

world record (five pounds 15 ounces) were established here. Great numbers are caught in tributary rivers, but many large fish are caught along the lake shoreline.

Great Bear anglers also get in some mighty fine Arctic charr fishing on the Tree and Coppermine Rivers via fly-outs. These rivers are covered separately in this book; in the case of the Tree, it should be noted that 95 per cent of sportfishing access is via a fly-out from Plummer's Great Bear Lake Lodge, making this an incredible triple whammy for great fishing. It is totally conceivable on one trip to catch a lake trout over 20 pounds, an Arctic charr over 15 pounds and a grayling over three pounds.

There is also a good population of northern pike in Great Bear. Many anglers enjoy a day of casting in bays for these fish, which are fairly numerous although not humongous. The odd large pike is caught at Great Bear, but this latitude is near the northern limit for that species. Pike are fun but not as compelling as catching a 50-pound laker that still has the tail of a five-pound trout sticking out of its stomach.

BELOW
Grayling are numerous, and large, in Great Bear and its tributaries.

Great Slave Lake

Northwest Territories, Canada

Northwest
Territories

Yellowknife

Fort Providence

Great Slave Lake

Fort Resolution

The 11th-largest lake in the world, Great Slave is 298 miles long and in some places over 2,000 feet deep. Containing over 11,000 square miles of water, it can hardly be missed on any map. This enormous lake has long been renowned for its lake trout, and in its post-World War II heyday, huge lakers were caught (and kept, unfortunately) regularly. Then it slumped in terms of producing large fish, but has been rebounding in recent years thanks to catch-and-release fishing efforts.

The prospect of catching big lake trout remains the lake's prime lure. A 74-pounder is reputed to have been netted at Great Slave many years ago, and anglers have caught

Lake Trout

Grayling

Northern Pike

Walleye

RIGHT
*Great Slave has lots
of water and not
much competition.*

them to 58½ pounds in more modern times. This mammoth body of water does contain some monsters, but it does not produce big trout with the same regularity as Great Bear Lake.

Nevertheless, Great Slave contains plenty of trout, and you do not have to be a veteran angler to catch fish. Trolling near shore around points, reefs and islands has long been the predominant tactic for lakers here. The water is always cold, and most trout are caught just ten to 20 feet deep. Many of them are in the ten- to 20-pound class.

The East Arm is blessed with islands and peninsulas, which make it geologically distinct from the wide-open remainder of the lake. This end has been reserved for sportfishing in recent years, with trophy fishing regulations in place. It has been made famous by Talteilei Narrows and the Stark and Lockhart Rivers, which are known for big lake trout, grayling, pike and whitefish.

Talteilei Narrows acts as a channel between McLeod and Christie Bays. Wind-driven currents on the big bays push the water back and forth through the Narrows creating eddies and backwaters, and the Talteilei area continues to produce spectacular trophies.

Remarkably good angling takes place at Stark River, using light spinning or fly gear for grayling up to three pounds, small trout, and the occasional whitefish. At the best of times it is a virtual bonanza, and there is good reason to understand why some have called the Stark the greatest grayling river in the world. The possibility of catching three- to four-pound grayling is very good.

The Stark is shallow, cold and swift. Pools, eddies, deep holes and the edges of riffles hold packs of grayling and some lake trout, and the mouth of the river contains a cornucopia of trout, grayling and whitefish. One of the positives of this location is the opportunity to fish five

ABOVE
A big laker is landed in Christie Bay.

Snowdrift River's volume attracts fish from the lake.

bodies of water in all: the Stark and Snowdrift Rivers as well as Stark, Great Slave and Murky Lakes, the latter having good northern pike fishing.

The North Arm is a maze of granite reefs that shelter some of the best northern pike in the NWT. Not only do the low islands and submerged structures provide great habitat, but they protect the pike waters around Trout Rock from casual boaters.

Fort Resolution is the jump-off point for fishing the Slave River Delta and the lower Taltson River. Local outfitters take clients out for northern pike, inconnu, walleye and whitefish. Road access allows Mackenzie Highway travelers to drive in and meet their guides.

The outlet of Great Slave Lake, where it enters the Mackenzie River, has some overlooked good fishing, with superb grayling, pike, whitefish and walleye angling around Brabant and Lobstick Islands. The Mackenzie Highway spur to the community of Hay River on the south shore of Great Slave Lake is a short bush flight from the lodge at Brabant Island. Adding to the value of the fishing here is the landscape, from the mountains that shield Wildbread Bay to the picturesque falls up the Snowdrift River. There are often spectacular sunsets, and you may (though rare in summer) observe the northern lights. For most of June and July it is light all night long, however, and you can fish late into the night.

Details

Great Slave Lake, Northwest Territories, Canada

Location/getting there: Great Slave Lake is located in the southcentral region of the Northwest Territories. Most anglers access it via chartered flights from Edmonton to Yellowknife, then via floatplane to the lodge. There is road access from the south through Alberta to Fort Resolution, Hay River and Yellowknife, but no road access further east.

Info sources: Contact Plummer's Arctic Lodges, 950 Bradford St., Winnipeg, MB R3H 0N5; call 204-774-5775 or 800-665-0240; or visit www.plummerslodges.com. Also contact Frontier Fishing Lodge, P.O. Box 32008, Edmonton, Alberta, T6K 4C2, Canada; call 780-465-6843; or visit www.frontierfishing.ab.ca/frontier.html. For Northwest Territories information, contact Northwest Territories

Tourism, Box 610, Yellowknife, NWT, Canada X1A 2N5; call 800-661-0788; or visit www.nwttravel.nt.ca.

Prime times: Many anglers prefer the first several weeks of the season, when the ice is departing, for concentrated trout and large fish that are shallow. For grayling, the middle and latter part of the season are best.

Gear needs: See the gear needs information for Great Bear Lake (see page 106).

Guide/tackle availability: Guides are part of the lodge package cost. Bring your own tackle, although some selection of lures and incidentals may be available at the lodges.

Accommodations/dining: There is good, ample food for breakfast and dinner at the lodges, with daily shore lunches for those who want them. Accommodations are motel-style, with private baths, heaters and daily housekeeping.

Etcetera: Fishing takes place at distant eastern lodges from mid-June through mid-September. Some visitors to Plummer's camp at Great Slave make a fly-out to fish for Arctic charr at the Tree River. Costs for a week are approximately $2,500, inclusive from Edmonton, excluding overnight accommodations in either Yellowknife or Edmonton.

Hudson River

New York, United States

The tidal Hudson River offers surprisingly good and diverse fishing from the Tappan Zee Bridge spanning Haverstraw Bay to the dam at Troy. The Hudson has enjoyed both a water quality comeback and a resurgence in top-rate angling that makes it a prime place in the northeastern U.S. to fish for largemouth and smallmouth bass, and an awesome spring hotspot for stripers, despite marginal shore fishing opportunities and the fact that transient boating is hampered by insufficient access.

A million or so stripers migrate into the Hudson each year to spawn, traversing 154 miles from Manhattan to Troy. These fish generally begin moving up the river in March, by mid-April have reached Newburgh and by late April have reached Kingston and beyond.

Spawning takes place when the water has warmed to the mid- to upper 50s, which is usually around mid- to late May. By mid-June, the main body of stripers has moved downstream and disperses in New York Harbor and along the coast. Some fish, mostly small schoolies, remain in the river through the summer. Fish over 50 pounds have been caught in the river.

Prominent striper fishing areas include Croton Point, Storm King Mountain, Denning Point, Esopus Meadows

BELOW
Spring morning scene on the Hudson River near Kingston.

Albany

New York

Catskill

Kingston

Newburgh

New York City

Striped Bass

Largemouth Bass

American Shad

due to the fact that virtually all bass are released. Shoals, sandbars, islands and rockpiles are main river spots, with the focus on assorted structure in creeks.

The Hudson River has other species as well. Crappie and trout are common in many creeks, and there are plenty of carp, some large, in the main river as well as white catfish and white perch. Sturgeon have historically been present, but there is no sportfishery for them. Bluefish range into the saline parts of the lower river, and provide excitement when available.

and the vicinity of Rondout, Esopus and Catskill Creeks. Very little casting is done, with most anglers drifting, anchoring or trolling. Tide changes are important, with most activity on a moving tide. The largest stripers regularly fall to bait; live herring, chunks of herring and live eels are mainstays.

Overshadowed by stripers lately are American shad. Hudson River shad were historically abundant and among the largest specimens on the East Coast. Their numbers have fluctuated in recent times and the expansiveness of the Hudson daunts would-be shad pursuers. Some anglers have success with flies and darts that are fished behind boats anchored in mid-river on the downstream edge of shoals, flats and islands. The run peaks between late April and early June.

From late spring through fall, there is action for largemouth and smallmouth bass on the Hudson. All of the major creeks, and portions of the main river from just south of Constitution Marsh near West Point to north of Coxsackie, produce bass.

Cover, current and tide are interrelated here, and sometimes so is salt content. The Hudson is slightly brackish or completely freshwater somewhere around Cornwall Bay, although the exact location may vary. Bass move and feed on tide changes, and fishing is usually best when the water is at peak movement rising or falling, with a falling tide prime. The average size of Hudson bass is fairly good, with two-pounders common. This is in spite of heavy fishing pressure and largely

RIGHT
A Hudson River striper.

Details

Hudson River, New York, United States

Location/getting there: The Hudson River is in eastern New York, with many adjacent major roadways and a busy commercial airport at Newburgh.

Info sources: For general area information, visit the web site of Hudson Valley Tourism, www.pojonews.com; from there you can contact and access the different county tourism agencies along the river.

Prime times: May is prime for striped bass, fall for largemouth and smallmouth bass.

Gear needs: Assorted depending on species and fishing method.

Guide/tackle availability: A number of charter boat operators fish in spring for striped bass. There is little guiding for other fish. Tackle and bait is available at local stores and some marinas.

Accommodations/dining: Lodging and dining options range widely throughout the area. One good facility favored by many anglers is Friar Tuck Resort and Convention Center, 4858 State Route 32, Catskill, NY 12414; call 800-832-7600; or visit

www.friartuck.com. Catskill, Saugerties, Kingston, and Newburgh are major fishing access areas.

Etcetera: Locating access points is difficult and requires some homework; check on ramps and general lower river information at www.hrfanj.org, the web site of the Hudson River Fishermens Association. Boaters need to exercise caution due to tidal flow and wave action, and the possibility of encountering floating objects. The prettiest section of river is the Hudson Highlands, which includes Bear Mountain north of Peekskill, and the U.S. Military Academy at West Point.

ABOVE
*Playing a fish on
the upper Hudson.*

ABOVE *Smallmouth bass are among the more popular species in the Kawarthas.*

Walleye

Smallmouth Bass

Largemouth Bass

Muskellunge

Kawartha Lakes

Ontario, Canada

The Kawartha Lakes is a group of 15 connected lakes in east-southcentral Ontario that are actually part of the lengthy, navigable Trent-Severn Waterway. The Kawarthas region is one of the greatest recreation playgrounds in Canada and is just two hours north-northeast of Toronto. Although the area is developed, it is not spoiled, and the fishing is fairly good. The area is particularly known as a place for family vacations; many people explore the area by houseboat camping and cruising, going from lake to lake through a system of locks.

The fishing attractions include largemouth and smallmouth bass, walleyes, muskies, yellow perch, rock bass, bluegills and catfish. Not only are these fish available in good numbers through the summer, but there is also a seemingly endless number of fishing spots.

Walleyes are the premier fish. Called pickerel here, they are abundant in virtually every lake. The heaviest walleye fishing occurs in the spring, especially for the first few weeks after the season opens on the first Saturday in May. Walleyes are well distributed in all sizes and range up to ten pounds, although a five-pounder is large enough to raise eyebrows and the average is a two-pounder.

Also popular in the Kawarthas, and no less abundant, are largemouth and smallmouth bass. The shallow, stumpy, weedy nature of all or parts of the Kawartha Lakes

Details

Kawartha Lakes, Ontario, Canada

Location/getting there: The city of Peterborough is a gateway to the Kawartha region, and can be accessed via major roads. It is about 140 miles from the Thousand Islands Bridge and about 160 miles from Niagara Falls.

Info sources: For area information, contact Kawartha Lakes Tourism, 175 George Street North, Peterborough, Ontario, Canada K9J 3G6; call 800-461-6424; or visit www.thekawarthas.net.

Prime times: Summer is the busiest season, with loads of boat traffic and powerboat activity; swimming is best then, but the better fishing, because of cooler temperatures and less boat traffic, is early for walleyes, and later for bass and muskies.

Gear needs: Assorted gear depending on species and methods.

Guide/tackle availability: There is little guided fishing locally; tackle is available at various outlets locally, although most visitors bring what they need.

Accommodations/dining: Lodging and dining options are numerous throughout the area.

Etcetera: This region is rich in history, having been a major travel route for the likes of Samuel de Champlain and other explorers, as well as the Iroquois and Huron Indians. Transformed into a system of natural and man-made lakes, linked by canals and locks, it was once a vehicle for commerce, but today is primarily a means of water control and a source for recreational navigation.

makes them especially good havens for largemouths. In the main sections of most of the lakes, there are enough rocky points, islands and reefs to find smallmouths. Panfish are available everywhere, though the bigger specimens are more likely to be caught away from the docks, locks and near-shore locales. Muskies are a popular target for dedicated muskie anglers and vary in availability; they range from 36 to 53 inches in size, with a 30-pounder being a large specimen.

The better fishing spots include Buckhorn, Pigeon and Stoney Lakes for largemouth bass; Balsam and Buckhorn for smallmouths; and Balsam, Pigeon, and Sturgeon for walleyes. Buckhorn, Lower Buckhorn, Pigeon, Chemong, Lovesick, Clear, Stoney and Rice are better locales for

muskies, many being shallower and having lots of vegetation. Rice and Scugog are noted for all species.

The eastern end of the Kawarthas, including Lakes Katchewanooka, Clear, Stoney and Lovesick, are the prettiest. The narrow and island-studded Hell's Gate junction of Clear and Stoney Lakes is particularly beautiful. With the possible exception of the main body of Sturgeon Lake, there are plenty of places to go if the wind kicks up. By studying navigation charts one can find an array of back bays, fingers, marshes and offtrack hideaways to fish or explore.

LEFT
Boaters queue up in the Rosedale Lock.

Kennebec River

Maine, United States

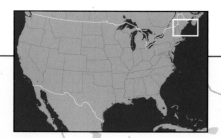

Maine

- Skowhegan
- Augusta
- Kennebec River Popham Beach
- Portland

Atlantic Ocean

The Kennebec River has long been an excellent fishery for diverse species, but things have really blossomed since the early 1990s, with the tremendous number of coastal striped bass that exist in the Northeast, plus the history-making removal of a dam on the lower river. Deliberately breached on July 1, 1999, the Edwards Dam in Augusta, erected in 1835, caused the extermination of most native Kennebec River striped bass. The stripers, and other anadromous species, were unable to go further upstream for all that time, although a small population survived by spawning in the marginal (for reproduction) water below the dam site.

Striped bass, which spawn locally in June, now have access to historic spawning grounds upstream of the dam site, and, just as importantly (since their numbers off the Maine coast are supplemented by fish spawned further south), provide delightful

RIGHT
Striped bass are abundant and very popular on the lower Kennebec River.

action in places where they were formerly unavailable. Anglers upriver are now catching stripers in places where they also tackle with smallmouth bass, sometimes on the same jigs, jerkbaits or flies.

The majority of the stripers, however, are caught in the lower reaches and in the tidewater section, where a world-class, small-boat sportfishery exists for stripers and thousands of bass are landed annually. There are 35 miles of striped bass fishing from Augusta to the river's mouth and to the waterways that connect it to the Sheepscot River. This includes the Sasanoa River with its Upper Hell's Gate, Hockomock Bay, the Cross River and Lower Hell's Gate. Live bait, plugs, jigs and flies all produce stripers locally, and much of the best fishing takes place during the outgoing tide and on rips. Fly fishing for stripers is especially productive. Launch ramps in the lower reach are available at Bath, Phippsburg and Hallowell (on the Kennebec), and Wiscasset (on the Sheepscot).

Popham Beach, on the western shore of the mouth of the Kennebec, is a popular and easily accessed surf fishing spot for stripers and bluefish. The coastline around the corner and stretching southwest to Small Point, which is mostly sand beach dotted with rocky islands and ledges, is good striper territory and can be worked from shore or boat. Seguin Island, two miles offshore, is surrounded by deeper waters which can produce bass and blues on trolled swimming plugs.

Moving upriver, the middle region of the Kennebec has very good smallmouth bass fishing, as well as wading, floating and motorized small-boat access opportunities. Some parts of the river are several hundred yards wide.

The section from Augusta to Skowhegan has been a good brown trout fishery in the past, although the

ABOVE
Upper Kennebec anglers land a smallmouth bass.

presence of striped bass has caused fisheries' biologists to change stocking schedules to coincide with the departure of stripers in order to minimize predation. Brown trout up to 16 inches are routine, and there are larger specimens, as well as some good-sized rainbow trout, but people catch fish all 12 months here.

Further north there is good fishing for trout, including wild rainbow trout as well as brook trout and the occasional landlocked salmon, especially in the tailwaters below several dams. Float fishing is popular in some stretches, as is wade fishing. The section below Wyman Dam is especially noteworthy for large fish. Water levels may rise quickly here due to releases, so anglers must be careful.

Details

Kennebec River, Maine, United States

Location/getting there: Located in westcentral Maine, the Kennebec flows south through Augusta to the coast northeast of Portland; it is paralleled by Route 201 for much of its length.

Info sources: For area information contact the Maine Office of Tourism at 888-624-6345; or visit www.visitmaine.com. Also contact the Bath Chamber of Commerce at 207-725-8797; or visit www.mainesmidcoast.com.

Prime times: Striped bass are caught from late May into early September, but prime time in the river is in June. For trout, June, early

July, and September are tops.

Gear needs: Varies depending on species and fishing methods.

Guide/tackle availability: A number of striper guides operate out of Bath, Phippsburg, Hallowell, Wiscasset, Boothbay Harbor and ports in Casco Bay. For upriver fishing, contact Northern Outdoors at 800-765-7238; or visit www.northernoutdoors.com.

Accommodations/dining: A wide array of lodging and dining options exist throughout the tidewater and upriver areas; a notable

upscale option in Freeport is Harraseeket Inn; call 800-342-6423; or visit www.www.stayfreeport.com. Owner Chip Gray runs an outfitting service out of the inn and can arrange for guides and transportation for guests.

Etcetera: You can observe bald eagles, ospreys, seals, and other wildlife, as well as lighthouses and plenty of lobster boats in the tidewater region of the Kennebec, so bring binoculars. Many tourists make a visit to the L.L. Bean store in Freeport.

Striped Bass

Smallmouth Bass

Brown Trout

Rainbow Trout

Kesagami Lake

Ontario, Canada

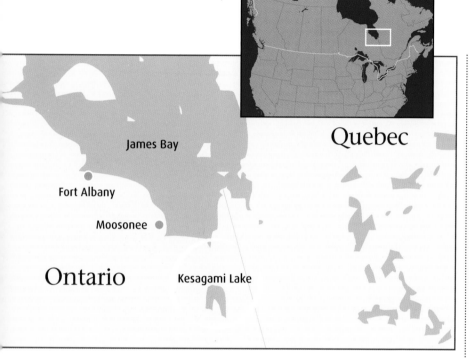

James Bay

Fort Albany

Moosonee

Ontario

Kesagami Lake

Quebec

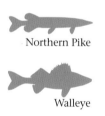

Northern Pike

Walleye

One of the finest and most unusual pike lakes in Canada is Kesagami, a little-known gem in the northwest corner of Ontario about 60 miles south of James Bay. By any standard, Kesagami fits the Ministry of Tourism appellation "Crown Jewel." An isolated water without road access, Kesagami Lake makes up most of Kesagami Provincial Park. Covering over 100 square miles, the lake is situated in a flat and poorly drained region of peat bog and muskeg. The surrounding terrain contains flora rare or unique to Canada and/or Ontario, including the fen meadow, and it is noted for high peat banks, some 13 feet deep.

Kesagami is an unusually shallow lake, with an average depth of seven feet and a maximum depth of 29. It has 180 miles of shoreline, many bays, and seven islands, one of which recently produced a 17th century French axe,

musket barrels and bone fragments. Speculation is that the island may have once been an aboriginal cemetery.

Being shallow, Kesagami warms early, contributing to a growth rate well above normal for the region. This, combined with a baitfish population of ciscoes, suckers and whitefish, produces a prodigious number of walleyes and many unusually plump northern pike. The Ministry of Natural Resources has netted a 35-inch pike here that weighed 25 pounds. While that is exceptional, it is common to see Kesagami pike with large shoulders and plenty of girth.

Details

Location/getting there: Kesagami Lake is located in Northern Ontario just below James Bay and northeast of Cochrane. Visitors drive to Cochrane via Highway 11, or fly to Timmins and take a 70-minute van shuttle to Cochrane. Cochrane Air Service flies people to the lake by floatplane.

Info sources: For lake fishing and lodging info, contact Kesagami Wilderness Lodge, c/o Michelbob's Restaurants, 371 Airport Rd. N., Naples, FL 34104; call 800-253-3474; or visit www.kesagami.com. For area info, contact the Northern Ontario Information and Reservation Centre, Suite 315, 1100c Memorial Ave., Thunder Bay, Ontario, Canada, P7B 4A3; call 800-947-8066; or visit www.getnorth.com.

Prime times: The entire June through September season is good; early season may have more bugs and later in the season is cooler.

Gear needs: Typical spinning, baitcasting and flycasting tackle. Large weedless spoons are especially good for pike, and jigs for walleyes.

Guide/tackle availability: Guides are available but not as part of the lodge package; many anglers fish unguided. The lodge has a limited selection of tackle available, but plan to bring your own.

Accommodations/dining: Kesagami Wilderness Lodge has deluxe lodge accommodations and private log cabins; food is excellent and at least one meal will be the owner's award-winning barbecue ribs.

Etcetera: Lodge rates range from $1,199 to $1,799 (from Cochrane) for three- to seven-day stays, not including guides, license and incidentals. There is self-guided, outpost-camp fishing for pike and walleye on six-mile-long Edgar Lake, and numerous other outpost lakes in the area. An interesting side excursion in the area is a trip to Moosonee on the southern end of James Bay aboard the Polar Bear Express. The train embarks from Cochrane, which is a jump-off point for northern adventure, from late June into September, and traverses 186 miles through the peat and muskeg forests, passing historic fur trade rivers like the Abitibi and Moose. This is one of the great rail excursions in North America, and draws railroad buffs from all over the world. For information contact Ontario Northland at 800-268-9281 or visit www.polarbearexpress.ca.

LEFT
Sunset fishing at Kesagami Lake.

Indeed, there are many pike here 15 pounds or better, and some in the 25- to 35-pound range. In many years the largest pike recorded (caught and released) at Kesagami has exceeded 50 inches; a 54-incher was released in 1999.

In the early 1990s, new owners purchased Kesagami Wilderness Lodge, a four-star Swiss Alpine facility, and instituted new conservation policies, including catch-and-release for pike and walleye (except for small shore lunch walleye), and the use of single barbless hooks. They shortened the fishing season to limit overall pressure, and in addition equipped each boat with a fish cradle instead of a landing net.

While the emphasis for many people is on pike at the lake, walleyes are truly abundant, and some guests do nothing but fish for walleyes, as it is often possible to catch a hundred or more per boat in a day. They mostly average two pounds, but range from three to six, and are so plentiful that a couple of hours of walleye fishing is sure to bring a successful diversion from hunting for trophy pike.

Other than occasional wilderness river paddlers, only the lodge and its guests have access to the lake, and only the lodge can use motorized boats, which is unusual in a provincial park. Anglers fish from 23-foot-long freighter canoes, which are a great stable vessel for casting lures or flies in the shallow back bays, or for drifting for walleyes.

Lac Beauchene

Quebec, Canada

One of the finest places in North America to fish for smallmouth bass is in southwestern Quebec brook trout country. Sounds a little strange, perhaps, but not if you have been to La Reserve Beauchene, which has not only good fishing for smallmouth bass and brook trout, but also plenty of walleyes and lake trout, plus action for northern pike.

Perhaps the most notable thing about La Reserve Beauchene is the place itself, because it signifies what many anglers today want from a high-quality, remote angling experience, and what some astute lodge owners and outfitters are striving to supply: good, well-managed fishing (it is catch-and-release except for shore lunch) in an aesthetically pleasing setting and attention to improving and preserving the resource so that it will last.

The heart of the fishing takes place on 12-mile-long Lac Beauchene. It is the largest of numerous lakes in the reserve, which includes 45,000 acres of land where the hunting and fishing rights are privately and exclusively leased from the provincial government. Recreation, which can be enjoyed by the public for a fee, is strictly managed.

The main attraction is smallmouth bass, which were reputedly stocked here over 70 years ago. They have thrived in excellent habitat, and as a result of catch-and-release fishing.

Beauchene's bass are hardy and chunky fish; many are in the three- to four-pound class, with some ranging higher. At times the bass can be rather elusive, and at other times almost too easy to catch. Various lures and methods produce bass here, with jigs, soft jerkbaits and minnow-imitating plugs especially favored, and with

Smallmouth Bass

Brook Trout

Walleye

Lake Trout

Northern Pike

LEFT
Casting for bass in a shallow bay on Lac Beauchene.

conditions being different (due to depth and temperature) on many of the smaller lakes from the main lake.

Lac Beauchene has plenty of lake trout, mainly in the three- to five-pound class, plus walleyes. In May, the lakers are very shallow and can be caught relatively easily. Five other lakes on the reserve also possess lakers. Walleyes in Lac Beauchene have been caught to 15 pounds, but are typically smaller, though plentiful, in certain areas. Walleyes are also in some of the other reserve lakes.

Northern pike are an incidental catch for the most part, and generally small, rarely exceeding 17 pounds, although larger fish were more common in the past. Both large and small brook trout (called speckled trout here) inhabit several reserve lakes. These are relatively

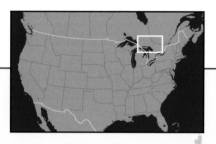

small waters, set aside for brook trout management and some have produced fish to eight pounds. A few are loaded with brookies in the 12- to 15-inch class. A few produce fewer numbers but a high average size, and there is a good chance of catching a four-pounder or better.

The reserve also has abundant wildlife. Anglers stand a good chance of spotting a moose, eagle, or otter, and will surely see and hear loons. The combination of wilderness, wildlife and top-quality fishing is indeed a fine one.

Details

Lac Beauchene, Quebec, Canada

Location/getting there: Located in the Kipawa region of southwestern Quebec, Beauchene is southwest of Temiscaming, a five-and-a-half-hour drive north of Toronto, and 75 minutes from North Bay.

Info sources: For general information, contact Quebec Tourism, 1010 rue Ste-Catherine Ouest, Bureau 400, Montreal, Quebec, Canada, H3B 1G2; call 877-266-5687; or visit www.bonjourquebec.com. For reserve fishing and lodging information, contact La Reserve Beauchene, C.P. 910, Temiscaming, Quebec, Canada, J0Z 3R0; call 888-627-3865; or visit www.beauchene.com.

Prime times: Fishing at Beauchene begins in early May and continues through early October; spring and early summer are preferred by many. Beauchene has an earlier opening season for bass than most Quebec waters, and a later closing date for trout.

Gear needs: Varies depending on species and fishing method. Bring portable sonar for lodge boats on back lakes, and bug repellent for spring blackflies.

Guide/tackle availability: Limited guide service is available; most anglers fish self-guided, using their own boats or lodge boats.

Bring whatever tackle you will need.

Accommodations/dining: There is an excellent main lodge building (which looks like a southern plantation house) as well as several log cabins and outpost housekeeping camps.

Etcetera: Three nights at the main lodge costs $825 Canadian, and seven nights $1,650 Canadian. There is also hunting for spring bear and fall grouse and moose. There is a launch ramp for anglers who tow their own boats, which are not used at the back lakes.

Lake Aguamilpa

Nayarit, Mexico

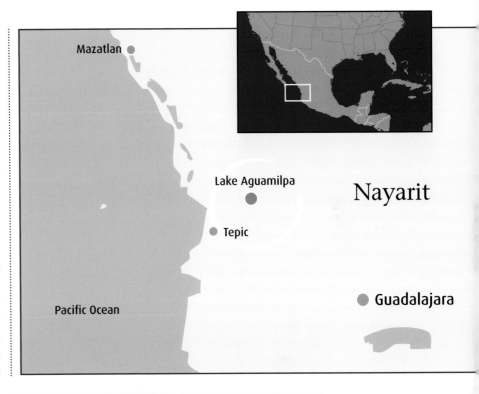

Mazatlan

Lake Aguamilpa

Nayarit

Tepic

Pacific Ocean

Guadalajara

Largemouth Bass

In Spanish, *Aguamilpa* means "water surrounded by corn." And while there is corn elsewhere in the state of Nayarit, along with sugar cane, agave (for tequila) and tobacco crops, there is no corn around this mountainous body of water. Perhaps the prettiest impoundment in all of Mexico, Aguamilpa is nestled 2,400 feet high in the mountains, and probably should be termed *Agualobina*, or "lake full of bass."

Finally impounded in 1994 by a dam that backed up the Santiago, Huaynamota and Chico Rivers, this sinewy, 70,000-acre lake was immediately stocked with Florida-strain largemouth bass, which have boomed here as they usually do in new lakes. Feeding heartily on shad and a huge population of two species of tilapia (one of which is frequently caught by anglers), Aguamilpa's bass are

LEFT
*Submerged brush
and trees add to
the challenge of
landing bass.*

RIGHT
*Sunrise fishing in
a cove off the
Santiago arm of
Lake Aguamilpa.*

BELOW
*Aguamilpa bass are
stout, deep-bellied
and vigorous.*

typically fat-bellied with a powerhouse disposition.

Bass are common in the three- to four- pound class, and frequently caught from five to seven pounds. The lake record, established in November 2000, is 12$\frac{1}{2}$ pounds, and fish in the ten-pound class are caught annually. If the lake does not suffer from an illegal commercial harvest of largemouths, as many Mexican lakes do, it could produce some monsters in the future. For the present, however, the calling card is a lot of action; sometimes 70 to 100 bass per boat in a day. That is a lot of great fishing when so many of the bass weigh three pounds or more.

One of the blessings that Aguamilpa enjoys is a comparatively stable water level. Many deep Mexican impoundments fluctuate widely, primarily due to irrigation

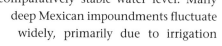

needs, but the Nayarit area receives abundant rainfall, irrigation is not a factor, and the lake is mainly used for hydroelectric purposes.

On the downside, it is a steep lake (605 feet by the dam), with few shallow flats and with shorelines that drop off precipitously. A lot of fishing is done in 20 or more feet of water, especially with plastic worms, and it takes a good plastic worm angler to handle that. However, spinnerbaits can produce some great results, fished deep in coves and especially for big fish around submerged tree clusters.

The lake gets bonus points for its beautiful surroundings; having loads of birdlife, including egrets, ibises and herons galore; great vistas in the folds of surrounding mountains; and a climate that produces pleasant weather nearly all year long. You might see deer in the area, which is populated by Coras and Huichols Indians, and there are jaguar in the mountains, although you will not see one. A three-day trip is almost guaranteed to produce some string-stretching.

Details

Lake Aguamilpa, Nayarit, Mexico

Location/getting there: Located in westcentral Mexico in the state of Nayarit, Lake Aguamilpa is a one-hour drive north of the city of Tepic, over a good two-lane road built to access the hydro dam, and a three-hour drive from Guadalajara via Tepic.

Info sources: Although tourists visiting Tepic can get transportation to the lake, and people with their own boats can drive to Aguamilpa, the only outfitter with a lodge on the lake is Chapman-Balderrama, which has operated facilities at several lakes in Mexico for many years. It is overseen by Bill Chapman, Sr. Contact Aguamilpa Lodge, c/o Anglers Inn, PMB 358, 2626 N. Mesa, El Paso, TX 79902; call their headquarters office in Mazatlan at 011-52-69-807474 or 800-408-2347; or visit www.anglersinn.com and www.chapmanbalderrama.com.

Prime times: January and February usually produce good topwater action; October into December has both good fishing and great weather.

Gear needs: Lean toward baitcasting rods with a heavy action, and line testing 15 pounds or more for big fish. Bring eight- to ten-inch worms, especially blue, plus 5/16- and 1/2-ounce weights; large white spinnerbaits with twin willowleaf blades and twin-tailed trailers; deep-diving crankbaits; and chrome or shad-colored poppers. Boats do not have sonar, so consider toting a portable unit.

Guide/tackle availability: Guides are provided by Aguamilpa Lodge as part of their package. Bring your own tackle.

Accommodations/dining: Aguamilpa Lodge is pleasant and comfortable, with good rooms and private baths/showers. Both the food and service are very good.

Etcetera: Expect to fish 15 to 25 or more feet deep, often among trees. The lake is currently closed to fishing (by law) from March through May, and the rainy season (rain four times a week) is from July through September. Some anglers combine a multi-day visit to this lake with several days on El Salto Lake to the north. Cost for three days at Aguamilpa is $1,295, plus transportation to the lodge, license and tips. Nayarit's coastal resort area is centered around the village of San Blas, 69 kilometers east of Tepic; Puerto Vallarta is 169 kilometers to the southeast.

Lake Athabasca

Saskatchewan, Canada

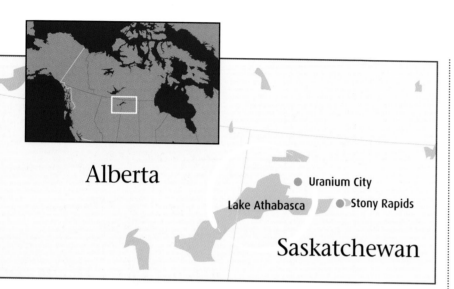

Alberta

Uranium City

Lake Athabasca • Stony Rapids

Saskatchewan

Lake Trout

Northern Pike

Little is heard about the fishing at Lake Athabasca, which is surprising considering that it is the fourth-largest lake entirely within Canada's borders, the ninth-largest lake on the continent and the 19th-largest in the world. That may be in part because it is reputed to be rough water, and has commercial fishing (mainly for walleyes). There are only a few lodges/fishing outfitters here, and collectively they bring a modest number of anglers annually, especially for a lake of this size. However, those anglers that do come find some of the best fishing in Saskatchewan.

Athabasca produces many pike that are 20 pounds or more, primarily in bays, and many lake trout from 20 pounds to the upper 30s, with some in the 40-pound and over class. There is plenty of grayling and walleye in certain areas, the latter being mainly in the western end of the lake.

Sportfishing efforts center on the northern and northcentral regions, the Precambrian Shield area which has many islands and reefs. The southern region, which is shallow and not known for its fish, has a more gradual slope and is made famous by the renowned Athabasca Sand Dunes. Constituting the largest active sand surface in Canada, these stretch about 100 kilometers along the southern shore of the lake and form a unique ecosystem.

The shoreline alone on the 200-mile-long Athabasca extends for 1,329 miles covering over 3,000 square miles of water, and although the maximum depth is 460 feet, the average depth is just 60 feet.

Details

Lake Athabasca, Saskatchewan, Canada

Location/getting there: About two-thirds of Lake Athabasca lies in Saskatchewan; the rest is in Alberta. Access is via chartered plane from Edmonton to Fort Chipewyan, then via floatplane to the lodge.

Info sources: A primary fishing outfitter here is Lakers Unlimited, Box 325, Tofield, Alberta T0B 4J0, Canada; call 780-662-3513; or visit www.lakersunlimited.com. For Saskatchewan information, contact Tourism Saskatchewan, 1922 Park St., Regina, Saskatchewan, S4P 3V7, Canada; call 877-237-2273; or visit www.sasktourism.com.

Prime times: Early and late in the season are preferred by many for shallow lake trout, although large fish are caught all season. Pike are most plentiful early in the shallows.

Gear needs: Lake trout: medium to heavy levelwind trolling tackle for deep fishing; lighter baitcasting, spinning and flycasting early in the season; heavy jigs, large trolling spoons and plugs. Pike: medium to medium-heavy spinning and baitcasting, with 12- to 20-pound line and nine- or ten-weight flycasting outfits; spoons, bucktail spinners, soft jerkbaits, and shallow-running plugs.

Guide/tackle availability: Guides are part of the package cost. Tackle is available plus some lures and terminal tackle.

Accommodations/dining: Lakers Unlimited has two lodges, 35 miles apart, which accommodate ten and eight people respectively and include a central dining building and rustic, unlit cabins with shared baths. Food is excellent and ample.

Etcetera: Fishing runs from early June through most of September, with the late season providing tough weather but the chance to cast for big spawning lakers on reefs. Cost for a week-long trip is $2,200, all-inclusive from Edmonton.

Lake Erie

Ohio/New York/Pennsylvania/Michigan, United States

All of the Great Lakes have some good bass and/or good walleye fishing, but none can top that of Lake Erie, which is the second smallest of the five and the shallowest, with an average depth over its 9,900 surface acres of only 62 feet. The western basin, in particular, is blessed with a generally shallow (35 feet and less) environment plus rocky islands and reefs.

Lake Erie is shared by four states plus Ontario, with the majority of angling occurring on the U.S. side. The deeper eastern basin of Lake Erie in New York has good numbers and size of walleyes and smallmouth bass, and also offers most of the lake's trout and salmon opportunities. Steelhead and rainbow trout have done especially well here.

Walleyes remain the main emphasis, however. Clear water has made Erie walleyes wary sight feeders that roam near the surface or at suspended depths. Big fish are common, mainly caught by long-line trolling. Big smallmouth bass are also present, with many specimens from three to five pounds and some larger, including a record-setting eight pound four ounce fish.

Pennsylvania has 42 miles of Erie shoreline and excellent fishing for walleyes, smallmouth bass, lake trout and steelhead. This is the only place in Pennsylvania where guiding anglers is big business. Charter boat businesses were first built on salmon, but now walleyes are the target, and there are lots of opportunities for six- to eight-pounders, with emphasis in July and August trolling for deeply suspended fish. Excellent steelhead fishing occurs in tributaries from late September through May, especially when creeks are rising. Presque Isle Bay and connecting lagoons in Presque Isle State Park offer bass, pike, muskie, panfish and steelhead.

Michigan has 50 miles of Lake Erie shoreline. Only 20 miles from the Michigan-Ohio border is Ohio's Maumee River, which has an annual spring walleye spawning run that averages an

LEFT
A typical fat Lake Erie walleye, this one caught near Buffalo.

Walleye

Smallmouth Bass

Steelhead

Chinook Salmon

Lake Trout

Details

Lake Erie, Ohio/New York/Pennsylvania/Michigan, United States

Location/getting there: Lake Erie is at the northernmost border of Ohio and Pennsylvania, and spans from eastern Michigan to western New York; it is readily accessed from many ports and locales.

Info sources: For general information, contact the appropriate state and county tourism agencies. In Ohio, contact the Department of Tourism at 800-282-5393; or visit www.ohiotourism.com. For fishing information from the Ohio Department of Natural Resources, call 888-466-5347; or visit www.dnr.state.oh.us/wildlife/lreport.html. An online fishing information source is Great Lakes Angler Online at www.fishlakeerie.com.

Prime times: See main text.

Gear needs: Varies widely with species and fishing methods.

Guide/tackle availability: Charter boats and stream/river guides are numerous; most provide tackle. Fishing equipment is widely available at shops.

Accommodations/dining: Lodging and dining options are extensive.

Etcetera: Lake Erie can get rough in a hurry and, therefore, requires big-water boats. Anglers unfamiliar with it need to be cautious.

incredible ten million fish. These walleyes, some in the eight-pound or better class, are later distributed along the coast and for miles offshore.

Smallmouth bass, largemouth bass and northern pike offer excellent fishing along Michigan's Lake Erie shoreline and offshore shallow reefs. This western area also has excellent populations of ten- to 15-pound steelhead and coho salmon, and chinooks that average 12 pounds and run to 20.

The Ohio portion of Lake Erie has a ton of good fishing opportunity for walleyes, smallmouth bass, steelhead and yellow perch. Walleye action begins in the western basin in March and April when these fish swarm around spawning reefs and head up the Maumee, Portage and Sandusky Rivers. In May, smallmouth bass move to the shallows as post-spawn walleye head for open water. Some walleye travel up the Detroit River to Lake St. Clair and beyond, while large schools roam the big lake, with June through August excellent. Smallmouth bass fishing is impressive all season along the shoreline and around the islands. Yellow perch are popular, but generally slightly smaller than their deep-water cousins in central Lake Erie.

In the central basin, spring and fall perch fishing attracts legions of boat anglers. Large schools of perch can provide non-stop action. Yellow perch populations

fluctuate over the years, but these fish remain the second-most popular Lake Erie catch. Flotillas of perch anglers can be found off Lorain, Cleveland, Fairport Harbor, Conneaut and Ashtabula.

In the central basin, large schools of walleye thrill anglers from Huron to Conneaut. Deep-water fish often suspend along the thermocline in summer, and are caught by trolling. A bonus catch is steelhead, often caught on walleye lures and at walleye depths. This region also has terrific near-shore smallmouth bass fishing, especially in harbors and on artificial reefs.

TOP RIGHT
Fishing boats assemble at the docks on South Bass Island, Ohio.

RIGHT
Lake Erie piers offer shore-based anglers good fishing at times for perch, walleye, steelhead and bass.

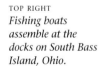

Lake Eufaula

Alabama/Georgia, United States

Lake Eufaula enjoyed a resurgence in its largemouth bass fishing in the mid-1990s, although not quite comparable to its legendary heyday of the late 1960s and early 1970s. Technically known as Walter F. George Reservoir, and straddling the Alabama/Georgia border, Lake Eufaula (pronounced "u-fall-ah") was one of the earliest big-bass lakes in the nation and helped usher in the era of modern bass fishing. However, good fishing today, along with many access sites, a national wildlife refuge and various parks and public-use areas, make this one of the more popular places for anglers from throughout the Southeast and Midwest to visit.

ABOVE
A good-sized largemouth bass is landed on Lake Eufaula.

Today, ten-pound-plus bass are caught each spring in Eufaula's tributary creeks, primarily with spinnerbaits and plastic worms. The most notable tributaries include Cowikee, Barbour, White Oak and Pataula, all of which include different types of stump, brush and vegetative cover as well as steep-sided channel drops. There are also many creeks, coves, points, flats and other good-looking spots to fish along its 640 miles of shoreline. And there are crappie, white bass and other species as well.

This lake is 85 miles long, so there are numerous places to get to know. The northern sector, above Cowikee Creek, has more riverine features to it, while the southern sector is rather typical of an impoundment environment, with more wide open areas. Created in 1963, Eufaula is a major hydroelectric and flood control reservoir; almost daily, current is created along the entire lake when power is being generated or water is being pulled for diversion.

The late winter and spring period is especially popular with both local and visiting anglers, and is known for producing large bass. However, there are frequent cold fronts that make fishing unpredictable, and fishing success drops off dramatically until several days of stable conditions prevail.

Fishing early in the season, especially when the bass are in spawning mode, is predominantly along shallow flats, especially those with stumps, brush rows and vegetation on them. Many of these are located in the major creeks. Some, however, are in the main lake, in the

open water sections, and extend for great distances. It also takes place along riprap banks. In mid- to late spring, the bass start moving to river and creek ledges and deeper water, and there is much reliance on vertical spoon jigging and worm fishing.

Hybrid striper fishing kicks into gear in the summer, with good fishing to be had in some locales (often the same daily) early and late in the day. The summer can be brutal on Eufaula, with high heat and humidity, and the mid-day fishing suffers as a result, in large part due to personal discomfort. Topwater activity is experienced in the fall from hybrids as well as white bass and also largemouths. The latter move to shallower water in the fall, and October and November provide good fishing again.

TOP LEFT
Launching a boat at one of Eufaula's many public access sites.

LEFT
Bass are the main attraction, with fishing best in spring.

Details

Lake Eufaula, Alabama/Georgia, United States

Location/getting there: Lake Eufaula is about a 75-minute drive southwest of Columbus, Georgia, on the Alabama-Georgia line.

Info sources: For area information, contact the Eufaula/Barbour County Chamber of Commerce and Tourism Council, 102 North Orange Avenue, P.O. Box 697, Eufaula, AL 36072; call 800-524-7529; or visit www.eufaula-barbourchamber.com.

Prime times: See main text.

Gear needs: Varies depending on species and methods.

Guide/tackle availability: Guides and fishing tackle are widely available in the area.

Accommodations/dining: A range of lodging and dining options exist, especially in Eufaula. An excellent facility is Lakepoint Resort State Park on the lake; call 800-544-5253; or visit www.dcnr.state.al.us/parks/state_parks_index_1a.html.

Etcetera: Check out the 38,000-gallon fish aquarium (with big bass), and other exhibits, at Tom Mann's Fish World, which is six miles north of Eufaula. Also visit the Walter F. George Lock and Dam; at 88-feet high it is the second-largest lock lift east of the Mississippi River. Plenty of other recreation, as well as wildlife viewing, is available at the 11,184-acre Eufaula National Wildlife Refuge, which borders the lake.

Largemouth Bass

Striped Bass

Crappie

Lake Fork

Texas, United States

Oklahoma

Sulphur Springs

Dallas ●

Lake Fork

Texas

Largemouth Bass

L ake Fork is probably the best public lake in the U.S. for catching a double-digit size largemouth bass. It is certainly the best lake in bass-crazed Texas for producing fish over ten pounds, and claims the 18.2-pound state record.

As appealing as this seems, it should be said that Lake Fork also gets a ton of fishing pressure; even some regulars who have fished the lake for many years have only caught a few bass over ten pounds. Lake Fork has also undergone some difficulties, the most significant being the death a few years ago of many large bass due to disease problems. Nevertheless, the lake dominates Texas's big bass records and attracts anglers from as far afield as Japan.

Built by the Sabine River Authority, this 27,690-acre impoundment has 315 miles of shoreline, is full of timber and opened in 1980 under the state's first restrictive bag limit. A strong catch-and-release ethic exists among regular anglers.

Lake Fork has an average depth of 12 to 15 feet, and constant water levels. The best fishing for large bass is in late winter and in summer. Although the February and March period is when there are many changing weather fronts, which can make fishing spotty, this is pre-spawn or spawning time, so bass are heavy and many 13-pound-and-better fish are caught then, especially on jigs.

Fishing is consistent from May through August. Daytime angling is best with Carolina-rigged worms, but night fishing produces well for larger bass, especially in the three-day period before and after the full moon. Big spinnerbaits, ten-inch black worms and large wobbling plugs are the ticket. In July and August, bass gather in schools; some are comprised of all six- to seven-pounders.

Details

Lake Fork, Texas, United States

Location/getting there: Easily reached by auto, Lake Fork is an hour east of Dallas and south of Sulphur Springs.

Info sources: For area information, contact the Lake Fork Chamber of Commerce at 888-265-1822; or visit www.ets-systems.com.

Prime times: See main text.

Gear needs: Medium to heavy baitcasting tackle is the norm, with heavy line for large fish amidst timber and assorted vegetation.

Guide/tackle availability: There are many guides on Lake Fork; tackle is widely available locally.

Accommodations/dining: There are numerous area lodging and dining options.

Etcetera: An excellent place to visit nearby is the Texas Freshwater Fisheries Center in Athens; call 903-676-2277; or visit www.tpwd.state.tx.us/fish/infish/hatchery/tfc/welcome.htm. This highly praised hatchery and aquarium houses over 40 species of freshwater fish native to Texas in natural-environment displays.

ABOVE RIGHT
Largemouth Bass are hungriest in the summer.

Lake Guerrero

Tamaulipas, Mexico

Lake Vicente Guerrero was the first of numerous lakes in Mexico to be called the "world's best bass fishing lake" by promoters. Its history is typical of many Mexican bass lakes: it became fished-out and dehydrated. Unusually, it has now staged a comeback and returned to the radar screen, in spite of its easy accessibility.

Largemouth Bass

Guerrero was formed in 1971 and was not supposed to be fishable for several years, but five incoming rivers filled the new reservoir quickly, flooding farmlands, ranches, roads and the village of Padilla. When completely full, the water covered 100,000 acres of brush and timber, with many flats, islands and creek beds. Half-submerged at full pool, Padilla's church was a dramatic and frequently used photographic background for anglers posing with their catch.

Throughout the 1970s, Guerrero had certifiably sensational bass fishing. If you could make a feeble cast with virtually any lure you could catch a bass. The early game was fishing for many small bass and lots of four- to seven-pounders.

But it was also nearly the ultimate in freshwater fishing excess. For at least a decade, with the exception of a ban on using live bait, it was no-holds-barred catching and keeping. The larger bass disappeared first, then even small bass dwindled, and camps closed. A prolonged drought drew Guerrero down drastically, at one point to half of its full size. Some camps, once at the water's edge, were left a mile or more from the shrunken lake, which was declared finished.

LEFT
Big bass, like this one caught on a jig, are a big attraction at Lake Guerrero.

Details

Location/getting there: Lake Vicente Guerrero is about 175 miles south of Brownsville, Texas, and about 20 miles from Ciudad Victoria. It is a three-and-a-half-hour drive from Harlingen, Texas. Some people drive their vehicles, some are picked up in Texas by lodges and others fly to Ciudad Victoria.

Info sources: There are a number of lodges on the lake and agents who represent them. Ricky Green fishes Guerrero often, is especially knowledgeable, and represents two lodges. Contact his company, International Outdoor Adventures, at 888-246-6798; or visit www.worldwidefishing.com/mexico/b901/.

Prime times: February and March, when the fish usually spawn, are favorite times. Some of the best big bass fishing has occurred in midsummer at night, although large fish are caught in all seasons.

Gear needs: Baitcasting tackle with 15- to 30-pound line is the mainstay; hard mesquite here is unforgiving on tackle. Top lures are ten-inch worms, $1/2$- to one-ounce spinnerbaits, large popping and walking topwater plugs, large soft jerkbaits and assorted crankbaits.

Guide/tackle availability: Guides are supplied with packages, but some people who have their own boats fish unguided. Bring your own tackle.

Accommodations/dining: The better lodges are accessed by paved roads and have good Tex-Mex food, services, electricity and purified water.

Etcetera: Inclusive package costs for three or four days of guided fishing is about $900 and $1,100 respectively. Many people drive to the lake with their own boats; some bring motorhomes. Check with customs and with your insurance company before driving into Mexico.

Nearly a decade later, big bass started showing up, thanks to the planting of Florida-strain fish, and the lake got a second angling life. The big bass were not the seven-pounders of years past, but fish over ten pounds. Fifteen- and 17-pound fish, and reputedly some larger, were caught in the early 1990s. There was again some goldmine fishing, this time for lunkers. Fishing for the huge monsters peaked, but the lake still produces ten-pound fish today, and is a good place to catch fish in the five- to eight-pound class, plus bass from ten to 12 pounds.

One of the reasons Guerrero continues to enjoy a resurgence is because of a prolonged drought in Tamaulipas, which has kept the lake 25 feet below normal and around half-full for about a decade. This produced a stability unusual for Mexican impoundments. Experienced anglers have had good success here in recent times, some fishing methodically in deep water, while those with lesser skills have varied results; being there when the fish are active, which is often hit or miss, can provide a lot of action. In recent years there has been a lot of rain, and the lake has been up, which has been good for fishing results.

Other developments that have helped, and which bode well for the future, are an increase here in catch-and-release fishing, the use of replica mounts for preserving trophies that are released and new government harvest restrictions.

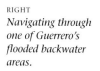

RIGHT
Navigating through one of Guerrero's flooded backwater areas.

Lake Huites

Sinaloa, Mexico

The village of Techobampo has a population of about 250 people, most of them Indian descendants whose previous houses are now underwater. All of Techobampo was relocated in 1994, when a dam on the Rio Fuerte was completed and a new impoundment, called Huites (pronounced "*we -tees*"), built for irrigation and hydroelectric purposes, started to fill.

That dam also backed up the Chinipas River, a serpentine watercourse that flows into Huites from rugged peaks near renowned Copper Canyon. *Barranca del Cobre*, Mexico's larger and deeper version of the Grand Canyon, is a nearby scenic wonder with a maximum depth of over 6,000 feet.

Southwest of canyon country, on the outskirts of the Sierra Madre Occidentals, Lake Huites is 22 miles long and covers 30,000 acres when full. It is so remote that most of the guides employed at the first fishing camp there had never seen a boat or outboard motor before, and the nearby villages only got electricity in the mid-1990s.

For a short while after Huites first opened for fishing, there were few camps and stupendous fishing, with fast-growing transplanted Florida-strain largemouth bass getting to the mid-teens in size. This exceptional growth rate produced football-shaped bass that have small heads and a large girth, plus a hot chili pepper disposition. Landing these dynamos is a 50–50 proposition and always a challenge.

Flooded *au naturel*, Huites is completely loaded with trees and brush, and the bass are found along the shorelines amidst this protective cover. When the fish

Largemouth Bass

ABOVE
The shoreline drops off sharply and has cover that strong bass can easily get tangled in.

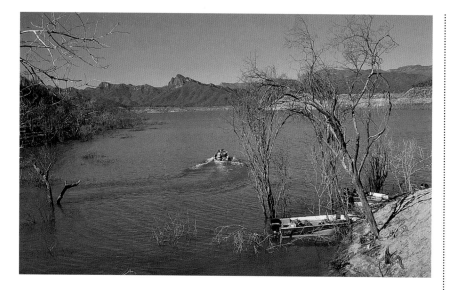

strike a lure, they dive for the nearest wood, often a multi-limbed cactus, and either break the line instantly or achieve freedom when an exasperated angler is unable to extract them.

When the fishing is at top form here, there are so many bass, and so many opportunities, that losing half the fish that strike is *no problema*. In fact, the bass often congregate in spots, usually off points near deep water, that can produce plenty of action.

The rub with Huites, however, is that it is subject to extreme water level fluctuations, especially in the middle of winter when most northern anglers (who prefer to

avoid the mid-summer heat) visit. When the lake water level is moved up and down quickly, it plays havoc with the bass, usually making them less aggressive and/or sending them into the depths. When that happens, only the most experienced anglers have the best success. Therefore, though still good, Huites has fallen a tad behind such lakes as El Salto and Aquamilpa, which produce more consistently.

However, Lake Huites may well be the prettiest of Mexico's mountain bass lakes. It is extremely still in the narrow sections of the lake, especially on the Chinipas. Boats travel through chasms so steep that the sun does not penetrate until mid-morning. Overhead, huge boulders hang on precipices hundreds of feet up, and every osprey that flies by has a fish in its talons. Below, the tips of 40-foot-tall trees barely make it to the water's surface, and the bass might pull your fishing rod into the water if you do not hold onto it.

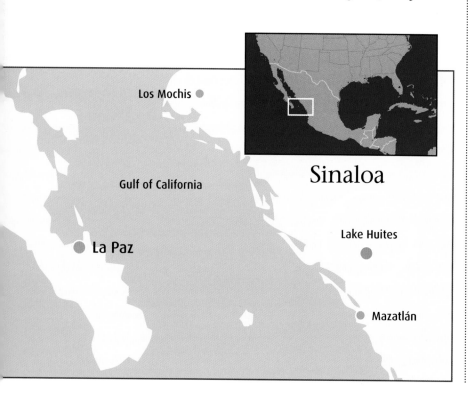

Sinaloa

Details

Lake Huites, Sinaloa, Mexico

Location/getting there: Lake Huites is in the mountains of western Mexico. Anglers fly into Los Mochis, then are driven to the lake, which is a good three hours away, some of it on a winding, rutted, mountain road.

Info sources: http://www.travelmanitoba.com/, http://www.anglersinn.com/ Campo Buena Vista at Lake Huites is an excellent full-service facility, featuring modern air-conditioned rooms with private baths, phone and fax service, fine dining and good boats. Contact Wet-A-Line Tours, 5592 Cool Springs Rd., Gainesville, GA 30506; call 888-295-4665 or visit www.wetaline.com

Prime times: Generally the preferred time is before and during the spawn; spawning time here is normally between mid-March and early April. October and November can be good months with stable water and good (but hot) weather.

Gear needs: Baitcasting tackle with 15- to 30-pound line is the mainstay; top lures are ten-inch plastic worms, 1/2- to one-ounce spinnerbaits and deep-diving crankbaits.

Guide/tackle availability: Guides are supplied. At most lodges you need to bring your own tackle, but Camp Buena Vista provides free use of quality Pflueger tackle.

Accommodations/dining: Three-day trips cost between $995 and $1,195 and four day-trips from $1,100 to $1,350, depending on the month. Longer trips are possible. If time permits, try to arrange a one-day side tour to visit the spectacular Copper Canyon.

ABOVE
Battling a typically hyper-frisky Lake Huites bass.

Lake Mead

Arizona/Nevada, United States

Nevada

Las Vegas ●

Lake Mead   Colorado River

California   Arizona

Striped Bass

Largemouth Bass

Crappie

Catfish

Carp

RIGHT
A small Mead striper caught at sunrise on a surface plug.

Ever since the Nevada legislature legalized it in 1931, gambling has been considered the lifeblood of Las Vegas. The real lifeblood, however, is water. Water for the falls and fountains in hotel lobbies. Water for the lagoons around housing developments. Water for the lush golf course fairways and greens. Water to harness the electricity...that powers the air conditioners and ice machines...that cool the gaming patrons...who spend the dough...that pays for life in such an extravagant playground.

Water here, as throughout most of the arid West, is the Colorado River, the seventh-longest river in the United States. More precisely for Las Vegas, water needs are satisfied by nearby Lake Mead, an impoundment of the Colorado contained by the 726-foot-high Hoover Dam, the western hemisphere's highest concrete dam and a structure that can hold back two years' worth of river flow.

Few people look upon Lake Mead for what it means to

their life, so long as it continues to supply about four billion kilowatt hours of electricity annually. But many look upon it for what it means to their bountiful recreation: sailboating, yachting, houseboating, water skiing, personal watercraft use by the hundreds, full-service lakeside marinas, swimming and fishing by all manner of boating enthusiasts.

Bare and desolate cactus country surrounds this lake, which stretches for roughly 110 miles when full, with 822 miles of shoreline snaking around red cliff canyons, coves and various hideaway basins; country where sometimes the only eyes watching you cast are those of a bighorn sheep. The lake forks on the upper reaches, one branch being the Overton Arm and the other being the Colorado River. All of this is part of the Lake Mead National Recreation Area.

Above the dam, Lake Mead's 162,000 surface acres offer diverse angling opportunities. The bounty includes striped bass, largemouth bass, channel catfish, crappie,

rainbow trout and bluegill. It also includes carp; in the summer, one of the more bizarre local attractions is the hundreds of carp that gather along the marina at Boulder Beach, grunting for bread and swimming over each other's backs to chase a crumb. Newcomers to the lake include tilapia and smallmouth bass.

Most angling attention (some 70 per cent, in fact) is focused on striped bass, however, which were introduced in 1968. Mead was noted for large stripers for a while, but the population is now comprised of an enormous amount of small fish. Lake Mead is known for its striper schooling activities, especially early and late in the day in the warmest months. This is considerate of these fish, as during a midsummer day it is routine for the temperature to soar past 100 degrees here. On a good August outing, a party of striped bass anglers have caught their fish by 9 o'clock in the morning and are headed off the water.

Largemouth bass have had ups and downs, but are doing better at Mead thanks to brush planting efforts. Fishing for largemouth bass on Mead usually picks up in March when fish move into the coves in preparation for spawning. Many lures, including spinnerbaits, jigs and swimming plugs, work then. By June, bass have moved to deeper water and you mostly have to fish along canyon walls using worms and jigs. However, some surface action is possible at first light.

BELOW
Fishing for stripers on Lake Mead.

Details

Lake Mead, Arizona/Nevada, United States

Location/getting there: Located near Las Vegas on the Colorado River, Lake Mead crosses both Arizona and Nevada.

Info sources: For Lake Mead fishing information, visit www.riverlakes.com /fishing.htm. For general tourism information, contact the Nevada Commission on Tourism, 800-638-2328; or visit www.travelnevada.com. For Lake Mead fishing reports and information about the Lake Mead National Recreation Area, contact the National Park Service, Lake Mead National Recreation Area, 601 Nevada Highway, Boulder City, NV 89005; call 702- 293-8990; or visit www.nps.gov/lame/index.htm.

Prime times: Spring for largemouth bass, late summer and fall for stripers.

Gear needs: Assorted depending on species.

Guide/tackle availability: Guides are available through marinas; tackle is available there and in area shops.

Accommodations/dining: There is plenty of both in the area; for information about the resorts and services on the lake, contact the National Park Service.

Etcetera: Survey reports indicate that 88 per cent of fishing effort on Lake Mead is in the Las Vegas Bay and Boulder Basin areas. Attractions nearby at Las Vegas need no comment, but for a piscatorial change from the big lake, note that the cold water released from the bottom of Lake Mead provides good temperature for rainbow trout, which are in good supply downriver in the vicinity of Willow Beach.

Lake Michigan

Michigan, United States

It is not far-fetched to say that Lake Michigan and its tributaries provide better fishing for Pacific salmon than most of the Pacific regions where these fish originated. The salmon runs in rivers like the St. Joseph, Grand, Big and Little Manistee, Pere Marquette, Platte and Betsie, which begin in late August and trickle off through

BELOW
A bright summer-time chinook from the offshore waters of Lake Michigan.

Lake Michigan is 307 miles long and 118 miles wide at its greatest point. It has a shoreline of over 1,600 miles and sports 22,300 surface acres of water that borders the states of Michigan, Illinois, Indiana and Wisconsin. Michigan has the lion's share of the lake, so this review concentrates on that state, which in itself is more than can be adequately addressed in this space.

October, provide excellent opportunities for numbers and size of chinook and coho. Lake Michigan salmon have rebounded from the decimation caused by bacterial kidney disease in the 1980s, and from a diminished baitfish population, to become the most abundant species in the daily catch of charter boats.

Steelhead fishing is outstanding as well. In addition to fishing for steelhead in the tributaries, there is also remarkable angling offshore, especially in the upper eastern end of the lake, where Michigan charter captains run 15 to 20 miles offshore to fish a scum line where current and wind concentrate enormous numbers of insects. There are huge numbers of steelhead here, and anglers catch ten- to 15-pounders on the surface.

The upper regions of Lake Michigan have notable fishing for smallmouth bass and walleyes. The coastline of the northwestern Lower Peninsula, for example, has fine smallmouth bass populations in rocky bays. Both arms of Grand Traverse Bay are excellent, and the annual appearance of spawning bass on the shallow rock reefs at Waugoshance Point off Wilderness State Park on the Lower Peninsula's extreme northwestern tip draws thousands of anglers. Across the lake to the northwest, Little Bay de Noc, near the town of Escanaba, is fabled for its numbers, and sizes, of walleye.

Southern Lake Michigan also has much to recommend it. Offshore waters here warm up early, and coho salmon move south along the Michigan shoreline through early June, then migrate west and north. Chinooks are offshore here all year. Skamania steelhead provide an offshore fishery all summer for Michigan and Indiana anglers in the southeastern area of the lake; rivers like the St. Joseph now get both spring, summer and fall runs.

There is also a good fishery for brown trout here, some of which are very large, like the 34-pound state record.

These fish are just offshore in spring, but are found later along reefs and bottom structure in 60 to 90 feet of water, less than a mile offshore along most of this shoreline.

Up the coast a short distance, Michigan's longest river (68 miles) is the Grand, which has fine fishing for salmon and steelhead, thanks to water quality improvements and fish ladders. There are spring and summer runs of big rainbows here. Many anglers fish the Grand in Lansing during lunchtime in jackets and ties, and many passers-by watch lucky anglers playing fish. The Grand also has plenty of smallmouth bass in riffles and largemouth in its backwaters; the Portland State Game area downstream from Lansing is especially notable, and is also good for channel catfish.

ABOVE
Many miles offshore, Lake Michigan anglers drift and cast for shallow-cruising steelhead.

Details

Lake Michigan, Michigan, United States

Location/getting there: The Michigan State portions of Lake Michigan are along the eastern, northern and northwestern shores, and are readily accessed from many ports and locales.

Info sources: For general information contact Travel Michigan for publications and county tourism bureau contacts; call 888-784-7328; or visit www.michigan.org. Online fishing information sources are Great Lakes Angler Online at www.fishlakemichigan.com, and Lake Michigan Angler at www.lakemichiganangler.com.

Prime times: Spring for brown trout and coho salmon; summer through early fall for chinook salmon; summer and fall for bass, walleye and lake trout.

Gear needs: Varies widely with species and fishing methods.

Guide/tackle availability: Charter boats and stream/river guides are numerous; most provide tackle. Recommended is Capt. Jim Karr; call 800-845-6095; or visit www.therapytoo.com. Tackle is widely available at shops.

Accommodations/dining: Lodging and dining options are extensive.

Etcetera: Not everyone favors salmonids, bass or walleyes on Lake Michigan. Ports like Grand Haven and St. Joseph were once renowned for party boats that garnered mighty catches of yellow perch, and may once again if the population rebounds. The population of these tasty fish has fallen off greatly, perhaps as a result of competition for food with a host of exotic invaders.

Chinook Salmon

Coho Salmon

Steelhead

Walleye

Smallmouth Bass

Lake Oahe

South Dakota, United States

North Dakota

Mobridge

Lake Oahe

South Dakota

Pierre

Walleye

Northern Pike

Chinook Salmon

In most of the fishing world at large, Lake Oahe is not very well known. This is hard to believe for a body of water that is 231 miles long with over 740,000 acres of water. But it is an angling Shangri-La if you are a walleye or pike devotee.

Oahe (pronounced "*oh-wah-he*") teems with marbleyes. In fact, there was a record harvest of this species in 2001, and there are so many that the state fisheries agency raised the catch limit significantly in recent years (42 in possession for 2001, for example) because the population has

doubled over the past few years. Just think of how many walleyes must live in this enormous lake.

This is not entirely good news, however, because there is a preponderance of small walleyes here due to a crash of their primary forage, rainbow smelt. Enormous predation, and the fact that floods washed 400 million of these baitfish out of the reservoir a few years ago, have both contributed to this.

Oahe had been known in the past for many walleyes in the six- to eight-pound range, and some in the ten-pound-or-better class. These big fish were prime in the fall, but the bigger fish are harder to come by currently, although they are expected again in greater numbers as the prey-predator ratio becomes more properly aligned. Nevertheless, fish over ten pounds, and up to 13 pounds, are caught here each season. In any case, spring and fall fishing is excellent, especially around tributaries in the spring. Good walleye angling also exists in the tailrace below the dam.

Lake Oahe is also a fine spot for big northern pike. Several hundred over 15 pounds are caught annually and 20- to 25-pounders are very possible. As with pike fishing in most locales, prime angling exists in the spring following ice-out, often caught on dead bait or while fishing with jigs tipped with bait. When ice fishing for pike, dead bait is very productive.

Oahe also has a strong population of chinook salmon. Most of these fish are in the mid-range sizes, but some from 15 to 20 pounds are caught, with spring fishing holding most excitement because the fish are shallow.

RIGHT
A typical Oahe walleye, caught on a jig.

INSET
Fishing scene on Lake Oahe.

Details

Lake Oahe, South Dakota, United States

Location/getting there: Lake Oahe is primarily accessed by traveling through Pierre, the capitol of South Dakota.

Info sources: For fishing and travel information, contact South Dakota Fishing Adventures, 711 E. Wells Ave., Pierre, SD 57501; call 800-732-5682; or visit www.travelsd.com.

Prime times: Depends on species, but spring is generally good for all species.

Gear needs: Assorted depending on species and technique.

Guide/tackle availability: Guide service is available at extra cost, but bring your own tackle and waders.

Accommodations/dining: Lodging and dining options are ample in Pierre.

Etcetera: In the fall, check out the salmon processing station and fish ladder off Highway 22 near Gettysburg.

Lake Okeechobee

Florida, United States

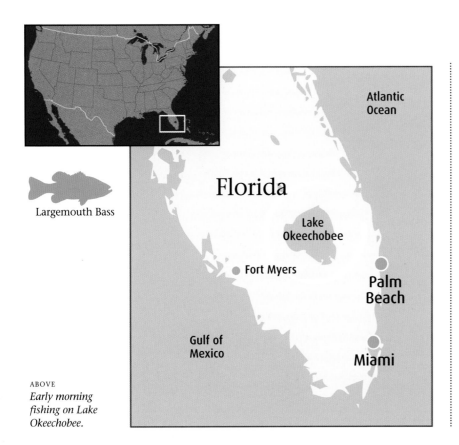

Largemouth Bass

ABOVE
Early morning fishing on Lake Okeechobee.

O ver the past few decades, the saga of Lake Okeechobee, one of the most-storied bass waters in the world, is one of cyclical ups and downs due to fluctuating water levels. Drought conditions, which briefly concentrate the fish and make them easier to find, generally hurt the bass population, but then higher waters turn the situation around.

Although the lake has been low of late, there are still loads of bass, with plenty of three- to six-pound fish. Tournaments, of which there are several on any weekend, are being won by anglers whose fish average four-and-a-half pounds apiece. However, the really big fish for which the "Big O" was once known—ten- to 12-pounders—are seldom caught these days, and then generally only on live shiners.

Lake Okeechobee's 200,00 surface acres and 730 square miles of water make it a little difficult to pinpoint specific

Details

Lake Okeechobee, Florida, United States

Location/getting there: Lake Okeechobee is in southcentral Florida, north of the Everglades, with many roads providing access. The southern city of Clewiston is a major jump-off for most angling activities.

Info sources: For information about lodging, marinas, guides, access, etc., contact the Clewiston Chamber of Commerce, 544 West Sugarland Highway, Clewiston, FL 33440; call 863-983-7979; or visit www.clewiston.org.

Prime times: Summer for bass and lack of crowds; November and December for good fishing and good weather; spring for big bluegills and shellcrackers.

Gear needs: Standard tackle is appropriate for bass and bluegills. Heavy line and stout rods are generally used for bigger bass in the thick vegetation. For bass, soft worms are very popular, as well as surface plugs and weedless spoons.

Guide/tackle availability: There are many guides at local marinas, and tackle is widely available.

Accommodations/dining: There are many lodging and dining options.

Etcetera: Due to its southern location, Okeechobee is often the least-affected Florida bass spot during late winter and early spring, when a lot of snowbirds are in the Sunshine State. It can offer fantastic fishing at that time, however, particularly when the weather is stable for a while. The fishing from September to December is also quite good.

BELOW
A largemouth bass, caught by flipping a worm into the Big O's abundant grasses.

places to devote your bass angling efforts. The Monkey Box area near Moonshine Bay is locally renowned, and the peppergrass flats between Observation Shoals and Clewiston, as well as the channels and cuts from Clewiston to Okeetantee, are among the more popular fishing locales. Biologists report that Okeechobee's bass populations move around a good deal, so this, plus the size of the lake, makes it a good idea for the newcomer to hire a guide, especially for the first visit.

Okeechobee's needlegrass and peppergrass flats concentrate largemouths during the spawning period (from February into April). The Big O is only 14 feet above sea level in normal conditions; it is not very deep, yet bass move off the shallow flats after spawning and go into slightly deeper water.

The lake can offer excellent fishing in late winter and early spring, particularly when the weather is stable for a while. The fishing from September to December is also quite good. Summer is the off-season for Florida's tourism trade yet it produces reliable, stable bass angling; it may be warm and humid, but there are few cold fronts and unstable weather conditions to alter bass behavior. The fish are much more predictable from mid-spring through mid-fall. This, plus the fact that you will find accommodations and facilities less crowded in the summer, make it a good idea to keep off-season fishing in mind.

Okeechobee also has good fishing for smaller species and something tasty for the pan. Bluegill (called copperhead bream here) fishing is prime in the spring, and often the shorelines of the lake's lengthy canals are lined with spawning beds. Shellcrackers, which are red ear sunfish, are also abundant and especially caught from March through the summer around the full moon. These panfish grow large here, and the action is so popular with

people from all over that there is even a South Carolina festival in honor of all the folks from that state who come just for the bluegill and shellcracker fishing. There are also plenty of catfish and black crappie (called speckled perch) taken throughout the year, especially during winter.

Lake Ontario

New York, United States

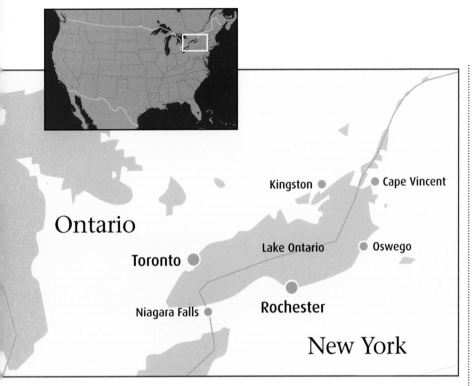

Niagara River established a modern-day Lake Ontario record. November anglers can jig and release scores of trout per day. However, the extreme eastern end of the lake is generally considered the prime laker habitat. Rocky reefs and islands make lakers a bread-and-butter fish for

Chinook Salmon

Lake Trout

Steelhead

Brown Trout

Walleye

RIGHT
This 24-pound brown trout was caught in Lake Ontario near Oswego.

The 19th-largest lake in the world, Lake Ontario is 193 miles long and 53 miles wide, with an average depth of 283 feet. No destination in the northeastern U.S. has been more distinctive in recent decades than Lake Ontario and its tributaries, providing angling that is among the best to be had throughout the Great Lakes.

Lake Ontario has arguably had the best angling and the largest chinook salmon of all the Great Lakes. The Oswego and Salmon Rivers in the eastern basin, which are small, narrow, shallow and generally slow, are magnets for salmon and anglers alike. But the western end of Lake Ontario, where the bottom drops off more steeply close to shore and where the incomparable Niagara River enters, has been the best big-water place to consistently catch these nomadic fish from April through September. It is the only section of the entire lake with dependable angling for chinooks in the spring and early summer.

The western basin also produces huge lake trout. In early 1994, a 39-pound laker caught at the mouth of the

boats departing from Henderson Harbor, Cape Vincent and Kingston.

Steelhead are highly prized, and are especially sought by winter and early spring anglers in the tributaries, especially the Salmon, Niagara, Black and Oswego Rivers. Fresh runs occur at various times and peak at spawning time in April. There is some early-season, near-shore fishing for steelhead, and also limited offshore fishing if, and when, there's a thermal bar.

Brown trout are spring mainstays in the lake, especially from Rochester to Pulaski, when they are inshore and shallow. They average several pounds, but it usually takes a 15-pounder to place in the top ten of contests, and a 20-pounder to win; fish over 30 pounds

ABOVE
A fly angler fishes for winter steelhead in the Salmon River.

Details

Lake Ontario, New York, United States

Location/getting there: Lake Ontario is the easternmost of the Great Lakes, borders northern New York and southeastern Ontario, and is readily accessed from many ports and locales.

Info sources: Information sources are varied and disjointed. Try contacting the Lake Ontario Sportfishing Promotion Council at 888-733-5246; or visit www.loc.org, which has links to, and contact information for, the tourism arms of all seven New York counties around the lake. An online fishing information source is Great Lakes Angler Online at www.fishlakeontario.com.

Prime times: Spring for brown trout; summer through early fall for chinook salmon; summer and fall for bass, walleye and lake trout.

Gear needs: Varies widely with species and fishing methods.

Guide/tackle availability: Charter boats and stream/river guides are numerous; most provide tackle. Recommended are Capt. Bob Cinelli of Olcott, 716-433-5210; Capt. Walt Boname of Cape Vincent, 315-654-2673; and Capt. John DeLorenzo of Niagara Falls, 716-297-9424 and www.niagarariverguides.com. Tackle is widely available at shops.

Accommodations/dining: Lodging and dining options are extensive.

Etcetera: If you are visiting the western end of the lake, a sidetrip to Niagara Falls is in order. In the fall, many people enjoy a short stop at the state fish hatchery, on the Salmon River near Altmar at the eastern end of the lake. Although Lake Ontario has shone for three decades, it is also a lake in transition, one that perplexes anglers and fisheries managers, and does not live up to expectations every year, often because of variable wind and weather patterns, as well as changing water conditions.

have also been landed. Most people troll, but in the early going, pier- and shore-based casters score well, too. Brown trout are widely dispersed along Lake Ontario, but the section from Mexico Bay to Fairhaven has been especially good for big fish.

These coldwater species, plus coho and Atlantic salmon, are the subject of most interest across the lake. Landlocked Atlantics have been stocked in greater numbers in recent years, especially in the eastern basin and in the Black River. Atlantic salmon were once native to Lake Ontario, the only Great Lake that had these fish.

On the warmwater front, walleye and smallmouth bass populations are generally good. These species are not nearly as widely dispersed as trout and salmon, but along the lake's 712 miles of shoreline there are many places to find them.

The far eastern region, especially from Cape Vincent to Henderson Harbor, is especially known for smallmouth bass, although the area has recently suffered from a poorly controlled predatory cormorant population. Bass habitat here is excellent, with plenty of rocky shoals, islands, points and weed-edged rocks. Walleyes are also abundant; eight- to ten-pounders once seemed common, although the big fish were heavily exploited. There are still many good-sized walleyes in this area, however.

There is also good smallmouth action to be found in the Sodus-to-Oswego area, and a good spring walleye fishery (some to ten pounds) at Oswego. Across the lake, Ontario's Bay of Quinte has an extraordinary population of walleyes that is targeted in spring, fall and winter.

Lake Powell

Utah/Arizona, United States

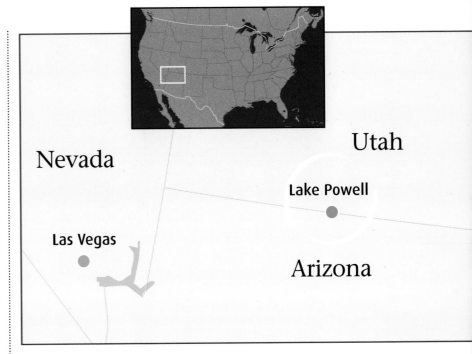

Although 186-mile-long Lake Powell used to be called the "bass capitol of the West," referring to largemouth bass, it might now be the "striper capitol of the West." There are so many striped bass here that for the past few years there has been a million-dollar fishing tournament for stripers in May, the object of which was to catch a specially tagged specimen that was worth the grand prize. No one caught it, but they caught loads of other stripers, which is what organizers wanted, as the huge lake is almost overrun with this saltwater transplant.

Lake Powell was the last of the Colorado River impoundments to get a striper fishery going, and the population has simply exploded, although large ones are

hard to come by because forage fish numbers (mainly shad) have been low. There are many small stripers, as well as fish from five to 15 pounds, and sometimes there's superb action for numbers of fish that boil up on the surface while chasing bait.

Lake Powell was created in 1963 with the completion of the Glen Canyon Dam across the Colorado River, extending the lake from Page, Arizona into Utah and causing it to be fed by the Colorado, San Juan and Escalante Rivers. It is also rimmed by many large canyons; there are 96 named, navigable tributary canyons, eight major bays, and dozens of smaller nameless waterways.

If you are a shore-oriented angler, you may be happy to learn that Lake Powell has more shoreline than Lake Michigan, although 1,900 miles of shoreline means far more good-looking places to fish than you can handle. It also means a place where one can get lost, accidently or on purpose, and find a hideaway that offers excellent relaxation, contemplation and fishing values.

Although there are trout, walleye, crappie, pike, catfish, bluegills and other fish species in Powell, it is the smallmouth bass, largemouth bass and striped bass that are

Striped Bass

Smallmouth Bass

Largemouth Bass

Crappie

RIGHT
Stripers are plentiful here, and several small ones make a great meal.

most popularly pursued. Fishing successfully for largemouth bass requires versatility and adaptability, as these fish have limited cover here and are not as numerous today as smallmouths. There is little vegetation in Lake Powell, although submerged trees are found in many spots, particularly in coves, and tree tops may come near the surface. Flooded or submerged brush offers inviting flipping targets, and flipping is a productive technique for largemouth bass along some rocky shores as well.

Smallmouth have flourished almost too well since they first came into prominence, and now the problem is that there are more smallmouth than food to feed them, meaning that they are generally small. The water is very clear in many places, often necessitating light tackle, yet it can be dirty back in some canyons, requiring heavier tackle.

Visiting anglers need sportfishing sonar on their boat to properly probe the Lake Powell shores. Many bluffs and sheer rock walls look inviting, but you can seldom tell what is below by simply looking at the shore. The underwater ledges, drop-offs and craggy cliffs often hold bass, and it is necessary to fish very close to cover. That may explain why jigs and plastic worms are especially favored throughout the season.

The Colorado River below the dam down to Lees Ferry offers some excellent fishing opportunities for rainbow, cutthroat and brook trout. The water here is continuously cold.

Details

Lake Powell, Utah/Arizona, United States

Location/getting there: Lake Powell is in northern Arizona and southern Utah. It is accessed from five locales, the most frequent being at Page, Arizona.

Info sources: Lake Powell is administered by the National Park Service in Glen Canyon National Recreation Area. Contact Lake Powell Resorts and Marinas, 2233 W. Dunlap, Suite 400, Phoenix, AZ 85012; call 800-528-6154; or visit www.visitlakepowell.com.

Prime times: The early part of the season is generally productive for bass and stripers.

Gear needs: Varies widely depending on species. Note that ultra-clear water in main areas may require delicate presentations for bass. Local bait anglers rely on live waterdogs (salamanders).

Guide/tackle availability: Limited guide service can be arranged at the marinas.

Accommodations/dining: Accommodations and dining can be found at each of the four full-service marinas on the lake.

Etcetera: Terrific scenery includes natural geological wonders, Indian ruins, petroglyphs, 100-foot-tall cliffs and towering mountains. The most famous natural attraction is Rainbow Bridge National Monument, which, at 290 feet high, is the world's tallest stone arch. Many of Lake Powell's visitors rent houseboats to tour and fish the lake for a week or more at a time, often bringing a fishing boat in tow.

Lake Sam Rayburn

Texas, United States

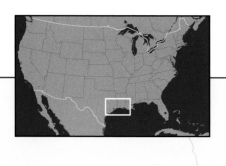

Lufkin
Lake Sam Rayburn
Jasper
Texas
Louisiana
Houston
Gulf of Mexico

Largemouth Bass

Crappie

Catfish

Striped Bass

Named after the noted politician, Lake Sam Rayburn is mammoth even by Texan standards, covering 114,000 acres, stretching for over 40 miles and encompassing some 560 miles of shoreline. Replete with flooded timber and enormous beds of aquatic vegetation, it hosts a tremendous population of largemouth bass, many of which are in the highly sought eight-to ten-pound class. Some rank Rayburn as the number one bass lake in the United States. It hosts competitive fishing events constantly, and its popularity is evidenced by a three-day spring big bass-only tournament in which 6,000 anglers participate.

RIGHT
This 13-pound bass was caught in the spring on Lake Sam Rayburn.

The largest lake entirely within Texas' boundaries, this east-Texas impoundment has gone through a boom-bust cycle of fish populations. Despite some droughts, it has recently been in a boom phase, with a lot of all-season angling opportunities, especially for largemouth bass, although the lake also produces excellent crappie and catfish action, and has good hybrid striper fishing and fair action for white bass in the spring.

What primarily attracts people to this lake, however, is bass of all sizes. There are plenty of three- and four-pound largemouths here, a good number of five- to eight-pounders, and there is always a chance of catching a ten-pounder. A 16.8-pounder caught in May 1997 is the lake record.

State stocking programs, especially of large-growing Florida-strain bass, restrictive bag limits and fluctuating water levels have all played a part in Rayburn's vitality. Periodic drawdowns from ten to 20 feet, primarily through drought, spur the growth of new, near-shore cover that helps create new habitat for baitfish and bass. The prominence of coontail moss, pond weed and hydrilla, which provide cover and feeding opportunities, has been good for fishing, too.

As is true of most big impoundments, creeks and submerged creek channels, the back ends of coves and bays, and the flats and drop-offs adjacent to deep water offer good places for anglers to start their efforts.

Bass normally spawn here in March and April, sometimes in stages, with shallower coves and southerly creeks warming up faster than other locations. However, some of the lake's best fishing is experienced in late February and early March, when bass are active and moving into staging areas to spawn.

The best early-season angling for big pre-spawn fish

takes place in the creeks and on the edges of creek channels. Coleman Creek, Ayish Bayou, Buck Bay and Five Fingers to the south, and the creeks off the Angelina and Atoyac Arms to the north, attract a lot of attention. Deeper edges-of-creek channels produce late in the year, and the vegetation is particularly worth fishing during the late spring and summer months. Hydrilla creates excellent bass cover, although fishing it frustrates most anglers. Bass can be tempted from this matted vegetation by fishing the edges with topwater plugs or buzzbaits. A heavy jig pitched into hydrilla will crash down through the growth and draw reaction strikes as it sinks.

Sam Rayburn is heavily timbered in many areas, especially in the creeks, with a lot of submerged trees and stumps. Fairly heavy line is the rule here. Jigs, adorned with pork or eel chunks, are especially favored, both for flipping and casting. Plastic worms and jigging spoons catch fish, too, as do spinnerbaits and surface lures.

ABOVE
Low water, as shown here near the Sam Rayburn dam, has been a major factor in the lake's bass fishing.

LEFT
Anglers admire a nice Rayburn largemouth, caught around deep weeds.

Details

Lake Sam Rayburn, Texas, United States

Location/getting there: Sam Rayburn Reservoir is in eastern Texas, east of Lufkin and north-northwest of Jasper, and can be reached by taking routes 69, 59 and 96.

Info sources: For general information contact the Jasper Chamber of Commerce, 246 E. Milam, Jasper, TX 75951; call 409-384-2762; or visit www.jaspercoc.org.

Prime times: See main text.

Gear needs: Standard tackle is used for bass, with medium to heavy baitcasting gear preferred. See the main text for lure information.

Guide/tackle availability: Guides and fishing tackle are widely available in the area.

Accommodations/dining: There is a wide range of lodging and dining options locally, with major emphasis on the city of Jasper.

Etcetera: Although this Corps of Engineers lake is very popular, its sheer size tends to disperse the crowds, and you can usually find a secluded cove. Camping facilities and boat ramps are abundant.

ABOVE *An angler poses with a fine Simcoe lake trout in front of his fish hut.*

Lake Simcoe

Ontario, Canada

If you lifted all the fishing huts off Ontario's Lake Simcoe on any winter weekend, and could view this large frozen gateway to Georgian Bay from the air, it would probably look like a chunk of Swiss cheese. With an average of perhaps four holes per angler, and up to six thousand anglers on a good weekend, there are a lot of circles and squares cut through that hard white lake.

From ice level, the collection of huts, vehicles and people looks more like a community on the move, or how you might imagine a ramshackle gold rush town in winter. Replace tents with thousands of huts, and replace horses and wagons with many hundreds of trucks, snowmobiles and ATVs, and you have a *large* temporary prospector's community.

The finny treasure being prospected is about as diverse as you could want. Simcoe has yellow perch, walleye, northern pike, lake trout, herring, whitefish, bass and even muskellunge among its fisheries, though perch (especially early in the winter), lake trout and whitefish have the biggest constituencies.

We are talking serious ice fishing here. This is where commercial hut operators cut tub-size holes with 36-inch-bar chainsaws. Where an auger is not worthy unless it is powered and capable of ten-inch-minimum circles. Where vehicular travel routes are marked like a highway and near-shore access areas are like deeply rutted dirt or sand roads. Where you drive five miles across the ice in a heated vehicle, then brave 20-below temperature for the time it takes to get into a heated hut with a pre-made hole.

Locally, folks used to call huge Lake Simcoe, which covers 287 square miles and is one of Ontario's largest non-Great Lakes waters, "The Ice Fishing Capitol of North America," but after the region successfully hosted the World Championships of Ice Fishing, and international participants said they had never seen anything like this place, they have since dubbed Simcoe "The Ice Fishing Capitol of the World."

Many non-local anglers are transported to the fishing by 20-foot-long, go-anywhere, motorized Bombardier caterpillars, which epitomize all-wheel drive. Such a vehicle becomes necessary not just for transport, but because Simcoe ice can be tricky. Pressure ridges build up in various spots on this 30-mile-wide lake and are not safe to cross just anywhere. Transporters regularly scout the

ice, check thickness and constantly establish safe routes. This changes because there is current in Simcoe, and because the places that they fish vary. Operators relocate huts as necessary according to fish movement, angling success and species sought.

Ice fishing on Simcoe normally starts in earnest around Christmas unless there is very mild weather. Huts, which must be registered and numbered, can be kept on the ice until mid-March.

For most of January and February, there is no lack of company on the ice. Vehicular travelers regularly pull in for progress reports and to see what you have available to eat or drink. With a cacophony of saws, augers, snowmobiles, ATVs, trucks, caterpillars, and even chair-bound anglers with radios, Simcoe in winter is an interesting fishing spectacle.

ABOVE
A Bombardier caterpillar, used to ferry ice anglers on Lake Simcoe.

Details

Lake Simcoe, Ontario, Canada

Location/getting there: Lake Simcoe is part of the navigable Trent-Severn Waterway connecting Lake Huron's Georgian Bay to the northwest and upper Lake Ontario at the Bay of Quinte to the southeast. It is about a 75-minute drive north of Toronto and is easily accessed.

Info sources: For general area information, contact Tourism Information in the town of Georgina at 888-436-7446; or visit the web site of the Huronia Tourist Association at www.county.simcoe.on.ca.

Prime times: Weekdays are best for beating the crowds.

Gear needs: You have to bring your own equipment, even when fishing with hut operators. Most ice angling is done with bait, primarily two- to three-inch shiners. Few local anglers use jigs; they prefer multiple-bait rigs for trout and whitefish, using a spreader to keep shiners apart, as well as having another shiner higher up. There is a lot of baiting and chumming in the holes. Two lines are allowed per angler.

Guide/tackle availability: Fishing is mostly self-guided; tackle and bait are available locally. Many people fish Simcoe with hut operators, who supply huts, pre-cut holes, transportation and bait. For a listing of hut operators, do a search on the Internet or visit this web page: http://notjustfishing. freeyellow.com/Ice/simcoeoperators.html.

Accommodations/dining: Assorted lodging and dining options exist around the lake.

Etcetera: Dress warm for outside, but you will be shedding outerwear inside the heated huts.

Lake Trout

Walleye

Lake Texoma

Oklahoma/Texas, United States

Oklahoma

Lake Texoma

● Denison

Dallas ●

Texas

Striped Bass

Largemouth Bass

Catfish

Crappie

Fed by the Red and Washita Rivers, and covering 88,000 acres, Texoma has a premier striped bass fishery. Although the lake does not yield monsters, some huge specimens are caught in the Red River below the dam, and the relatively clear waters of the lake proper have supported a self-sustaining striper population that has numbered in the millions for more than two decades.

Some of the hottest striper fishing takes place during fall and winter, when large schools of fish actively chase shad. These are readily located by looking for flocks of seagulls diving into the water to capture shad injured by marauding stripers. Anglers use heavy slab spoons, as well as crankbaits and soft-bodied jigs, to catch the fish, in sometimes frenetic moments.

Some of the most reliable and varied striper fishing occurs in summer. Flatline trolling with crankbaits and plugs commonly takes large numbers of fish from ten to 30 feet deep, while downriggers are used to catch stripers suspended in deep water off points and creek channels. Many anglers use a cast net to catch live shad for bait, although it can sometimes be difficult to locate these baitfish. Summer also offers exciting topwater action. Stripers can often be seen breaking the surface of the water, particularly on calm days.

F ormed in 1944, Lake Texoma sprawls along the Oklahoma/Texas border and is one of the most popular vacation destinations in the Southwest. It ranks as the second most heavily visited Corps of Engineers Lake in the U.S..

RIGHT
Fishing at sunrise on Lake Texoma.

Details

Lake Texoma, Oklahoma/Texas, United States

Location/getting there: Lake Texoma is situated on the Oklahoma-Texas border, about 75 miles north of Dallas and 121 miles south of Oklahoma City.

Info sources: For area information, contact The Lake Texoma Association, P.O. Box 610, Kingston, OK 73439; call 580-564-2334; or visit www.laketexomaonline.com.

Prime times: See main text.

Gear needs: Varies with species and fishing method; many striper guides provide tackle.

Guide/tackle availability: There are literally hundreds of guides on Lake Texoma; tackle is widely available.

Accommodations/dining: Marinas, resorts, motels and over 50 campgrounds exist in the area; dining options are equally diverse.

Etcetera: This immense area provides lots of recreation and outdoor enjoyment beyond fishing. Bald eagle watching in the fall is very popular. Boating is immensely popular, and over 80 public ramps exist. There are also two wildlife refuges here, two state parks, over 50 parks managed by the Corps of Engineers, dozens of resorts and hundreds of campgrounds.

Texoma is also known for good crappie, white bass and largemouth bass fishing. Crappies enter the shallow water to spawn in late March and early April; anglers who dabble small jigs or soak live minnows in and around shoreline cover do well then. White bass, called "sandies" here, are popular targets in spring when they spawn in tributaries, and in summer when they school near the surface. Largemouth bass anglers score well by fishing in and around flooded cover during the spring months; an 11.8-pounder established a new lake record in 2000.

Texoma stripers typically run between 12 and 22 inches, although fish up to 15 pounds are not uncommon. Trophy fish can be found in the Red River below the dam. During heavy water releases, stripers move up below the dam to feed on stunned baitfish that have gone through the dam's turbines. Free-lining live bait is an effective tactic, but many large fish are caught on jigs and topwater plugs. The Red River record is a 43-pounder.

There is also excellent smallmouth bass fishing to be found on Texoma. Fish in the five- to seven-pound class are possible, especially in February and March. Good action can also be had from late spring through early summer. Smallmouths congregate on the lake's many rocky points, with the top fishing locations offering deep water close to shore.

Blue and channel catfish are also numerous here, and a variety of fishing techniques is used. Drifting with live or cut shad, a tactic also employed by striper anglers, is excellent for catfish. Drifters usually concentrate on flats adjacent to deeper creek channels. Platter Flats, Willafa Wood and Willow Springs are favorite drift-fishing areas. The lake record blue cat is a 116-pounder.

LEFT
A fisherman lands a small Texoma striper as other boats gather to cast around a surfacing school.

BELOW
A good-sized rainy day striped bass from Lake Texoma.

Lake of the Woods

Minnesota, United States, and Ontario, Canada

Lake of the Woods has the size and fish that befit its status as the pre-eminent northcentral warmwater fishery of North America. It is roughly 66 miles long (from Baudette, Minnesota to Kenora, Ontario) and 52 miles wide (from Northwest Angle, Minnesota to Nestor Falls, Ontario), with about 65,000 miles of shoreline. There are over 14,500 islands—most in the Canadian sector—and to say that one can get lost quite easily on Lake of the Woods, or spend a lot of time searching for fishing hotspots, is an understatement.

This is truly a picture-postcard lake, characterized by rocky shores, some weedy bays and a hearty shoreline mixture of conifers and hardwoods. Its rough-woods wilderness profile is only occasionally punctuated by houses, camps or boat docks, and you can travel in some portions of the lake without seeing any signs of civilization. The central and northern sectors house nearly all of the islands. The wide-open southern expanse of Big Traverse Bay, situated in Minnesota, is fairly shallow with few reefs and islands.

Angling in general throughout the lake is among the best to be found in North America for several species of fish, most notably smallmouth bass, walleye, pike and muskie.

The bass do not run particularly large but they are plentiful. The best smallmouth are in the central and northern half of the lake. Most angling is in relatively shallow water throughout the season. Jigs are the main lure, but spinners, some crankbaits and surface plugs are useful. Largemouth bass are present here, too, but are greatly outnumbered by their cousins.

Walleyes are plentiful throughout the lake, with the possibility of getting some in the seven-pound-and-up class and sometimes over ten pounds. Walleyes get a lot of attention here in mid-May when the season opens and the fishing is both fast and relatively easy. The mayfly hatch of late spring and early summer drops walleye fishing success for a while. They then leave the bays and

Details

Lake of the Woods, Minnesota, United States, and Ontario, Canada

Location/getting there: Lake of the Woods borders northern Minnesota and southwestern Ontario and is readily accessed by major roads. Baudette, Northwest Angle, Kenora and Sioux Narrows provide major access. Floatplanes fly from Baudette to distant areas.

Info sources: For area information, contact Lake of the Woods Vacation Area; call 800-535-4549; or visit www.lakeofthewoods.com. Also contact Lake of the Woods Tourism, P.O. Box 518, Baudette, MN 56623; call 800-382-3474; or visit www.lakeofthewoodsmn.com.

Prime times: Fall for muskies; summer for bass; spring and fall for walleyes.

Gear needs: Varies depending on species and fishing methods.

Guide/tackle availability: Guides are available through many lodges, although most anglers fish unguided. Tackle is available at stores and camps, but bring most of what you will need.

Accommodations/dining: Lodging and dining options are plentiful. Two fishing camps

of note are Totem Lodge, Box 180, Sioux Narrows, Ontario, Canada, P0X 1N0 (call 807-226-5275 or visit www.totemresorts.com) and Centre Island South, P.O. Box 31, Oak Island, MN 56741 (call 218-766-2025 and 807-543-4030 or visit www.centreislandsouth.com).

Etcetera: Another notable fishery in the area is the outflowing Rainy River, at the southeast corner of the lake. Lake of the Woods is big water that demands suitable boats and navigational equipment. A good navigational chart and GPS are very helpful.

Smallmouth Bass

Walleye

Muskellunge

Northern Pike

Largemouth Bass

head for rocky reefs and, to a lesser degree, deep-water points and rocky islands. Near the end of summer the walleyes leave the reefs, moving into weedy bays that have mud and sand bottoms.

If you are walleye fishing regularly, you will surely catch a few northern pike; while jigging you will undoubtedly be cut off a few times each day as well. If you pursue pike expressly, you will find plenty. Leader-linked lures such as spinners, spinnerbaits, spoons and some muskie plugs will catch pike in their favored weedy haunts, though the bigger fish seem to be off rocky points or reefs. Four- to five-pounders are common, and there are opportunities for much larger ones, including the occasional pike in the 18- to 25-pound range.

The muskie population is extraordinary. Lake of the Woods offers an excellent chance of catching a specimen of 30 pounds or better. The average size is about 18 pounds, but a lot of 20- to 30-pounders are caught and released

annually. The muskie season opens in mid-June, and fishing is good through the fall. August may be the best month because the fish are very active and shallow, and will even strike surface lures. Bucktail spinners are the foremost lure, followed by jerkbaits, swimming plugs and crankbaits. This is almost entirely a casting fishery. Shallow water, rocky reefs and submerged weed growth are everywhere.

Early in the summer, muskies are found in the same locales as walleyes, which are their primary forage. By midsummer they have moved onto reefs with good weed cover. The midsection of the lake, from Monument Bay to Sabaskosing Bay, is prime muskie territory, and there is a lot of ground to cover.

Lake of the Woods also has an excellent fishery in places for crappies, has plenty of sauger, and contains lake trout in fair numbers. Ice fishing for perch, walleye and pike is popular from late December into April.

LEFT
A mid-lake view of Lake of the Woods as a summer thunderstorm approaches.

OPPOSITE
Smallmouth bass fishing on Lake of the Woods.

ABOVE *Stable, square-sterned wooden canoes are used by Miramichi fishing camps.*

Miramichi River

New Brunswick, Canada

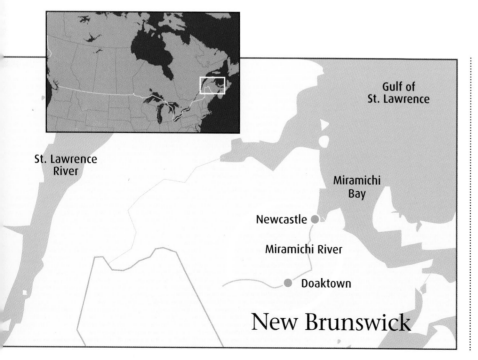

Gulf of
St. Lawrence

St. Lawrence
River

Miramichi
Bay

Newcastle

Miramichi River

Doaktown

New Brunswick

Although Atlantic salmon fishing in most North American rivers is far from what it once was, a few waters still attract the passionate and dedicated salmon angler. Arguably the most notable of these is New Brunswick's fabled Miramichi. There are several stems to the Miramichi, with the main Southwest Miramichi being the focal point for gentrified salmon angling efforts from July through September.

Although big salmon are an infrequent catch on the Miramichi, as they are elsewhere in North America, fish of 20 pounds and up to 30 are occasionally taken, and make big news. No large salmon can be kept here; any salmon over 63 centimeters fork length, or about 25 inches, must be released, which effectively limits the seasonal take (eight in total and one per day) to grilse.

Anadromous Atlantic salmon that spend only one year at sea and weigh from three to six pounds are called grilse when they return to freshwater to spawn. Most are males. Salmon that return after two winters spent at sea usually weigh from six to 15 pounds.

The Southwest Miramichi is a long, winding, relatively shallow river with many bars and pools. It is an easy river to wade under most circumstances. Wide by the standards of most trout anglers, it is known for long casting, although that is not an absolute necessity.

The established fishing season on the Miramichi for bright (fresh-run) salmon is primarily from mid-May through mid-October. June angling is often spotty, with July usually having a good number of fish. September has produced excellent angling, although there is often some fluctuation in fish numbers due to water levels, rainfall and the weather. Lately, good numbers of fish, and some in the 30-pound class, have been available into October.

The Miramichi has excellent sport for "black" or "spring" salmon, which are Atlantics returning to sea after wintering in the river. Darker than incoming fish, these salmon are readily caught on the fly, and provide an especially good introduction to Atlantic salmon fishing and/or to fly fishing. This has been a much-overlooked opportunity on the Miramichi, although it is one that is disdained by many salmon traditionalists. However, more lodges and camps are promoting it. The period for this catch-and-release fishery is mid-April through mid-May.

The major pools on the Miramichi are in private hands, being leased or owned predominantly by clubs or sporting camps. Some own many miles of water. Non-resident anglers must have a licensed guide everywhere on this river, as well as on other New Brunswick waters that are "designated." Some sections of the river are also categorized as hook-and-release only.

The Miramichi also hosts an excellent run of American shad in late May–early June. This is virtually neglected, and is done by fly fishing with unweighted flies only, primarily by casting from anchored canoes. The fish run from two-and-a-half to five pounds on average, but there are much larger ones present. When the run is strong, an angler can get into some very fast action with these fish.

BELOW
*Fishing a Miramichi
salmon pool.*

Details

Miramichi River, New Brunswick, Canada

Location/getting there: The Miramichi is located in eastcentral New Brunswick, with Doaktown being the hub of information and activity. Visitors access the area by flying to Fredericton and by driving from Highway 2 to Highway 8. Doaktown is about 65 miles from Fredericton.

Info sources: For area information, contact Tourism New Brunswick, P.O. Box 12345, Campbellton, New Brunswick, Canada E3N 1T6; call 800-561-0123; or visit www.tourismnbcanada.com.

Prime times: See text.

Gear needs: Atlantic salmon fishing here by law is fly fishing with an unweighted artificial fly. Most of this is dry fly fishing, using large deer-haired flies, many brightly colored, on nine-foot rods with eight- or nine-weight lines, although wet flies on floating lines are also employed.

Guide/tackle availability: Non-residents require guides. Some camps provide one guide per two anglers and boat, while others spread a guide over several people. Flies are available locally, and there may be tackle at some camps, although most anglers bring their own.

Accommodations/dining: Established lodges and camps provide excellent dining and good, rustic accommodations.

Etcetera: The southwest Miramichi produces more salmon consistently throughout the angling season than any of its tributaries, yet other area waters are also worth a visit. The Dungarvon, for example, usually provides good early-season fishing; the Renous and the Cains are often good in the fall.

Atlantic Salmon

American Shad

Mississippi River (Lower)

Arkansas/Mississippi, United States

The lower Mississippi is large, roiled and intimidating. It has loads of big vessels, many of which leave ocean wave-like wakes, and rolls along at a good clip when it is high. You would not call it a very inviting fishing spot. But get off on the fringe, into the backwaters, up the oxbows and into tributary sloughs, and it is another world: inviting and productive for catching largemouth bass, crappies, bream, catfish and striped bass, plus encounters with gar, drum, bowfin and carp.

The region in Arkansas and Mississippi from just below Memphis south to the Arkansas-Louisiana border is especially notable. In Mississippi, there are dozens of oxbow lakes, formed when the silt-laden river changed course and isolated a curve. Sometimes the oxbows are completely separated from the main river; other times

Details

Mississippi River (Lower), Arkansas/Mississippi, United States

Location/getting there: This area is along the Arkansas and Mississippi portions of the lower Mississippi River from south of Memphis to the Arkansas-Louisiana border. Some oxbows are accessed from major roads, but most are reached only by water. Good highway maps, topographic maps and navigation charts are a necessity.

Info sources: For general area information in Arkansas, contact the Arkansas Department of Parks and Tourism at 800-628-8725; or visit www.arkansas.com. For general area information in Mississippi, contact the Mississippi Division of Tourism at 800-927-6378; or visit www.visitmississippi.org. Also

contact the White River National Wildlife Refuge, P.O. Box 308, Dewitt, AR 72042; call 870-946-1468; or visit www.fws.gov/~r4eao.

Prime times: Whenever the water level is stable.

Gear needs: Varies depending on species and fishing methods. Using a larger boat to ferry a pair of lightweight fishing kayaks is a good means of getting to remote places.

Guide/tackle availability: Limited guide service is available in the area. Tackle is available at shops, which are widely scattered.

Accommodations/dining: There is a wide range of lodging and dining options throughout the region.

Etcetera: Fishing on the big river and its oxbows is subject to changing water levels due to weather, both locally and especially upriver. The best fishing conditions occur with a stable water level, which makes the fish more predictable. A steady fall is better than a steady rise. In some places, local river rats know exactly at what river stages certain sloughs become accessible to large boats or become inaccessible to anything but a kayak. When the water has been rising and falling a good deal, it will be especially dirty, which is poor for fishing.

Largemouth Bass

Crappie

Catfish

Striped Bass

they are open at one or both ends. Size can vary from less than 100 to several thousand acres in size. Most oxbows usually sport standing willow and/or cypress trees, and have deep channels as well as shallow flats.

Among the largest and best-known oxbows in Mississippi are Tunica Cut-Off in northern Mississippi near the city of Tunica, DeSoto Lake near Clarksdale and Lake Ferguson near Greenville. All three offer 2,500 or more acres of bass, crappie, bream, catfish and striped bass action. Largemouth bass, as well as striped bass, are especially favored.

Arkansas may have even more oxbows. Bream, channel catfish, crappie, hybrid striped bass and largemouth bass are prime at Lake Chicot, a 5,300-acre Mississippi River oxbow south of Greenville, which is said to be the largest oxbow lake in the world. Action starts here earlier in the year than on most large Arkansas lakes, thanks to Chicot's extreme southern location. The best fishing is generally around cypress trees, willows, buckbrush, dead timber and private docks along the

shore, except for open-water stripers.

Moving south along the Mississippi River, other large (over 900 acres) top-notch oxbow lakes in Arkansas include Horseshoe, Wapanocca, Dacus, Midway, Mellwood, Old Town and Grand. These have well-deserved reputations for producing numerous big crappie, largemouth bass, bream and catfish.

Hundreds of oxbow lakes, most less than 100 acres, are open to fishing during portions of the year in White River National Wildlife Refuge in southeast Arkansas. This refuge spans 157,000 acres and includes 356 natural and man-made lakes as well as 90 miles of the White River.

The White empties into the Arkansas River, which joins the Mississippi. Backwaters along the White vary in accessibility depending on the water level, meaning that adventurous anglers (using small boats or kayaks) have opportunities to reach places that few others can go. That gets them fishing around flooded cypress and tupelo trees in a wild and secluded pond-like bayou, where the water looks like pure tea and where there is plenty of birdlife.

OPPOSITE PAGE
Fishing around flooded cypress deep in the Arkansas National Wildlife Refuge.

FAR LEFT
An angler casts to flooded timber back in an Arkansas oxbow.

LEFT
Landing a nice largemouth bass from a kayak near Tunica, Mississippi.

Moose Lake/ Blackwater River

British Columbia, Canada

Moose Lake is British Columbia's premier jump-off spot for fishing in the real wilderness, where the air, the woods, the game and the fish are pure, wild and plentiful, and where the scenery is more compelling than any tourism brochure.

The region surrounding Moose Lake is just remote enough to have been spared from extensive logging and access roads, and is probably not too different from when Alexander Mackenzie first explored this region over 200 years ago. Having already traveled the great Arctic river that bears his name, Mackenzie struck westward from the Northwest Territories in 1793 searching for an overland route to the Pacific for the fur-trading North West

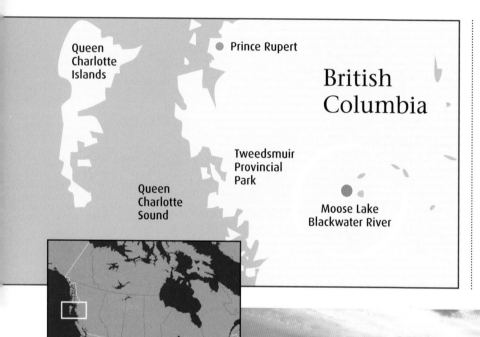

Queen Charlotte Islands

Prince Rupert

British Columbia

Tweedsmuir Provincial Park

Queen Charlotte Sound

Moose Lake Blackwater River

Rainbow Trout

RIGHT
Sunrise scene at Moose Lake.

Company. After passing through this region, he ultimately found a low pass to the sea near Bella Coola.

He evidently never visited Moose Lake, however, and never saw its grandeur. Primarily anglers and hunters come to this lake now and, when they stand on the shore of this six-mile-long lake and watch the sun set, casting an alpen glow on the jackpine mountains and the distant snow-topped peaks, they can watch an eagle on its nest, listen to calling loons, view a moose feeding along the shore and see rainbow trout jumping within casting distance.

This mountainous interior of British Columbia is a land of glaciers, thick pine forests, mosquitoes, lakes, rivers, moose, grizzly bears, eagles, wolves, coyotes and colorful wild trout. It is 30 minutes by floatplane to the nearest community, Anahim Lake, which, with a few stores and an Indian reservation, is not exactly Gotham.

And the fish really do jump freely out of the water here. At Moose Lake, rainbow trout have free-leaped into a boat, and once a fisherman was hit in the face with an unhooked leaper. Such behavior is partly due to profuse bug life and loads of freshwater shrimp. The abundance of food is not only good for trout, but also for squawfish and suckers, which you will catch frequently, and which often become eagle prey in shallow, weedy locations.

It is almost enough to stay at Moose Lake and catch oodles of willing rainbow trout, but there are richer and varied opportunities throughout the region. Many of the lakes and rivers in the region hold rainbow or cutthroat trout or Dolly Varden. Visiting via foot, horseback, or (most likely) floatplane, one can easily connect with scrappy fish. They are plentiful in most places.

In all of British Columbia, one of the finest of these places is the Blackwater River, a small, swift, brush- and tree-lined gem, parts of which are very close to the

ABOVE
A Moose Lake angler casts for trout.

INSET
Dining room view from Moose Lake Lodge.

Mackenzie Trail. There is excellent action to be found in the Blackwater's pools and eddies for brilliantly colored wild fish.

There is also superb fishing in turquoise-colored, high-altitude lakes among the Coast Mountains, which include the tallest peaks in British Columbia. They provide a marvelous distant vista, but when you fly by and through them in a floatplane, you get close to glaciers, gorges, ravines, valleys, falls, sheer rock cliffs and lush mountain bowls. Fishing takes place at the inlet to fjord-like lakes with sparkling clear water that courses through gravel and empties into a greenish-blue pool.

Here, the mountains rise steeply all around, furrowed by wide glacial cuts that narrow up high, where the snow begins and blends into light clouds. The cutthroat trout are so abundant and careless that you can stand downstream and watch a companion's fly float by and observe trout after trout dart from cover to pounce on it.

Details

Moose Lake/Blackwater River, British Columbia, Canada

Location/getting there: Located in the Chilcotin region of B.C., Moose Lake is not shown on many maps. To reach it by commercial travel, it is necessary to connect through Vancouver to Anahim Lake, where you transfer to a floatplane for a 30-minute trip to the lodge.

Info sources: Contact Moose Lake Lodge, Box 3310, Anahim Lake, B.C. V0L 1C0, Canada; call 250-742-3535; or visit www.mooselake lodge.ca. Contact the Sport Fishing Institute of British Columbia, 200-1676 Duranleau St., Granville Island, Vancouver, B.C., V6H 3S4, Canada; call 1-800-HELLO-BC for a free Sport Fishing Planning Guide or visit www.sportfishing.bc.ca.

Prime times: All summer for trout.

Gear needs: Light flycasting and spinning tackle; most flycasting is with a floating line and dry flies, although wet flies are also used. Waders are a necessity.

Guide/tackle availability: Guide service is available at extra cost. Some flies are available at the lodge, but bring your own tackle and waders.

Accommodations/dining: The main lodge is rustic and used both for dining and gathering; it has a spectacular view of Moose Lake. Guests stay in eight wood-stove-heated log cabins with private baths that overlook the lake. Food is excellent and plentiful.

Etcetera: The sights and scenery are so compelling everywhere here that you will need lots of film. Take a visit to an abandoned Indian community at Gotchko Lake along the Mackenzie Trail. Moose Lake Lodge is open from mid-May to mid-October and offers horseback trail rides as well as hiking; it also has one of Canada's premier moose hunting operations in the fall. Costs for five days at Moose Lake are $2,100, all inclusive from Vancouver; fly-out trips are extra. They also have a lodge and fly-out fishing for steelhead and salmon on the Dean River.

ABOVE
*Landing a chinook
salmon on the
lower Niagara
River.*

 # Niagara River

New York, United States

Derived from the Indian word *Ongiara*, meaning "thundering water," Niagara is certainly an appropriate name for this body of water, whose famous falls inspire awe in everyone. Much of the world knows this river for its thundering main attraction, plus the ***Maid of the Mist*** boat rides, the Cave of the Catacombs walk, the wax museum, casino gambling and all the other attractions and treasures that contribute to making this locale one of the honeymoon capitols of North America. Many anglers, however, have a different type of romance with this body of water and its fish. These anglers know that the Niagara River has some of the best and most varied of all angling on the Great Lakes and its tributaries.

Most of this resource is below the great falls, where much of the entire volume of the Great Lakes that is headed to the sea flushes amidst a tumultuous spray, then courses by the Niagara Power Project, one of the world's largest hydroelectric power-producing facilities. This structure is adjacent to Devil's Hole, a dangerous piece of whirlpooling water that acts as a magnet for migrating salmon, attracting one of the Great Lakes' best runs of large chinook salmon (15 to 35 pounds) each year in late summer and early fall.

From Niagara Falls to miles below past Lewiston, the lower Niagara River is a steep, forbidding gorge. But it can yield some awesome fishing to the diligent and careful angler. Drifting with preserved salmon egg clusters is most productive for salmon, but flatline trolling with deep-diving plugs is a strong hot second, especially when it happens early in the day.

From mid-October through April, steelhead are present in the lower Niagara in good numbers, with the best action in February and March; the clearer the water

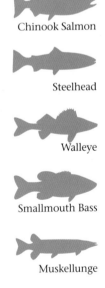

Chinook Salmon

Steelhead

Walleye

Smallmouth Bass

Muskellunge

LEFT
A big walleye is netted on the Niagara.

that comes down the river from Lake Erie, the better the steelhead fishing. Drifting with eggs is the main technique, but other methods are possible, including fly fishing.

The river gets a good run of lake trout in May, and angling for this species is surprisingly good. In the spring, some huge lakers—including a record 39-pounder—are caught at the mouth of the river off the Niagara Bar. This is also a hotspot for chinook salmon in the spring, and a great place for brown trout.

Walleyes and smallmouth bass are bountiful in the lower river, and are caught in both numbers and size; some walleyes have been caught up to 15 pounds; seven-pound walleyes are common, and it is possible to catch many dozens of smallmouths. Both of these species are also caught in the upper Niagara—the section from Lake Erie to just above the falls—but the bigger news here is an unheralded muskellunge fishery, especially in fall. The upper Niagara water is usually clear, and fishing for muskies is by flatline trolling with large plugs.

Details

Niagara River, New York, United States

Location/getting there: The Niagara River forms a boundary between southeastern Ontario and western New York. The primary fishing and boating access is at Lewiston, New York.

Info sources: For area and general sportfishing information, contact Niagara County Sportfishing, 139 Niagara St., Lockport, NY 14094; call 800-338-7890; or visit www.niagara_usa.com/pages/sportfishing/htm. For guided fishing contact Capt. John DeLorenzo, 716-297-9424 and www.niagarariverguides.com. Capt. Bob Cinelli, 716-433-5210 and www.cinellissport-fishing.websitegalaxy.com and Capt. Ernie Calandrelli, 716-284-2335.

Prime times: August through September for river salmon; February and March for steelhead; summer through fall for walleye and bass; fall for muskie.

Gear needs: Assorted depending on species.

Guide/tackle availability: Guides are widely available, and provide tackle; supplies are available in local shops.

Accommodations/dining: A range of lodging and dining options exist in the area.

Etcetera: After fishing in the river, there is always the Falls and related attractions, or a visit to Fort Niagara. And the fishing is not too shabby in Lake Ontario or in eastern Lake Erie.

North Seal River

Manitoba, Canada

The North Seal River and connected lakes encompass a region that provides remarkable scenery—from sub-tundra jackpine to treeless barrenlands—and equally commendable fishing. Covering nearly 100 miles from north to south, this watershed includes dozens of lakes, scores of tributaries to those lakes, plus the main stems of the North Seal River, and results in opportunities galore for northern pike, grayling, lake trout and walleye.

Northern pike are the most highly sought species and are plentiful in a full range of sizes in many waters. The only outfitter in this area, North Seal Lake Lodge, registers an impressive number of Manitoba-citation trophy catches (all released) annually, with some pike having reached the 48-inch class.

Grayling likewise are caught in both numbers and size, with some record-class fish having been landed; the Manitoba record grayling came from the North Seal River. Walleyes are abundant in all of the lakes of this area. This is the most northerly range in the province for walleyes, yet some here grow to 30-inch size. The lakes in this area also provide good action for lake trout, and these have

recently been yielding numerous Manitoba-trophy specimens, incuding a few in the 40-pound range.

What especially appeals to many visitors to this area is the diversity and the plentitude. Abundant populations of four species, plus lakes and rivers with different looks, features and personalities, make it possible to have a constant stream of new adventures. Furthermore, you can do most of this is without long boat rides or having to fish rough water.

Details

North Seal River, Manitoba, Canada

Location/getting there: The North Seal River and connected lakes are in northern Manitoba, and are accessed by chartered plane from Winnipeg, landing at the lodge's own airstrip.

Info sources: For information, contact North Seal River Lodge at 800-235-6343; or visit www.ganglers.com. For Manitoba information, contact Travel Manitoba, 7-155 Carlton St., Winnipeg, Manitoba R3C 3H8, Canada; call 800-665-0040; or visit www.travelmanitoba.com.

Prime times: Early season is preferred by some pike and lake trout anglers for shallow fishing.

Gear needs: See the information on this topic for Selwyn Lake (see page 198).

Guide/tackle availability: Guides are part of the package at the main lodge; fishing is self-guided at outposts. A limited selection of gear is available at the main lodges.

Accommodations/dining: Accommodations, food and service are excellent.

Etcetera: Anglers who visit North Seal River Lodge are based at Egenolf Lake, but have the opportunity to explore a few nearby (via portage) lakes and 16 fly-out lakes, some barely fished and with exceptional action. There are also outpost camps at certain lakes. Cost for seven days is $3,195, which is all-inclusive from Winnipeg.

Northern Pike

Grayling

Lake Trout

Walleye

Nueltin Lake

Manitoba, Canada

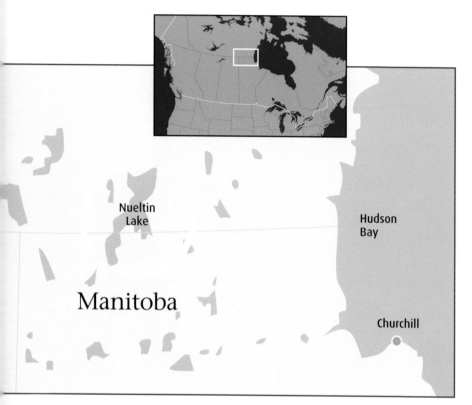

Known as the first lake in Canada to voluntarily adopt a total catch-and-release ethic (except for small lunch fish), which it did in 1978, Nueltin Lake is one of Canada's premier lake trout, pike and grayling destinations. Only a few dozen people fish this 125-mile-long lake each week during a short season, and some places are too distant to be reached by boat on day trips, so they have rarely been visited.

Nueltin Fly-In Lodges has one of the foremost fly-in lodges in all of Canada here (Treeline Lodge) and helps maintain such a high-quality fishery by virtue of the fact that it has exclusive access not only to Nueltin Lake, which straddles northern Manitoba and southern Nunavut Territory, but to scores of large and small lakes and rivers throughout the region. Some 130 boats are scattered about to access these places; many are only visited for occasional one-day trips, some have overnight cabins and a few are outpost camps.

Lake Trout

Northern Pike

Grayling

RIGHT
Anglers ready for a day of fishing at Nueltin Lake.

OPPOSITE
Thirty-five pounds of Nueltin Lake trout is a great catch. INSET: *Evening fishing at Kasmere Lake.*

One of their sites is 24-mile-long Kasmere Lake, newly opened in 2000 with a deluxe lodge. It has good fishing in the lake and also in the exciting Thlewiaza River, which begins at Kasmere and empties into Nueltin Lake some 25 air miles away. A few people each year make a partial float from Kasmere down the Thlewiaza, fishing for pike in several small bays and two small lakes, and traversing three Class III or better whitewater rapids. The fish have hardly seen any lures and the chances of seeing moose on this wilderness float trip are very good.

Nueltin Lake is the crown jewel, however. Lots of trout and pike, including specimens of enormous size, are an honest-to-goodness possibility for any visitor who is even a moderately skilled angler. The Manitoba Master Angler program is testimony to the lake's great pike and lake trout fishing and, if it was not for the fact that two-thirds of Nueltin lies in Nunavut Territory and trophy fish caught in those waters are not registered in the Manitoba program, then Nueltin would dominate the stat sheet far more than it does presently.

Fifty-six pounds is the largest laker on record for Nueltin. Specimens in the 15- to 25-pound class are fairly common, with good opportunities for catching trout that range from 20 to 40 pounds. Many of the biggest lakers could be caught late in the season when they come up on reefs to spawn, but the camp closes then because of bad weather, so few people fish it in September.

Most lake trout fishing is done by trolling; flatlining is effective early, but in midsummer, when the fish are usually deep, it is necessary to use large spoons near or on the bottom. Sonar units are on all boats; downriggers and three-way rigs with heavy sinkers are used, but some trout are also caught using deep-diving planers. Jigging opportunities do exist, and two- to four-ounce leadheads with bucktail and soft-plastic bodies are needed. Early season can provide light-tackle trout fishing.

For pike, the period of late June through early July offers probably the most action, with plenty of fish in shallow water which are eager to strike surface lures, spinnerbaits, plugs and weedless spoons that are cast into the shore in the backs of countless bays. They move to deeper weeds once the water warms. Many pike in the 15- to 22-pound range are available, with some larger ones caught annually.

Grayling fishing is also good at Nueltin. Some large fish, in the three-pound-range, are caught here, especially by anglers fishing the swifter waters around Nueltin Narrows.

Nueltin is as remote as one can get in Manitoba, with wild unspoiled beauty, countless islands and bays, many incoming rivers and plenty of sandy beach where you might see the tracks of a moose, wolf or bear if not the animal itself. The southern portion is amply treed with spruce and tamarack, and the terrain tapers to stark tundra at the northern end by Sealhole Lake, where caribou are occasionally seen. Some visitors have spotted caribou by the thousands from the air.

BELOW
A young angler fishes late in the day at Sealhole Lake.

Details

Nueltin Lake, Manitoba, Canada

Location/getting there: Nueltin Lake straddles the 60th Parallel about 850 miles north of Winnipeg. It is accessed by charter plane from Winnipeg that lands at a private airstrip at Treeline Lodge.

Info sources: For information contact, Nueltin Fly-In Lodges, Box 500, Alonsa, Manitoba R0H 0A0, Canada; call 800-361-7177; or visit www.nueltin.com. For Manitoba information, contact Travel Manitoba, 7-155 Carlton St., Winnipeg, Manitoba R3C 3H8, Canada; call 800-665-0040; or visit www.travel manitoba.com.

Prime times: Many regulars prefer the first three weeks after ice-out for shallow fishing.

Gear needs: Lake trout: medium to heavy levelwind trolling tackle for deep fishing;

lighter baitcasting, spinning and flycasting early in the season; heavy jigs, large trolling spoons and plugs. Pike: medium to medium-heavy spinning and baitcasting, with 12- to 20-pound line and nine- or ten-weight flycasting outfits; spoons, bucktail spinners, soft jerkbaits and shallow-running plugs. Grayling: light spinning and five-weight flycasting; small jigs, spinners, dry flies and wet flies. All hooks must be barbless.

Guide/tackle availability: Guides are part of the package at the main lodges; fishing is self-guided at outposts. A limited selection of spoons, plugs, terminal gear and incidentals is available at the main lodges.

Accommodations/dining: Accommodations at the main lodges are excellent, with motel-like rooms equipped with heat and private

showers. The main lodges at Treeline and Kasmere are spacious and have all the amenities. Service is excellent, overseen by the Gurke family, and dining is first-rate at morning and evening. Shore lunches, featuring freshly cooked pike or lake trout, are a daily staple.

Etcetera: The cost for a seven-day trip is $3,595 at Treeline Lodge and $2,295 at outpost camps; a four-day stay at Kasmere is $2,595. These prices are inclusive from Winnipeg but exclude overnight accommodations there. If you tire of catching fish at Nueltin, you can try their new golf driving range, but it is probably best to do so when the wind can keep the flies and mosquitoes at bay.

ABOVE
A dusting of late-August snow greets sunrise at Treeline Lodge.

Ottawa River

Ontario, Canada

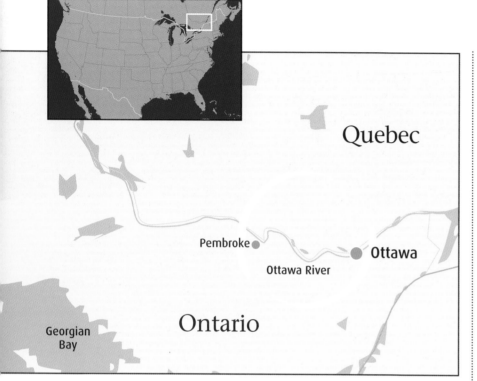

The water of the Ottawa River is somewhat stained, since it comes from northern bogs and swamps. Two decades ago it was heavily polluted by effluent from sewage treatment plants and paper mills, a problem that has been greatly alleviated. The river also used to be covered in places with floating logs from timbering operations. Logs were contained in great rafts, which sometimes broke up in storms; unrecovered runaway logs were plentiful. The river is no longer used for floating timber, however. Although some deadheads exist and require careful boating, many have been removed; each year there are larger boats on sections of the river where once only

The Ottawa River is 250 miles long and forms a border between the provinces of Ontario and Quebec. In the wild, remote-but-accessible upper Ottawa Valley, especially in the area from Mattawa to a few miles south of Pembroke, it is loaded with good fishing opportunities. In the lower valley, the Ottawa River has some of the best muskie fishing in North America, right in the shadows of Ottawa, Canada's capitol city.

RIGHT
A nice muskie from the lower Ottawa.

smaller aluminum craft could be seen.

Muskies have been prospering near the city of Ottawa from Arnprior to Hawkesbury and even further downriver, yet there is only a relatively small group of people fishing for them. There is abundant vegetation here, as well as well-defined breaklines, a variety of islands and bays, and other typical muskie habitat.

This area has excellent muskie angling for the first three weeks of the season, from mid-June into early July. Vegetation is not too dense then, and muskies stage on those weeds that are present. The best muskie fishing, as well as the chance for big fish, is from mid-September until the mid-November, perhaps later if both weather and access (no ice on the launch ramps) cooperate.

Muskies over 55 inches are not common here at any time, and experts say that the genetics of the fish in most of the river indicate that 21 years is where the bigger muskies top out (muskies can live for 30 years). Nevertheless, a 58-incher and a 60-incher (possibly 50

pounds) have been caught in the river, the latter back in the late 1990s closer to Montreal. Muskies here are caught in many ways, including high-speed trolling with various lures, and casting.

Upriver, the foremost draw for anglers is walleye, and there is no better time for fast action than when the provincial season opener occurs on the second Saturday of May. The standard catch is in the two- and three-pound range, but some trophies in the eight- to ten-pound class are caught.

There is also a plentiful supply of northern pike here, plus smallmouth bass. There are no muskies in this section, but, surprisingly, there are largemouths in backwater locales, and they are virtually overlooked by anglers concentrating on walleye and smallmouth in the main flowage. In recent years there has been a surge in the population of channel catfish in the river, and much more fishing has been done for them, so much so that even the tourism agencies are promoting it.

ABOVE
A fisherman gets ready to explore the lower Ottawa River on a fall morning.

Details

Ottawa River, Ontario, Canada

Location/getting there: Readily reached by major roads, the Ottawa River borders Ontario and Quebec and joins the St. Lawrence River above Montreal.

Info sources: For area information, contact the Ottawa Valley Tourist Association, 9 International Dr., Pembroke, Ontario, Canada K8A 6W5; call 800-757-6580; or visit www.ottawavalley.org.

Prime times: Fall for muskies; spring for walleyes; summer for bass.

Gear needs: Varies depending on species and method of fishing.

Guide/tackle availability: There are a few guides who fish for muskies in the section of the Ottawa from Arnprior to Hawkesbury, though most muskie anglers fish self-guided and bring their own tackle. Most fishing on

the upper river is done by anglers using their own boats, or boats provided by a camp.

Accommodations/dining: Assorted lodging and dining options exist along the river.

Etcetera: A newcomer to this area will have to do some sleuthing to find topographic maps, navigational charts and access points. There are various other waters to fish in the area, some with brook trout.

Muskellunge

Walleye

Northern Pike

Smallmouth Bass

ABOVE *Landing a chinook salmon on the Pere Marquette.*

Pere Marquette River

Michigan, United States

There are few places in the Midwest where you can see more anglers with nine-foot rods fully bent over while playing 20- to 40-pound fish than Michigan's Pere Marquette River. The big fish are fall-run chinook salmon, and when they come into the net these bruisers form a sagging semicircle. In the latter part of the run, you can spot dark torpedo shapes all over the river, many in water so shallow that it barely covers the fish's dorsal fin.

Salmon and steelhead are the main attractions in the Pere Marquette, drawing anglers from afar, although the river also has a respectable fishery for brown trout and some rainbows. Beginning in late August, salmon migrate from

Details

Pere Marquette River, Michigan, United States

Location/getting there: The Pere Marquette is in westcentral Michigan, flowing westerly into Lake Michigan near Ludington. Out-of-area visitors generally fly to Grand Rapids.

Info sources: For lodging, river and fly fishing information, contact the Pere Marquette River Lodge, 8841 S. M-37, Baldwin, Michigan 49304; call 231-745-3972; or visit www.pmlodge.com. This is both a lodge and full-service fly fishing shop.

Prime times: September for salmon; November and April for steelhead.

Gear needs: Guides provide fishing tackle, especially terminal gear and flies/bait. Long rods and reels with good drags and plenty of

capacity are the norm. Flycasters use nine-foot rods in eight- and nine-weight models, generally with floating or sink-tip lines. Bring chest waders.

Guide/tackle availability: For guided fishing, contact Jon Kolehouse of Grand Rapids at 231-652-4967. In addition to the Pere Marquette, he guides on the Muskegon, Manistee and Grand Rivers using all types of tackle, and fishing either from a drift boat or an 18-foot jet sled. Costs for a ten-hour, door-to-door day are about $300 for two anglers, and includes tackle, grilled shore lunch and transportation; the only extra is fly costs, since you will lose a lot of flies in a day. Tackle is available locally.

Accommodations/dining: There are assorted lodging and dining options in the area; plan well ahead in peak season. The Pere Marquette River Lodge is an excellent facility with lodge and motel-style rooms.

Etcetera: Launching at the popular Green Cottage launch of the fly-fishing-only section is an interesting phenomenon in itself. One boat wide and 40-degree steep, it features about 20 fiberglass-coated steps. Anglers back their trailer to the top of the steps, then roll the boat off the back and push it down the steps into the water. If you are in the area in summer, try evening fishing for brown trout, as prolific insect hatches occur then and provide good dry fly action.

Chinook Salmon

Steelhead

Brown Trout

Rainbow Trout

eastern Lake Michigan into the Pere Marquette, sometimes in waves and often spurred on by new rainfall.

September is generally prime for salmon, which are in peak condition then; they are darker and more fatigued as they get closer to spawning. By the end of October, if not sooner, all of the Pere Marquette's salmon will be dead—they all die after spawning—and then steelhead migrate in.

There is 100 per cent natural salmon reproduction in the Pere Marquette, meaning that these fish are not the result of repeated stocking. So there is an emphasis on releasing fish (mandatory in some sections) to spawn, which is more beneficial here than in other rivers. In most other Great Lakes tributaries, stocking by state fisheries agencies is what keeps salmon and steelhead numbers high. But the Pere Marquette is loaded with shallow gravel, which makes perfect spawning grounds; using polarized sunglasses, it is possible to occasionally spot a hen salmon turn on its side and thrash its tail as she scoops out a reed and deposits eggs.

Steelhead are in the river all winter. November is a prime steelhead fishing month, not only because the fish are powerful and colorful, but because the weather is still tolerable; later, ice, snow, and extreme cold make this a game for the hardiest anglers. These fish, which average ten pounds, spawn in late winter/early spring, and March and April also provide good fishing.

There is a seven-mile long fly-fishing-only section of the Pere Marquette about 60 miles upstream from where the river enters the eastern shore of Lake Michigan. While the majority of anglers here cast with fly rods, some use

spinning tackle, employing flies beneath casting floats and weights. This section has also been designated completely catch-and-release.

There is plenty of river to fish with whatever weapons you choose. Salmon fishing here is not especially difficult. Short casts or flips are the norm, and with fly rods, it is just a matter of making a good roll cast with a long and fairly strong fly rod, since you fish with a weighted fly and a light piece of lead. Varying amounts of lead are necessary to get down and drift your offering along the river bottom; a lightweight float or indicator is pegged some four to six feet above the hook to help detect strikes.

The Pere Marquette is shallow and fished by wading most of the time, even by those who use a drift boat to access pools and runs (boaters anchor and get out to fish).

LEFT
Salmon darken the longer they are in the river, and before spawning.

Platte River (North & South)

Colorado/Wyoming, United States

Nebraska

Wyoming

Colorado

South Platte River

Casper

North Platte River

Denver

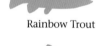

Rainbow Trout

Brown Trout

Cutthroat Trout

Walleye

the Pike National Forest and above. The South Platte originates near Fairplay, about 100 miles west of Denver. Three upriver reservoirs—Antero, Spinney Mountain and Elevenmile—produce large, fast-growing rainbows, browns and Snake River cutthroats. Fifty miles southwest of Denver, the Platte offers world-class tailwater angling in Cheesman Canyon for selective rainbows and browns.

The North Platte begins in Routt National Forest in Colorado, where there is excellent summer fly fishing for browns and rainbows, as well as fishing for brook and cutthroat trout. Notable tributary streams here include Norris, Roaring and Grizzly Creeks, the North Fork of the North Platte and the Michigan and Illinois Rivers.

In southeastern Wyoming, nearly 90 miles of the North Platte River is designated as class I, or blue ribbon, waters. Float trips for rainbow and brown trout down the undisturbed upper river are exceptional adventures, especially from mid-June through July.

The most renowned trout angling is for large rainbows and browns in two tailwater sections, the "Miracle Mile" between Seminoe and Pathfinder Reservoirs, and the Gray Reef area below Alcova Reservoir. The Mile is actually five to eight miles long in non-drought years. However, it rarely offers a solitary experience. The clear tailwaters of Gray Reef Dam are excellent all year round, with large trout caught between November and March.

T he North and South Platte Rivers, as well as their tributaries and numerous impoundments, offer excellent trout fishing.

The majority of the better angling on Colorado's South Platte, as well as the larger fish, is upstream of Denver in

Details

Platte River (North & South), Colorado/Wyoming, United States

Location/getting there: The best trout waters of the South Platte are south-southwest of Denver, while those of the North Platte are south of Casper, Wyoming.

Info sources: For general information, contact the Colorado Tourism Office at 800-265-6723; visit www.colorado.com and www.CentralColorado.com. Also contact the Casper (WY) Area CVB at 800-852-1889; or visit www.casperwyoming.info.

Prime times: Spring and fall, with some exceptions.

Gear needs: Flycasting gear is the main tackle, with five-weight rods for smaller water and six- to eight-weight rods for larger, wind-blown water.

Guide/tackle availability: Guides and tackle are available locally.

Accommodations/dining: A range of lodging and dining options exist.

Etcetera: There is also good fishing on the North Platte in a big-water stretch from Alcova Reservoir to Edness Kimball Wilkins State Park at Casper. This area has good rainbow trout and some big browns; high trout densities are in the stretch from Lusby to Gray Reef and at The Narrows.

OPPOSITE
Fly fishing in the Routt National Forest.

Red River

Manitoba, Canada

Lake
Winnipeg

Lockport

Winnipeg

Manitoba

Red River

North Dakota

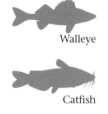

Walleye

Catfish

To many anglers a walleye over four or five pounds is a nice fish, but avid walleye chasers know that they really have something to brag about if they catch a fish in the eight-pound-and-over class. Walleyes this size are caught in a number of places in the United States and Canada, but there are only a few locations where your chances of doing so are better than average.

Details

Red River, Manitoba, Canada

Location/getting there: The Red River is in the vicinity of Lockport, Manitoba, not far from the city of Winnipeg, and is easily accessed by vehicle.

Info sources: For information, contact Travel Manitoba, 7-155 Carlton St., Winnipeg, Manitoba R3C 3H8, Canada; call 800-665-0040; or visit www.travelmanitoba.com.

Prime times: Summer and fall.

Gear needs: Walleyes: spinning and baitcasting tackle with eight- through 15-pound line. Catfish: baitcasting gear with a wide spool/large capacity and 20- to 30-pound line.

Guide/tackle availability: Guides and tackle are available in the area.

Accommodations/dining: Lodging and dining options are extensive.

Etcetera: Do not plan a visit if there has been a lot of rain, which swells the river and makes it even muddier than usual.

RIGHT
Landing a big walleye on the Red River.

Located in southern Manitoba and, with water flowing northward, the Red River is one of the best bets in North America for catching a large walleye. The Red produces an awesome number of walleyes that are ten pounds or heavier (over 100 Master Angler citations in some years, for example), not to mention all of the fish from six to ten pounds. These fish are migrants from Lake Winnipeg, which, surprisingly, does not have much of a sportfishery itself.

Generally dirty and roily, especially in spring and early summer, the Red River flows northward through farm country from the Dakotas through southern Manitoba into Lake Winnipeg. The hotbed of big-fish activity is in the Selkirk area of Manitoba, just north of the city of Winnipeg below the Lockport Dam. This is not a particularly scenic or wild locale, but the kind of fish caught here seems to override such matters. However, big walleyes can be caught anywhere in the river and fall for a variety of presentations, with slow trolling one of the more reliable techniques for newcomers to this waterway.

October generally seems to be the best time to fish because of the tremendous run of big walleyes migrating out of Lake Winnipeg. That run starts in mid-September,

when the water cools and the north winds blow. The Winnipeg River, incidentally, which is about 60 miles away from Lockport, is another good producer of walleye. It does not seem to have as many large fish, but they are more aesthetically appealing, having an emerald green coloration in the fall. Winnipeg River fish are locally called "greenbacks."

Actually, all walleye here are called "pickerel" and fishing by local anglers is mostly done with so-called "pickerel rigs," which sport a long-shanked bait hook for a nightcrawler and a small spinner blade. Drifting and stillfishing with live bait or jigs tipped with bait is also popular. Some plug trolling is done, mostly by visitors from the U.S., and this also merits attention.

The Red River is also known as one of the premier spots in North America for giant catfish. In Manitoba, the Red dominates the Master Angler citation list, and it rates as one of the best places to have a chance of catching a 20-pound-or-better specimen. The huge cats are almost exclusively taken on bait, predominantly chicken liver or gizzard shad chunks, fished along the bottom. Many smaller cats are available as well, both on the Red and on its tributary, the Assiniboine.

ABOVE
Big catfish are caught deep in the tailwater of the Selkirk dam.

Saginaw Bay

Michigan, United States

Walleye

Smallmouth Bass

Chinook Salmon

Steelhead

Lake Trout

ABOVE RIGHT
*Large walleyes are
common in
Saginaw Bay and
major tributaries.*

Saginaw Bay is one of the finest fishing sites in North America, and definitely one of the most venerated places to fish for trophy walleyes. This big bay, and its tributaries, also boast huge numbers of perch and bass in its interior, as well as white bass and catfish, plus chinook salmon, steelhead, lake trout and brown trout in the exterior where it mingles with the clear open water of Lake Huron.

About 60 miles long and 30 miles wide, Saginaw Bay is like a huge lake itself, although still not as large as Georgian Bay on the opposite side of Lake Huron. The south shore sports assorted canals and creeks that provide shore fishing opportunities and places for boaters to seek a respite from wind-whipped water. These canals often have very good angling for perch and panfish, and in spring they have a tremendous number of carp, which are an under-utilized resource in the bay and throughout the lake.

National acclaim has been heaped on Saginaw Bay for its fabulous walleye fishery. During the spring spawning run in April and May, when fish run into the Tittabawassee and Saginaw Rivers, anglers routinely cull seven-pounders. Forty or more pounds of walleye can often be boated in a couple of hours. Walleye fishing continues right through the winter, and ice anglers on snow machines will rival summer-time anglers in productivity on a sunny winter weekend. In fall, trophy-sized fish, many from ten to 12 pounds, are caught on their river runs.

However, the prime period in the lake for big walleyes is from June through August. Schools of fish are encountered then, often roaming open waters throughout the bay to feed on baitfish. Trolling via planer boards with crankbaits and spinners is usually effective, although

Details

Saginaw Bay, Michigan, United States

Location/getting there: Saginaw Bay is part of western Lake Huron, and is accessed from eastern Michigan. Access points exist around the bay, and there is an airport in Saginaw.

Info sources: For area information contact the Bay County Convention and Visitors Bureau, 901 Saginaw Street, Bay City, MI 48708; call 888-229-8696; or visit www.tourbaycitymi.org. Also visit the Saginaw Bay Network website at www.saginawbay.com.

Prime times: Spring for brown trout; summer through early fall for chinook salmon and lake trout; summer and fall for bass. Spring and fall are prime for big walleyes in the rivers, while summer is the season for lake fishing.

Gear needs: Varies depending on species and fishing methods.

Guide/tackle availability: There are many charter boats around the bay; most provide tackle. Tackle is widely available at shops.

Accommodations/dining: Lodging and dining options are extensive.

Etcetera: Saginaw Bay is huge and requires big-water boats and prudent navigation. It can get very rough under the right wind conditions, which is especially dangerous when the water is cold. That said, ice fishing is popular here when conditions are right, with walleye and perch the major targets.

there is also fishing along shallow southwestern-bay reefs with bottom rigs, jigging spoons and spinners.

Big pike are occasionally caught here, even out in the open bay where walleyes roam. Smallmouth bass are abundant, and also large, and are complemented by a good population of largemouth bass. The western shore of the bay has good summer catches of walleye, perch, pike and bass.

The more open eastern end of Saginaw Bay, as well as the area to the south, is mainly trout and salmon country. South of Saginaw Bay, the shoreline lacks many streams and refuge spots. This big-water region from the mouth of the bay south to Port Huron at the head of the St. Clair River is mostly a place for salmon trolling; steelhead, lake trout and brown trout are also caught seasonally here, as well as some walleyes.

BELOW
A nice pike, caught from open-bay waters, is released.

El Salto Lake

Sinaloa, Mexico

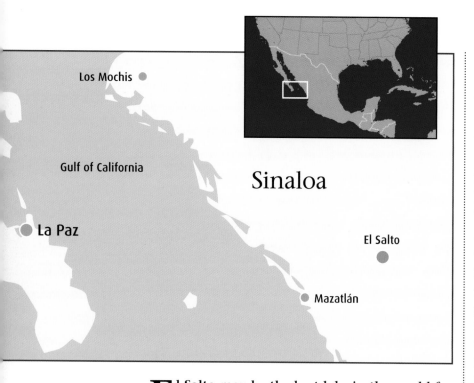

Los Mochis

Gulf of California

Sinaloa

La Paz

El Salto

Mazatlán

Largemouth Bass

that include protruding tombstones and a church. Parts of the surrounding area are farmed, and when you get back into some nooks you will see and hear (because of neck bells) cows along the shore. Sometimes they are calf-deep in water hyacinths. The lake has a lot of hyacinths, some of it clogged in backwater places and some of it in floating islands. When the water level drops, many hyacinths are left high and get burned for control purposes.

The lake also has a ton of brush and trees in it, some that reach up to the surface from 40 feet deep or more. This provides great cover and terrific ambush opportunity, but also makes it hard to land the big bruisers. Fast-moving and broad-shouldered bass are virtually guaranteed to streak into a submerged cactus or mesquite tree as soon as they are hooked. Many anglers have lost the biggest bass of their lives at El Salto when their line proved no match for jalapeno-hot fish and wooden underwater booby traps.

The routine at El Salto is that you get up early in the morning, when coffee or juice is brought to your door,

El Salto may be the best lake in the world for catching largemouth bass over eight pounds. In recent years, nearly 90 per cent of the visitors caught a bass that was six pounds or better, a high number caught a fish that was eight pounds or more and many got a ten-pounder. There are also much bigger fish at El Salto. The 24,000-acre lake produced a lake-record 18½-pounder in May 2001, besting the previous record, a 16-pounder. A few years ago, a 16-pound-three-ounce bass was found dead in the lake; it had choked to death with a tilapia wedged in its throat. Even if a huge bass does not happen, there is often plenty of opportunity to struggle with frisky fat-bellied fish, especially when they are caught among the trees.

RIGHT
Big largemouth bass are the calling card at El Salto.

OPPOSITE
Bass grow large on ample food at El Salto and all are released.

Nestled in the mountains, El Salto is an impoundment created to provide water for farmland irrigation. Some of the shoreline is cliff-like, and you can find flooded areas

have an ample breakfast in the main dining area, then head out with your guide just as it is getting light enough to see. In ten to 15 minutes you are fishing; you return to the lodge for lunch and a siesta, which you actually come to appreciate on scorching hot days, and then you go back out at two, fishing until darkness sets in. Surface fishing chances are best at first and last light.

Ten-inch worms fished Texas rig style or on Carolina rigs work well, as do large soft jerkbaits. Minnow-style plugs and rattling divers produce good results, and spinnerbaits are favored for big fish, sometimes fished deep and slow-rolled. Deep-diving crankbaits at times are also a good option.

One of the things in El Salto's fishing favor is that it has very stable water levels. Unlike some other Mexican lakes, especially those in the mountains, El Salto does not have wild up-and-down cycles. The fact that bass are present at all is because the lake was stocked with 200,000 Florida-strain bass in 1985 when it was filling. These fish, which have formed the cornerstone of much-heralded trophy bass stocking programs in California and Texas, are noted for growing fast and achieving huge (ten- to 20-pound) sizes. This has paid off with big bass in recent years.

Another plus is that El Salto has an enormous population of food fish. In addition to shad, the lake is

absolutely loaded with tilapia, an exotic species imported to Mexico many years ago to provide food and commercial fishing opportunity. Tilapia are netted in many lakes and sold to market. In El Salto, these prolific fish spawn twice a year and are netted by the tens of thousands monthly by commercial fishermen. Small tilapia are a prominent food source for bass, and are undoubtedly a major reason for the fast growth of El Salto's largemouths.

Some people have speculated that El Salto is a candidate to produce the next world record largemouth, and they could be right.

Details

El Salto Lake, Sinaloa, Mexico

Location/getting there: El Salto is about a 90-minute drive northeast of Mazatlán. Anglers Inn meets guests at Mazatlán airport and takes them to the lake.

Info sources: Contact Anglers Inn, PMB 358, 2626 N. Mesa, El Paso, TX 79902; call their headquarters office in Mazatlán at 011-52-69-807474 or 800-408-2347; or visit www.anglersinn.com.

Prime times: The lodge is open from October 1 through June 20. Fishing is good all season, but October through December is when the lake's biggest bass have been caught.

Gear needs: Baitcasting tackle with 15- to 30-pound line is the mainstay; spinning and fly gear can also be used; ten-inch plastic worms, $1/2$- to one-ounce spinnerbaits, deep-diving crankbaits, seven-inch soft jerkbaits and large poppers are especially good.

Guide/tackle availability: Guides are supplied. Bring your own tackle, although there is a moderate selection of lures and line at the lodge.

Accommodations/dining: There is excellent lodging, dining and service at the lodge. Accommodations include high-quality trailers and permanent structures, with private showers, air conditioners and a twice-daily

housekeeping service. There is electricity at the camp and standard outlets for electrical devices, as well as limited satellite telephone service. Tex-Mex meals are family and buffet style; ask the chef to make a bass ceviche appetizer one night.

Etcetera: Cost for a four-day fishing stay is $1,995, all inclusive from Mazatlán. Anglers Inn also offers inshore and offshore saltwater fishing excursions from Mazatlán, and they accommodate dove and duck hunters at El Salto from November through February. Birdlife, by the way, is also exceptional here. You almost cannot go any distance without seeing an osprey, and all kinds of long-legged birds prowl the shallows and shorelines.

Santee Cooper

South Carolina, United States

Columbia

South
Carolina

Lake
Marion

Lake
Moultrie

Atlantic
Ocean

Charleston

Georgia

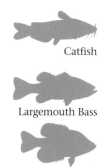

Striped Bass

Catfish

Largemouth Bass

Crappie

entirely freshwater existence. Thus was born the phenomenon of inland striped bass fishing. From this stock of fish, over 30 states ultimately received stripers to plant in impoundments that were full of baitfish and had suitable deep, open-water habitat.

Striped bass fishing peaks in the spring when these fish head to the six-and-a-half-mile-long Diversion Canal in spawning runs. Summer fishing is not especially productive; stripers move deep and are harder to locate and catch, though some anglers troll the old river channels with success. Action can be dynamic in fall and winter, when schooling fish "herd" baitfish to the surface and then smash them in savage flurries of feeding.

One of the most noted angling destinations in the southeastern U.S. is the vast, interlocking complex in South Carolina formed by Lakes Marion and Moultrie and their connecting Diversion Canal. Commonly known as Santee Cooper, this vast inland sea of 171,000 acres features a mixture of flooded timber, cypress swamps and huge stretches of open water. Over the years, world records for several species of fish, including striped bass, channel catfish and blue catfish, have been produced here, and fishing remains good for these premier species as well as for largemouth bass and crappie.

The Santee Cooper waterway was also responsible for creating modern inland striper fishing. When the Santee and Cooper Rivers were dammed in 1941, striped bass migrating from the ocean were trapped in newly formed Lakes Marion and Moultrie, and thrived, proving that this anadromous species was adaptable enough to live an

RIGHT
Big catfish are a major calling card at Santee Cooper; this one was caught in Lake Marion.

Circling seagulls are a visual index to such frenzies. All manner of jigs, jigging spoons, lead-bodied lures and popping plugs or stickbaits will catch surface-schooling fish. Angling is frenzied as boats race to the fish, which are sometimes located by looking for seagulls working the commotion for scraps.

When it comes to big catfish, Santee Cooper may be in a class by itself. It takes specimens above 50 pounds even to raise eyebrows, and every year whiskered giants in the 80-pound range are landed. In the winter months, smaller cats, mostly channels and blues, are caught in large numbers around the riprap at the base of the dam. Catfish in the ten- to 20-pound class are routine, and no doubt this area is one of the top spots in North America for catching a catfish that is 20 pounds or better.

Catfishing here is almost entirely a matter of stillfishing or drifting along the bottom using dead bait, primarily chunked herring. The Diversion Canal, which has current, is one of the better big cat locales, but monsters reside in the lake as well; sometimes an unstoppable brute will thoroughly surprise an unsuspecting crappie or bass angler in one of the lakes.

Vast areas of flooded timber and cypress swamps offer ideal topwater or shallow-running lure fishing for bass in the spring and fall. The plentiful structure also lends itself to prime bream and crappie fishing, with the latter usually spawning in late March and April, while bream go on the beds in May. Fishing for largemouths is best in spring and fall; plastic worms, spinnerbaits, crankbaits and surface lures all have merit, but worms and spinnerbaits fished around wood and vegetation are the prominent lures.

LEFT
A typical Santee Cooper striped bass, caught in the fall by trolling a diving plug.

ABOVE
Evening in the summer is a good time for fishing at Santee Cooper.

Details

Santee Cooper, South Carolina, United States

Location/getting there: Southeast of Columbia, Santee Cooper is bisected by the major north-south artery I-95. From Columbia, it is reached by taking I-26 to U.S. 301.

Info sources: For area information, contact Santee Cooper Country, P.O. Drawer 40, Santee, SC 29142; call 800-227-8510; or visit www.santeecoopercountry.org.

Prime times: See main text.

Gear needs: Varies depending on species and fishing method.

Guide/tackle availability: Guides are widely available. Tackle is also available at marinas and local shops.

Accommodations/dining: A range of lodging and dining options exists, and there are many camping facilities as well as dozens of marinas around the lake.

Etcetera: The five-county region here has diverse recreational and general-interest activities. Nearby Santee National Wildlife Refuge (call 803-478-2217; or visit www.fws.gov/r4rw_sc.snt) is especially popular for bird viewing. There are state and federal fish hatcheries in the area, as well as plantation homes, nature trails, historic battlegrounds and waterway tours. Boaters can be lowered down Lake Moultrie's 75-foot-high Pinopolis Lock to the Tailrace Canal, which leads to the Cooper River and eventually to Charleston.

Scott Lake

Saskatchewan, Canada

ABOVE
*Anglers head out
for deep holes to
fish for lake trout.*

Scott Lake, in northernmost Saskatchewan, is an exceptional place with excellent pike and lake trout fishing, plus a fly-out to one of the world's most scenic grayling waters. It sports a five-star camp that became one of the premier lodges in all of Canada when it was expanded in the mid-1990s, and the guides here enhance the experience by using modern fishing equipment and methods.

Details

Scott Lake, Saskatchewan, Canada

Location/getting there: Scott Lake straddles the Saskatchewan-Northwest Territories border. Guests at Scott Lake Lodge, the only facility on the lake, arrive via charter plane from Saskatoon to Stony Rapids, followed by a 25-minute floatplane trip to the lodge.

Info sources: Contact Scott Lake Lodge at 888-830-9525 and visit www.scottlake lodge.com. For Saskatchewan information, contact Tourism Saskatchewan, 1922 Park St., Regina, Saskatchewan, S4P 3V7, Canada; call 877-237-2273; or visit www.sasktourism.com.

Prime times: Early summer is preferred for pike and midsummer for trout; grayling are best from mid-July on.

Gear needs: Lake trout: medium to heavy levelwind trolling tackle for deep fishing; lighter baitcasting, spinning and flycasting early in the season; heavy jigs, large trolling spoons and plugs. Pike: medium to medium-heavy spinning and baitcasting, with 12- to 20-pound line and nine- or ten-weight flycasting outfits; spoons, bucktail spinners, soft jerkbaits and shallow-running plugs. Grayling: light spinning and five-weight flycasting; small jigs, spinners, dry flies and wet flies. All hooks must be barbless.

Guide/tackle availability: Guides are part of the package for Scott Lake and fly-out trips, but the outpost camp is self-guided. Good-quality fishing tackle is available on loan at the camp, including fly gear.

Accommodations/dining: Accommodations are excellent, with motel-like rooms equipped with heat and private showers. The main lodge area is excellent, as is the service, and there is a new recreation center, plus hot tub, at the main lodge, and canoes and kayaks are available for evening paddling. Shore lunches, featuring freshly cooked pike or lake trout, are a daily staple.

Etcetera: The cost for a five-day trip is $3,000 from Saskatoon, and includes guide, licenses, northbound lodging in Saskatoon and use of lodge tackle. It does not include airfare to/from Saskatoon.

BELOW
Trophy northern pike are a hallmark of Scott Lake.

This jewel has been lightly fished over the years, thanks in part to an early designation as catch-and-release lake trout water by the original owners, who started a small camp there in the mid-1960s and served a limited clientele. The lake is 40 miles long and 40 miles wide at its greatest points, with northern parts spilling over into the Northwest Territories.

Just 100 miles below the Arctic treeline, the lake bears some tundra influence in the north, yet in the south it is distinctly reminiscent of southern Ontario, with craggy cliffs, jackpine shorelines and plenty of birch trees. It has five long arms, an extraordinary number of bays, and all of the islands, nooks, crannies and shoreline that you can possibly imagine.

This makes for great northern pike habitat. Scott has an abundant population of these fish, and is an excellent place to catch a trophy. A lot of visitors will land a 20-pounder if they work at it, and some will do far better. Each season something is caught in the 30-pound-plus range, with some having been in the 36- to 38-pound class—estimated according to length and girth measurements.

There are lots of lake trout, too, including trophy specimens in the 20- to 40-pound class. These are especially clustered in deep-water areas through the

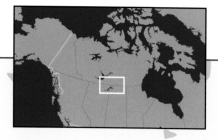

Northwest Territories

Scott Lake

Uranium City
Lake Athabasca
Stony Rapids

Saskatchewan

Northern Pike

Lake Trout

Grayling

summer. Many of the biggest lakers are caught when the fish are deep and hard to access, using more sophisticated angling methods than most far-northern camps.

The guides are all trained in sonar use and every boat is equipped for diverse fishing. Camp boats are 18-footers, with a carpeted bow deck and pedestal seat, in-transit rod holders, dry storage, floorboards, padded seats with backrest and liquid crystal recording sonar. The sonar is critical for lake trout fishing, especially in the summer.

In the early part of the season, trout are near the surface and are caught by flatline trolling with conventional light to medium tackle. As the water warms they go deeper, and the guides use heavier gear with wire line and ball weights to reach the appropriate depths. The trout stack up in midsummer and many can be caught once they have been located and the proper trolling depth established.

For pike, guides take anglers on the customary spoon, spinner and plug casting forays, but explore other avenues as well, working not just obvious weeds, but points, breaklines and shallow bay mouths. When the fishing is slow, they have been successful using soft plastic jerk worms

RIGHT
Morning coffee on the deck of the main lodge overlooking the lake.

to tease up pike, and they have developed a following for fly fishing. For both pike and lake trout, the camp policy is entirely catch-and-release, using only barbless hooks.

As if this good pike and lake trout angling is not enough, the lake has other endearing attributes. Wildlife is plentiful, including many bald eagles, and the occasional wolf or bear is sighted. Caribou sometimes migrate by the camp when the lake is frozen, and you may see trails, carcasses and antlers ashore.

Scott Lake Lodge has numerous top-quality fly-out experiences, too, including eight destinations in Saskatchewan and 12 in the Northwest Territories. Some of them are for grayling, including large specimens on the Dubawnt River. The crown jewel is a daytrip fly-out to Hunt Falls, locally called Lefty Falls. Hunt Falls is the tallest waterfall in central Canada, and stretches about 150 yards across the Griese River in Saskatchewan. A short distance downstream are hundreds, if not thousands, of Arctic grayling. The grayling are not as large here as in other local waters, but none could be caught in a more magnificent place. Also of note is an outpost camp at Wignes Lakes, which has both lake trout and pike fisheries.

ABOVE
Reviving a large pike for release in one of Scott Lake's back bays.

Selwyn Lake

Saskatchewan, Canada

Northwest Territories

Selwyn Lake

Uranium City

Lake Athabasca

Stony Rapids

Saskatchewan

Northern Pike

Lake Trout

Grayling

OPPOSITE
*Stalking shallow
pike in Selwyn's
bays is sure to
bring success.*

RIGHT
*Trophy-class
northern pike bring
a smile, even in the
rain and cold.*

Primarily in Saskatchewan, Selwyn Lake is one of Canada's premier waters for northern pike and lake trout. Some 45 miles long and 18 miles wide, it covers 135,000 acres, nearly all of it packed with islands and treacherous reefs, and despite having untold miles of shoreline and countless bays, it also has plenty of deep water, some of it down to 300 feet. An assortment of rivers and streams feed the lake, and two rivers flow out, eventually into Lake Athabasca and north to the Arctic Ocean.

This is well-forested country, with rocky shores accompanied by muskeg, marshy peat bogs, and plenty of low- to medium-growth tamarack, spruce, birch and poplar. Moose, bear, wolves and caribou range here, and it is common to see and hear loons. The only full-scale facility on the lake, Selwyn Lake Lodge, was erected in 1993 and expanded in 2000, and attracts anglers from all over North America. With the exception of one or two kept for daily shore lunch, all fish are released.

Shore lunch is a daily ritual here. There is never any problem with not catching a fish for lunch. If anything there is sometimes a problem in catching one that is small enough (no kidding).

There is nothing like starting off an angling adventure with slam-bang action. And that is often the case with visitors to Selwyn Lake, especially if they are fishing early in the season for northern pike when they are shallow in the back of bays. In fact, you can often spot and stalk the fish. Within two hours of your early morning arrival from Saskatoon, and after a hearty breakfast and short boat ride, you are casting and setting the hook.

By the time the day is done, you have probably hooked a couple of dozen pike, some up to 20 pounds, lost a bunch that swiped and did not get hooked, had a number of fish slam the lure so close to the boat that it startled you, and generally had enough excitement to make for great stories at dinner.

Selwyn Lake produces many pike that meet Saskatchewan's official "trophy" designation—41 inches—worthy of a provincial recognition certificate. Such a fish would likely range from 17 to just under 20 pounds. Pike are caught regularly up to 44 inches, or about 25 pounds, and a few are landed each year in the 25- to 30-pound range. Many pike over 35 inches long are caught, and all of these specimens are released. Most angling is done by casting spoons and spinners, but flycasting with streamers and poppers is also excellent, especially early in the season.

Selwyn is somewhat unique in that it has recently produced several specimens of silver pike. The silver pike is not a separate species, but a true northern pike with a color mutation that results in a steely blue appearance. A couple of specimens in the 28- to 30-inch range were caught in the past two years.

Lake trout up to 50 pounds have been caught at Selwyn, and at least one a year is landed that meets or exceeds 40 pounds. Many are caught that exceed 20 pounds. Early season provides good fishing for lakers of various sizes, and they are fairly shallow, as the near surface waters are still cold. That lasts for two or three weeks and then the trout scatter and move deeper.

By mid-July, the trout are from 60 to 100 feet deep, and often congregated. Some people have caught up to a hundred in a day by deep jigging, especially using a large jig tipped with a piece of the belly strip from a shore-lunch fish. However, the larger trout are seldom caught by deep jigging here; trolling with large spoons, either behind a downrigger weight or via a round sinker and three-way swivel rig, is preferred.

Plenty of grayling exist in several rivers, and Selwyn has produced specimens over three pounds. There is one spot on the lake where anglers can fish from a boat for these frisky, high-dorsal-finned fish, but elsewhere it is necessary to get out of the boat and either wade or walk along shoreline rocks.

One of the blessings of Selwyn is that its countless islands offer protection from the wind. So when the lake gets rough in spots, it is usually possible for the guide to

find a good, protected fishing place. This is a mixed benefit, as protection from the wind often means the presence of mosquitoes and/or blackflies, of which this northern country has more than its fair share. When the time comes for guests to leave, the Indian guides often ask them to take the mosquitoes back with them.

Details

Selwyn Lake, Saskatchewan, Canada

Location/getting there: Selwyn Lake is on the 60th Parallel about 650 miles north of Saskatoon straddling Saskatchewan and the Northwest Territories. Guests at Selwyn Lake Lodge arrive via charter plane from Saskatoon to Stony Rapids, followed by a 45-minute floatplane trip to the lodge.

Info sources: Contact Selwyn Lake Lodge, 255 Robin Crescent, Saskatoon, Saskatchewan, S7L 6M8 Canada; call 800-667-9556; or visit www.selwynlake.com. For Saskatchewan information, contact Tourism Saskatchewan, 1922 Park St., Regina, Saskatchewan, S4P 3V7, Canada; call 877-237-2273; or visit www.sasktourism.com.

Prime times: The lodge is open for fishing from June 10 through the first week of September. Dedicated lake trout anglers prefer from mid-July through August, when the trout are concentrated in deep water. The top pike action is from early June through the first week of July. Grayling action is best from mid-July on, when there is shallower water and more stream insect life.

Gear needs: Lake trout: medium to heavy levelwind trolling tackle for deep fishing; lighter baitcasting, spinning and flycasting early in the season; heavy jigs, large trolling spoons and plugs. Pike: medium to medium-heavy spinning and baitcasting, with 12- to 20-pound line and nine- or ten-weight flycasting outfits; spoons, bucktail spinners, soft jerkbaits and shallow-running plugs. Grayling: light spinning and five-weight flycasting; small jigs, spinners, dry flies and wet flies. All hooks must be barbless.

Guide/tackle availability: Guides are part of the package cost, but are not provided at the outpost camp. The main lodge is fully equipped with good baitcasting, spinning and flycasting tackle. Lures, flies, leaders, insect repellent and a few other incidentals are available at the lodge, although some supplies may be limited later in the season.

Accommodations/dining: Accommodations are excellent, with motel-like rooms equipped with heating and private showers. The new main lodge area is spacious with amenities, and there is a screened gazebo by the water.

Service is excellent, overseen by owners Gord Wallace and Mary Daigneault-Wallace, and dining is first-rate in the morning and evening. Shore lunches, featuring freshly cooked pike or lake trout, are a daily staple.

Etcetera: The cost for a three-day trip to Selwyn Lake ranges from $2,195 to $2,595 depending on the time of visit, for four days from $2,495 to $2,895, and for seven days from $3,295 to $3,795. These prices are from Saskatoon and do not include licenses, motel room in Saskatoon and airfare to/from Saskatoon. There is also an outpost camp on the lake. Day and overnight fly-out trips by floatplane are available.
In Saskatoon, most anglers stay at the Travel Lodge, which is close to the airport, but it often attracts a crowd who enjoy their pool and waterslide. Ask for a room away from these. With time to kill, visit Muskokwin, an Indian heritage park about ten minutes away. Downtown restaurants to try include Crawdaddy's for Cajun fare, Mykonos for Greek food, and Mr. Johns steakhouse.

St. Croix River

Maine, United States

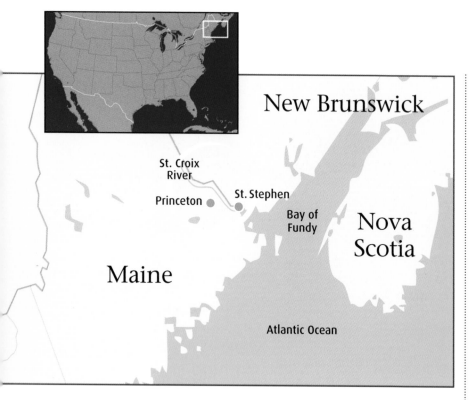

New Brunswick

St. Croix River

Princeton

St. Stephen

Bay of Fundy

Nova Scotia

Maine

Atlantic Ocean

Smallmouth Bass

Atlantic Salmon

Brook Trout

relatively undeveloped, moderately used, lovely and not too difficult to float and fish. The St. Croix is not known for large fish, but with 25 miles of water from Vanceboro to Grand Falls Flowage, there are many good smallmouth of ten to 12 inches to be caught, as well as some opportunities for three-pounders and the occasional landlocked salmon or brook trout in a tributary flow.

This is canoe or kayak paddling water, with the exception of the larger area downstream, and it affords nice two- or three-day overnight fish-camping opportunities. There are a few Class II rapids, and one Class III, at Little Falls, which makes a great spot for an overnight visit and provides good evening fly fishing opportunities in the flatwater upstream. Once used for floating logs, this crystal-clear river still has easily spotted and well preserved sunken logs along its bottom, and provides the occasional chance to see or hear a moose.

Better opportunities for bigger river bass are below

Northeastern Maine has almost an embarrassment of riches when it comes to fishing opportunities and scenic splendor. The St. Croix River and its headwater lakes have excellent opportunities for smallmouth bass and landlocked Atlantic salmon, as well as good fishing for brook trout, lake trout (called "togue" here), and chain pickerel. Just as diverse as the species is the water, which includes large and occasionally rough lakes, small placid backwaters, wadeable tributary streams and the main river.

A close look at a good map will show a lot of blue lines snaking to the international border with New Brunswick; on the west near the village of Grand Lake Stream and Princeton, and on the east and north near the villages of Forest City and Vanceboro.

Perhaps the most adventurous and interesting opportunity here is the St. Croix River, which is remote,

RIGHT
A fall morning at Little Falls on the St. Croix River.

Loon Bay and in the Grand Falls Flowage area, where the St. Croix widens and the water becomes deeper and slower. Larger bass, and different fishing, exists in headwater lakes.

On the east branch of the St. Croix are two well-known lakes, Spednic, which is just above Vanceboro, and Grand Lake upstream (also called East Grand Lake). On the West Branch of the St. Croix are Big Lake, West Grand Lake, Junior Lake and others.

This is not trophy salmon water, although some large specimens do exist. West Grand and East Grand Lakes are two of Maine's best salmon lakes. Ice-out is late April or early May and landlocks cruise near the surface until June, then come back to the surface in September. Both waters also have bass and togue. Grand Lake Stream is one of

Maine's premier landlocked salmon streams, and fly anglers congregate there in May, early June, September and early October.

Top bass waters feeding into the St. Croix include Meddybemps Lake west of Calais, Big Lake west of Princeton, and Junior Lake northwest of West Grand Lake. Fifteen-inch smallmouths are average, four-pounders are possible, and there is the odd fish to six pounds. Old flooded timber in the Grand Falls Flowage provides some excellent stump fishing for large bass on summer evenings.

Many area waters also have excellent pickerel fishing, and there are myriad streams with brook trout, many of which are underfished. This is a wonderful place to catch native brookies in secluded woodland settings.

ABOVE LEFT
A nice smallmouth caught from one of the St. Croix's slow pools.

ABOVE RIGHT
A few rapids on the St. Croix provide mild excitement for canoeists and kayakers.

Details

St. Croix River, Maine, United States

Location/getting there: The St. Croix River and its headwater lakes are located in Washington County, Maine, on the border with New Brunswick, and are accessed via Routes 1 and 6.

Info sources: For area information contact the Maine Office of Tourism at 888-624-6345 or visit www.visitmaine.com. Also visit the Downeast Regional Tourism site at www.downeastregion.com.

Prime times: Spring and fall for salmon; summer for brook trout; summer and fall for brook trout and bass.

Gear needs: Varies with species and fishing methods, although light spinning and flycasting tackle predominate.

Guide/tackle availability: Guides are available throughout the area. An excellent all-around ("wicked good" as they say in Maine) operation is Wilds of Maine Guide Service; call 207-338-3932; or visit www.wildsofmaine.com. Tackle is available in local shops.

Accommodations/dining: A modest range of lodging and dining options exist, with more opportunities at larger towns further from the

river. Many lodges and camps exist on headwater lakes.

Etcetera: A short drive to the southeast is Quoddy Head, the easternmost point of land in the United States. About 90 minutes southwest of Vanceboro, en route to Bangor, is the city of Old Town, home to the Old Town Canoe Company (call 207-827-5513; or visit www.oldtowncanoe.com). Near the banks of the Penobscot River, this 104-year-old company is the world's leading canoe manufacturer, and has a well-stocked paddling store with bargain-priced (due to cosmetic irregularities) canoes and kayaks.

St. Lawrence River/ 1,000 Islands

New York, United States and Ontario, Canada

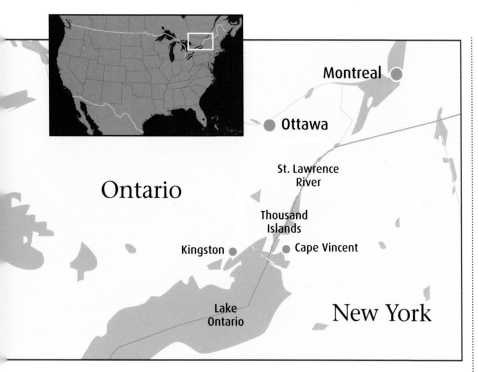

If you are not familiar with the St. Lawrence River, you might be inclined to think of it as a typical river, featuring pools, eddies and riffles. Think again. It is more like a mammoth lake, holding half a million surface acres of water. Also known as the St. Lawrence Seaway, the river flows northeasterly from Lake Ontario for 700 miles and is used as a shipping channel for colossal freighters carrying assorted cargo from Great Lakes ports. It is 200 feet deep in spots, several miles wide at most points, and there are over 1,600 islands in The Thousand Islands sector, the largest of which is 21 miles long.

The prime angling interests in this great body of water are smallmouth bass, largemouth bass, walleye, northern pike and muskellunge. The St. Lawrence is a fabled muskie water, and has historically been renowned for large

Steeped in history, tradition and fishing renown, the St. Lawrence River is a place that has been in the sportfishing limelight since ever there was a limelight. Its natural resources were of tremendous value as long ago as 1535, when French explorer Jacques Cartier discovered it while looking for the Northwest Passage to the Orient.

But it is the 52-mile-long section of the St. Lawrence called The Thousand Islands—known to the Mohawk Indians as the "Garden of the Great Spirit"—which has produced not only the famous salad dressing of that name, but some of the continent's foremost bass and muskellunge fishing. The St. Lawrence River borders eastern Ontario and northern New York, with the most prominent locales for fishing being at Cape Vincent, Clayton, and Alexandria Bay in New York, and Kingston and Gananoque in Ontario.

RIGHT
A fine walleye from the head of the St. Lawrence River near Lake Ontario.

years, however, but a few 30- to 40-pound muskies are landed every year by devoted trollers, with much emphasis still placed on traditional locales, such as Hinckley Shoal off Carleton Island and Forty Acre Shoals off Gananoque. This is almost exclusively a trolling fishery, best experienced from September through November.

Many more people ply the St. Lawrence for bass. The river has a tremendous population of smallmouths, thanks in part to a phenomenal quantity of rocky bars, shoals, bluffs and island heads near deep water with plenty of current. Largemouths, too, are abundant in the main river along deep grassbeds and weedlines, as well as back in the weed- and lily-filled bays and creeks. Lake of the Isles at Wellesley Island is one of the most noted largemouth areas; another is Chippewa Bay above the town of Alexandria Bay. Jigs and live bait are the foremost presentations here for bass, but the entire gamut of tactics and tackle is applicable. Good fishing can be had almost all season long from mid-June till November.

Northern pike, though not particularly large here, are abundant, and are a good spring and winter quarry; ice fishing (when sufficient ice allows) in the bays for pike is quite popular. Walleyes reappeared two decades ago in both numbers and sizes. Walleyes over ten pounds were caught regularly at the head of the river where it meets eastern Lake Ontario, but the bigger fish have been less frequent recently.

Water clarification by zebra mussels, threats to fisheries (especially smallmouths) from over-abundant cormorants, and the proliferation of spiny water fleas have been issues that have altered angling tactics in recent years, but for many anglers the biggest problem is having pike or muskie cut their line when fishing for other species.

muskellunge. The former all-tackle world record muskie (disputed by some angling revisionists and stripped of its record status in the 1990s), weighed 69 pounds 15 ounces and was caught somewhere in The Thousand Islands stretch in 1957. Several 60-pounders were caught here during the heyday of the 1950s. No other single locale in North America has been as closely identified with mighty muskellunge as the St. Lawrence.

The huge fish have not been caught here in recent

Details

St. Lawrence River/1,000 Islands
New York, United States and Ontario, Canada

Location/getting there: The St. Lawrence River borders northern New York and southeastern Ontario and is readily accessed by major roads.

Info sources: For area information, contact 1,000 Islands International Tourism Council, 43373 Collins Landing, P.O. Box 400, Alexandria Bay, NY 13607; call 800-847-5263; or visit www.visit1000islands.com.

Prime times: Bass fishing is generally good all season, but does not open until late June. Fall is best for muskies and walleyes.

Gear needs: Varies depending on species and angling methods.

Guide/tackle availability: There are numerous guides (charter boats) along the river locally; some do a shore lunch. Recommended are Capt. Walt Boname, Linda-Vue Adventures, 36783 Maloney Road, Clayton, NY 13624 (315-654-2673); and Capt. Jim Brabant, Clayton Fishing Charters, P.O. Box 123, Clayton, NY 13624 (315-686-5118). Larger boats may be unable to get into the shallow water that is sometimes necessary for bass fishing, so inquire about boat type and fishing methods before committing. Tackle is widely available.

Accommodations/dining: There are numerous lodging and dining options along the river.

Etcetera: This is big water that can get very rough, especially when the wind comes straight across Lake Ontario, although there are many places to fish out of the wind in the river proper. Get a good navigational chart and be careful when motoring. Wind, weather, and proper boat permitting, you might venture onto Lake Ontario for trout, salmon, walleye and smallmouth bass. Heading downriver toward Massena brings you another good stretch of water.

Smallmouth Bass

Largemouth Bass

Muskellunge

Walleye

Northern Pike

Table Rock Lake

Missouri, United States

impoundments as Truman Lake, Lake of the Ozarks, Bull Shoals and Stockton Lake. Among these jewels is Table Rock Lake, a 43,100-acre impoundment considered to be one of the top bass lakes in the United States.

Situated in far southwestern Missouri near Branson, and partly spilling south into Arkansas, this is a popular lake for varied recreation, yet one that annually supports excellent bass fishing. A highland reservoir with deep structure and rocky shoreline, Table Rock is 70 miles long and has 745 miles of shoreline at full pool.

Viewed on a map, Table Rock is serpentine in character, with countless nooks, crannies and bends that befit its location in the up-and-down Ozark hills. The diversity of its landscape is reflected in the diversity of its fishery. Bass, for example, include largemouth, smallmouth and spotted species, which can not only be

Anglers who live in or visit southern Missouri have almost too many good fishing options, from the White River to such notable large

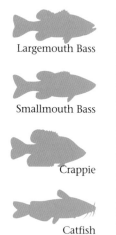

Largemouth Bass

Smallmouth Bass

Crappie

Catfish

RIGHT
Fishing in a timbered cove on Table Rock during a low-water period.

caught in the same places on the same patterns at times, but can also be caught on different patterns in different parts of the lake at the same time.

Table Rock is the second impoundment along the White River, and was created in 1958. Lots of cedar and hardwood trees were left standing, some of which poke through the surface in 60 feet of water. The lake's structure includes gravel banks, bluffs, sloping points and rocky coves, and there are five major river or creek arms.

In addition to bass, the lake holds good fishing for white bass, usually up the various arms, and crappies, and also has channel catfish and paddlefish, although there is no sportfishing for the latter. Bass reign supreme for local and visiting anglers, and fishing can be good throughout the year.

A lot of deep bass fishing is done at Table Rock. Winter fishing for spotted bass and largemouths is very good, even when the water temperature is in the mid-40s; jigging spoons are especially favored, and fish are caught 30 to 60 feet deep. Larger bass are caught from February through April, with deep crankbaits and stickbaits popular, as well as soft jerkbaits. Bass spawn in April and May. In June they move deeper and are mainly caught on Carolina-rigged worms, and at night. Fishing is shallower in the fall, with surface lures and spinnerbaits often prevailing. A minimum size limit of 15 inches for all of the bass species has helped keep the average size good, with three- to six-pounders quite available.

Tailwaters below Table Rock Dam lead to narrow and small Lake Taneycomo, and support a popular year-round coldwater fishery. Regularly stocked rainbow and brown trout are abundant here, though seldom of large size.

ABOVE
A typical Table Rock largemouth bass.

Details

Table Rock Lake, Missouri, United States

Location/getting there: Table Rock Lake is in southwestern Missouri, 45 miles south of Springfield via U.S. 65 and a short distance west of Branson.

Info sources: For general information, contact the Missouri Division of Tourism at 800-877-1234; or visit www.visitmo.com. Also contact the Table Rock Lake Chamber of Commerce at 800-595-0393; or visit www.tablerock lake.com/chamber.

Prime times: Fishing is good here all year, but spring is best for big fish.

Gear needs: Varies depending on species and fishing methods, although standard bass tackle predominates.

Guide/tackle availability: Guides and fishing tackle are widely available.

Accommodations/dining: There is a wide range of lodging and dining options around the lake and the area, including Branson and Springfield. A popular lakeside resort, owned by Bass Pro Shops, is Big Cedar Lodge; call 417-335-2777; or visit www.big-cedar.com.

Etcetera: There are many local attractions, including museums, caves and resorts. Nearby Branson is dubbed the "Live Music Capitol of the World," and is full of resorts, shows and attractions. Sixteen miles west of Big Cedar Lodge on Highway 86 is Dogwood Canyon Nature Park (417-779-5983); this 10,000-acre park has pay-to-fish stream and pond trout fishing, with some large fish available. In Springfield, the huge store for Bass Pro Shops, which is headquartered in this city, is the top tourist attraction in the state. Near the store is the new Wonders of Wildlife Museum.

Toledo Bend Reservoir

Louisiana/Texas, United States

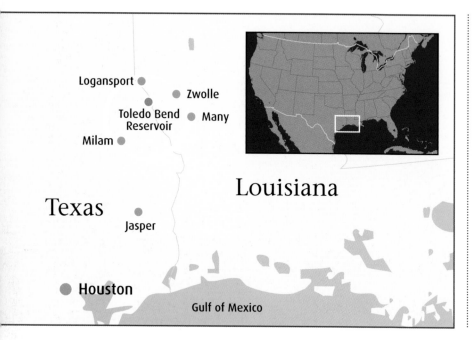

Logansport

Zwolle

Toledo Bend
Reservoir

Many

Milam

Louisiana

Texas

Jasper

Houston

Gulf of Mexico

Toledo Bend Reservoir is the fifth-largest man-made reservoir in the United States, and one of the most well-known bass fishing destinations in North America. Impounded in 1967 along the Sabine River, Toledo Bend spans 185,000 acres, stretches for 65 miles and has 1,200 miles of shoreline. It is more like three lakes than one, yet has good fishing for largemouth bass, crappie, bluegills, catfish and striped bass.

The water levels of this impoundment do not usually fluctuate more than five feet, and the water is usually clearer in the middle and lower regions, while slightly turbid in the upper region. A lot of timber was left standing, and much of this is now below the surface, making for

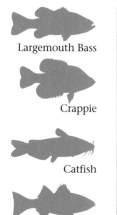

Largemouth Bass

Crappie

Catfish

Striped Bass

RIGHT
Largemouth bass have been a top quarry at Toledo Bend Reservoir since its impoundment.

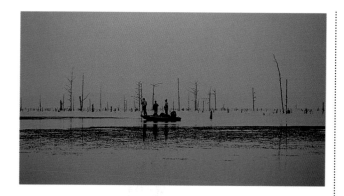

tricky boating if you are not careful, although a good, marked navigational system is now in place that allows for safe high-speed motoring as well as more leisurely cruising.

There is lots of vegetation, especially hydrilla, in the lake, providing an extraordinary amount of cover for largemouth bass. The middle and lower regions have more vegetation than the upper. Fishing in and around the vegetation is important at almost all times of the year. In periods of high water, flooded terrestrial bushes and trees provide good bass fishing throughout the lake.

Prime time on Toledo Bend has usually been from late February through the first few weeks of April, which constitutes the normal spawning season and the time when big bass are in the shallows and on the flats. Toledo Bend regulars catch a lengthy spawning season for largemouth bass by first concentrating on the upper reaches of the lake, which warms before the more southern waters. Spawning action begins as early as February in the northern end, and continues through April down near the dam. Big fish are possible in this period; a former 14-pound lake-record largemouth was caught in March of 1998.

The current lake-record bass, 15.32 pounds, was caught in July 2000 on a jig. Summer months are very hot,

however, and, with thick vegetation growth, many anglers struggle to catch bass during the day, having to work ledges and channel drop-offs, primarily with worms and jigs. Fall provides some of the best bass fishing of the season; the weather is cooler then and more stable, fish are shallower and bass behavior is predictable.

Toledo Bend has a good population of striped bass, though these are not as readily pursued as largemouths. Concentrations of stripers are found along the old Sabine River channel. In summer and fall these fish may school off points, humps and near-channel flats. Hybrid stripers have been caught here to 15 pounds. Below the dam are large pure-strain stripers, some to 20 and 30 pounds, in the swift tailrace waters. Winter through April is best there.

There are also big blue catfish and flathead catfish in Toledo Bend, and good fishing in the spring for spawning-run white bass. Spring is tops for crappies, when they are spawning and caught on jigs and minnows. In mid-winter, crappies suspend over the Sabine River channel in huge numbers above the Pendleton Bridge at mid-lake.

Details

Toledo Bend Reservoir, Louisiana/Texas, United States

Location/getting there: On the Louisiana-Texas border, Toledo Bend is accessed from Many, Zwolle and Logansport in Louisiana, and Hemphill and Milam in Texas. The dam is 24 miles northeast of Jasper, Texas.

Info sources: For area information, contact the Sabine Parish Chamber of Commerce, 920 Fisher Road, Many, Louisiana 71449; call 318-256-3523; or visit www.sabineparish.com; and the Sabine County Texas Chamber of Commerce, Hwy. 87 N, P.O. Box 717, Hemphill, TX 75948; call 409-787-2732; or visit

www.sabinecountytexas.com. An excellent source of online info can be found at www.toledo-bend.com/index.asp.

Prime times: See main text.

Gear needs: Varies with species and fishing method; standard tackle is used for bass, with medium to heavy baitcasting gear preferred.

Guide/tackle availability: Guides and fishing tackle are widely available.

Accommodations/dining: There is an extensive range of lodging, camping and dining options; about 50 private facilities exist on the Texas side and 40 on the Louisiana side.

Etcetera: Toledo Bend is situated amidst the eastern portion of the 160,000-acre Sabine National Forest, which provides extensive and diverse recreation opportunities; for information, call the regional office of the USDA Forest Service at 936-639-8501; or visit www.southernregion.fs.fed.us/texas/index.html.

Tree River

Nunavut Territory, Canada

Arctic Charr

Lake Trout

The Tree River is arguably North America's greatest charr water. It sees the most angling of any top Canadian charr destination (about 400 people in an eight-week season, most of them for just a one- or two-day visit), annually produces big fish (20- to 28-pounders), and lays claim to the all-tackle world record (32 pound 9 ounces, caught in 1981) plus several line-class/fly-tippet records.

Located in Nunavut Territory, northeast of Great Bear Lake and 75 miles east of the village of Kugluktuk (formerly known as Coppermine), the Tree River flows out of Inulik Lake northerly into Coronation Gulf, an adjunct to the Arctic Ocean. The section fished by anglers is relatively short, as the distance from the river mouth upstream to the impassable Third Falls is just seven miles.

Visiting anglers almost all come via fly-outs from Plummer's Arctic Lodges at Great Bear or Great Slave Lakes, which owns the only lodge on the river, Tree River Lodge. It is

RIGHT
Fishing below Third Falls on the Tree River.

BELOW
A setting midnight sun lights up the sky over Tree River Lodge.

an interesting journey; you take an old school bus from Great Bear to a dirt airstrip, you then fly on a DC-3 plane to a dirt airstrip at the Tree River, and then walk to the river for a short boat ride to the camp. Sometimes the plane stops in Kugluktuk.

Charr spawn in the Tree River in late fall, and migrate into the river beginning in mid- to late June in a normal year. An abnormal year—one in which there is an unusual amount of late snow and sustained run-off—causes charr to arrive two to four weeks late because of high and

muddy water, and this can make for disappointing fishing. This happened in 2001, and the result was the poorest July charr fishing in decades. However, in a normal year, the charr arriving in mid-July have a lot of color and become even more colorful in August.

Almost all of the charr are caught in the river; a few are landed at the river mouth in the ocean. Most charr are found below the camp in early July, and are then scattered both below and above camp in late July and primarily above the camp for two miles up to Third Falls in August. When the charr run is thick, at least one 20-pounder is averaged a day, and every year there is at least one in the 28-pound range.

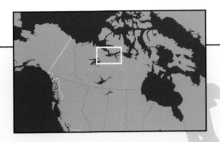

Victoria Island

Coronation Gulf

Kugluktuk (Coppermine)

Tree River

Nunavut

Great Bear Lake

The Tree is swift and slippery, and most charr are caught in its pools and along current seams, mainly by casting with spoons, spinners and flies; however, some large charr are caught in the bigger pools below camp by trolling with spoons. There have also been more lake trout in this portion of the river in recent years than in the past, and some surprised anglers have landed these up to 30 pounds.

The lower river is accessed from camp by boat, with anglers fishing from either the shore or from the boat; the upper river is partly accessed by boat, but most fishing is done from shore and by wading, and it takes a lot of hiking to reach the upper pools. One of these is named Presidential Pool, where a rock bears a plaque with an inscription citing the 1995 occasion when former president George Bush caught a charr.

There are no trees in the tundra region here, which means that visitors often see caribou and musk ox in the distance. There are occasional sightings of grizzly bear and wolf, the latter no doubt interested in the area's large Arctic hare. Summer nights are long here, providing an opportunity for both late and early fishing (even through the night in August), and some terrific sunrise and sunset scenes.

ABOVE LEFT
Twenty-three pounds of colorful charr is the fish of a lifetime.

FOLLOWING PAGES
Landing a charr in the river directly above camp.

INSET
A charr in pre-spawning color.

Details

Tree River, Nunavut Territory, Canada

Location/getting there: The Tree River is 75 miles east of Kugluktuk. Most anglers come via fly-outs from Great Bear or Great Slave Lakes.

Info sources: Contact Plummer's Arctic Lodges, 950 Bradford St., Winnipeg, MB R3H 0N5; call 800-665-0240; or visit www.plummerslodges.com. For Nunavut information, contact Nunavut Tourism, P.O. Box 1450, Iqaluit, Nunavut, Canada X0A 0H0; call 800-491-7910; or visit www.nunatour.nt.ca.

Prime times: August for the most colorful charr.

Gear needs: Light to medium spinning and baitcasting gear with six- through 15-pound line; seven- to ten-weight flycasting tackle, a reel with a good drag and assorted line types

(sink-tip and full-sinking may be needed depending on circumstances). Terminal gear includes streamer flies and weighted bead heads, Thompson Original spoons, Eppinger Rocket Devil spoons, Blue Fox Pixie spoons and Mepps or Blue Fox spinners; No. 5 spinners work especially well, and spoons may need to be as heavy as 3/4-ounce. Note that a big charr caught in fast water may take a ton of line and require a reel with plenty of backing.

Guide/tackle availability: Guides are supplied; lures and flies are available at Tree River Lodge. Waders are necessary, and are available at the lodge.

Accommodations/dining: Framed-tent cabins exist at Tree River, with outdoor plumbing and a central cookhouse/kitchen that serves excellent, and hearty, meals.

Etcetera: Bring good footwear for hiking. Note that the weather can change in an instant here. Many visitors to Tree River come for just one day, some opt for a two-day stay, and some wind up delayed for a longer period because of bad flying weather. A few people go to Tree River Lodge for four days or the week (including those with private aircraft), solely interested in fishing for charr. Fishing is entirely catch-and-release, with barbless hooks. Please note that sometimes the plane needs to pick up a passenger or refuel in Kugluktuk, which has a population of 1,200, where you can visit the Co-op store and the Visitor Center, which is an outpost for Inuit arts and crafts.

ABOVE *Anglers net a northern pike caught by a stream entering Dozois Reservoir.*

Verendrye Reserve/ Dozois Reservoir

Quebec, Canada

Walleye

Northern Pike

Smallmouth Bass

Northeastern anglers looking for diversified drive-to angling can find it in southwestern Quebec in Verendrye Wildlife Reserve and scenic Dozois Reservoir. North of Ottawa, Verendrye is a huge wilderness provincial reserve in the land of Algonquin fur traders and it contains lots of water, including Dozois (pronounced "*dose-wah*") Reservoir, a large serpentine impoundment with northern pike, walleyes, smallmouth bass, yellow perch and sturgeon.

Dozois is mainly known for its walleye fishing, and anglers have good success here fishing with jigs and worms off river mouths and island points. The average walleye is from one-and-a-half to two pounds, and there are plenty of these, as well as some three- to eight-pounders. The big-water section of the western region of Dozois, known locally as Birch Lake, is a prime walleye area. The Outaouais (Ottawa), Whiskey and Capitachouane Rivers on the east are scenic and productive as well.

Northern pike in the ten- to 20-pound class are caught here, although the average is much smaller and the fishing is not like that found in inaccessible lakes to the

Details

Dozois Reservoir / Verendrye Reserve, Quebec, Canada

Location/getting there: Verendrye Wildlife Reserve is located in southwestern Quebec. It is about 250 kilometers from Ottawa, accessed via Highway 105 north through Maniwaki to Grand-Remous, then northwest on Highway 117.

Info sources: For general information, contact Quebec Tourism, 1010 rue Ste-Catherine Ouest, Bureau 400, Montreal, Quebec, Canada, H3B 1G2; call 877-266-5687; or visit www.bonjourquebec.com. For information about Vérendrye, contact Réserve Faunique La Vérendrye, Outaouais Sector, South Entrance, RR1 Montcerf, Québec, Canada, J0W 1N0; call 819-438-2017; or visit www.sepaq.com/LaVerendrye/En.

Prime times: May and June for walleyes and pike; early summer for bass.

Gear needs: Varies according to species and fishing method.

Guide/tackle availability: Limited guide service is available, mainly through fishing camps; some tackle is available, but plan to bring what you will need.

Accommodations/dining: There are assorted facilities in the area, with modest dining options. Contact Auberge Dorval Lodge, P.O. Box 340, Maniwaki, Quebec, Canada, J9E 3C9; call 888-449-4789; or visit www.quebec-outfitters.net/dorval. They have efficiency cottages, dining room, gas, boats, launch ramp, dockage, bait and licenses/permits.

Etcetera: Verendrye Wildlife Reserve also contains Cabonga Reservoir, which is larger than Dozois and features the same species plus lake trout. The reserve, which is enormous, reputedly contains over 4,000 lakes and 2,000 kilometers of canoe trails; some of the southern waters have brook trout (called speckled trout). There is a good chance of spotting moose, and possibly black bear. The reserve is separated into Abitibi-Temiscamingue and Outaouais sections, and contains wilderness camping and established campgrounds. Le Domaine is the main service center and offers guides, restaurant facilities, accommodations and a service station.

BELOW LEFT
A walleye is landed in a timbered bay.

north and west. Pike are primarily caught here as an adjunct to walleye fishing.

Because it is an impoundment that was first built to help float logs to and down the Ottawa River, Dozois is full of stumps and standing timber and requires careful boating. Spare propellers and a good sonar are helpful for self-guided anglers, as there are unmarked rock shoals, trees and occasional deadhead logs just under the surface.

Additionally, Dozois covers over 13,615 square kilometers and about 2,000 miles of shoreline, so to navigate its countless bays, islands and backwaters, you must have a compass, appropriate maps, a hardy spirit and a good sense of direction. GPS would be a big help in preventing you from getting lost.

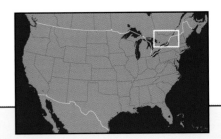

Dozois Reservoir/ Verendrye Reserve

Quebec

St. Lawrence River

Montreal

Ottawa

Victoria Island

Nunavut Territory, Canada

Arctic Charr

Lake Trout

Nunavut

Prince Albert Sound

Victoria Island

Ikaluktutiak
(Cambridge Bay)

Coronation Gulf

RIGHT
This bright, ocean-caught charr contrasts with its colorful spawning brethren.

OPPOSITE
Large and colorful charr like this are the main draw for Victoria Island.

Above the mainland Nunavut Territory, 250 miles north of the Arctic Circle and in the lower reaches of the Arctic Ocean, Victoria Island is a long way from anywhere. It is a particularly long way to go to wade waist-deep in water that never gets above 40 degrees and cast for a fish that may not be there. Much of the time there is only the whistling of wind for company, or an occasional caribou a half-mile away on the horizon. Other than caribou, musk ox and rocks, nothing rises here more than a few inches off the ground. The nearest tree is 400 miles to the south, across a spongy, moss-covered, nearly level plain that hides an always-frozen substrata.

In this apparently desolate spot, however, are treasures that only several dozen anglers a summer are able to enjoy. In some of Victoria Island's rivers, which flow north to the Viscount Melville Sound and south to the Coronation and Queen Maud Gulfs, not far from the permanent polar icecap and the hunting grounds of polar bears (sometimes spotted from the air), the lucky ones will intercept the elusive, brilliantly colored Arctic charr on the way to its spawning grounds.

Victoria Island is one of the premier spots in all of North America for having a chance at catching a trophy-sized (15 pounds or better) member of a coveted, hard-fighting and elusive species that few people ever see in person. While Arctic charr occur all across the North American Arctic, the largest individuals come regularly from Victoria Island and the Tree River on the mainland. Geographically, these places are not that far apart, but their charr are different, and come from strains that have long migrated to particular areas of this region.

The biggest record-book charr caught at Victoria Island's only fishing camp, High Arctic Lodge, was a line-class world record 24-pounder taken in 1982. Several other line class world records have been established here

BELOW
Fighting charr on a noodle rod on the shallow flats of the Beaufort Sea.

RIGHT
High Arctic Lodge sits on the tundra by Merkley Lake.

as well. Summer charr here run from 12 to 20 pounds, a weight well above that found in most other regions.

Charr spawn approximately every three years, and it is the spawning fish that change color and which are the largest and the most prized. Silver charr, those descending lakes and rivers and running out to the ocean for the summer, are smaller and bright, though a lot of fun to catch. Fishing is done on Victoria Island for silver charr in July and holdover (spawning) charr in August. The season, which is just six weeks long, begins in mid-July and runs through mid-August, after which time the weather becomes problematic.

In addition to having tremendous charr fishing, Victoria Island has some exceptional lake trout angling. Lakers up to 44 pounds have been caught in the relatively shallow, 15-mile-long Merkley Lake, which is the base camp for High Arctic Lodge, the only established lodge outfitter on the island. A few anglers venture here strictly for lake trout, especially when the camp opens.

Details

Location/getting there: Victoria Island is 250 miles north of the Arctic Circle at the 70th Parallel and is accessed by scheduled air service from Yellowknife to Ikaluktutiak (formerly called Cambridge Bay). The lodge transports guests inland via floatplane.

Info sources: Contact High Arctic Lodge, P.O. Box 280, Penticton, BC V2A 6K4, Canada; call 800-661-3880; or visit www.higharctic.com. For Nunavut information contact Nunavut Tourism, P.O. Box 1450, Iqaluit, Nunavut X0A 0H0, Canada; call 800-491-7910 or visit www.nunatour.nt.ca.

Prime times: The last few weeks in August generally produce the more colorful fish.

Gear needs: You must bring chest waders, preferably neoprene. Charr: light to medium spinning and baitcasting gear with six- through 14-pound line; seven- to nine-weight flycasting tackle, a reel with ample backing, and assorted line types (sink-tip and full-sinking may be needed depending on circumstances), plus silver/red and silver/chartreuse streamer flies. Lake trout: assorted spinning, baitcasting and fly tackle; see Nueltin Lake (page 174) for trout tackle information.

Guide/tackle availability: Guides are provided; some rods and reels are available at the lodge, as are lures.

Accommodations/dining: The lodge accommodates 12 people in five cabins and has a central dining building and rustic cabins with shared baths. Food is both good and ample.

Etcetera: Musk ox hunting, canoe/kayak adventures and naturalist tours are also available. Visitors should take some time to explore this barren countryside, hiking the eskers and looking for fossil remains. In Ikaluktutiak, check out the wreck of the Maud, the round-hulled vessel used by Norwegian explorer Roald Amundsen to make the first east-west crossing of the Canadian Arctic at the turn of this century. A few yards from that is the site of the first church here, a Roman Catholic building made of double stone walls, with caribou hides for insulation. Cost for a week is $3,495 from Ikaluktutiak.

The larger lakers are usually taken right after ice-out during the first two or three weeks of fishing. Throughout the season, small lake trout can be taken in shallow water by sight-casting to feeding/cruising pods.

At High Arctic Lodge, anglers fish strictly with barbless hooks, mainly single hooks on spoons and spinners, and no more than one set of treble hooks on plugs. The camp policy is catch-and-release.

Access to the charr fishing is done by floatplane, so anglers head north to Hadley Bay, or west to various outflows, where charr tend to concentrate. Most fishing is done at the foot of rapids or the head of pools, but some charr can be caught on ocean flats. Here, the floatplane is tied up while anglers wade the crystal clear shallows and make long casts, not into a foaming surf, but into a lake-like section of ocean shore. Some charr, though usually smaller, are also caught in interior lakes.

Victoria Island has various fishing locales that are rarely fished. This is partly due to the fact that some waters here open up only every few years, usually after a mild winter. Char Inlet, for example, which is a gorgeous spot with 350-foot cliffs, off Hadley Bay, can sometimes only be visited a couple of times a season because of ice.

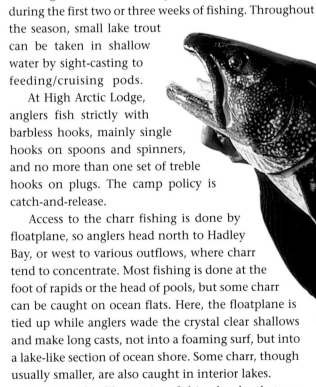

LEFT
Thirty-plus pounds of Victoria Island lake trout.

White River

Arkansas/Missouri, United States

Missouri

● Springfield

White River

Arkansas

The perpetually cold-water outflow of Bull Shoals, Table Rock and Norfolk Lakes, plus Lake Taneycomo, give trout the comfort level they need year-round, and their presence is sustained by aggressive fish stocking. A good food source is provided by the slightly alkaline water, and the presence of many small cousins no doubt helps fuel big-fish growth. Once the big browns get a taste of juvenile rainbow trout meat, they are off an insect diet.

Without argument the White River and its main tributaries are the most frequent producers of really big river brown trout in North America. Certainly some of the Great Lakes produce huge browns annually, but seldom do their tributaries. The White River, and its four-mile-long tributary, the North Fork, have yielded many brown trout in the 20- to 30-pound range, several over 30 pounds,

Brown Trout

Rainbow Trout

When the White River is high, it does not look like much of a trout stream. When the water is low and you can see every boulder and pebble from a long distance away, you have to marvel at the fact that huge brown trout dwell in it and that many have escaped capture for years in order to reach gargantuan proportions. And when the meteorologist predicts a scorching mid-South summer day, a visitor cannot help but marvel at the fact that the river is densely shrouded in fog every morning and that a light jacket is needed to ward off the chill.

However, the White River, which was once a free-flowing smallmouth bass stream, is indeed premier trout water, although not in the sense of a storied Rocky Mountain river. The docks, motorboats and fish-cleaning stations that line many portions of the White make that distinction very clear, not to mention the impoundments in between cold streams.

RIGHT
A typical White River rainbow is landed above Lake Taneycomo.

a 40-pound four-ounce 1992 all-tackle world record, a previous unofficial world record of 38 pounds nine ounces (not recognized as a record because a treble hook was used with bait), plus previous and current line-class world records, two of which were 33 and 34 pounds.

It is estimated that 90 per cent of the trout, however, are rainbows, and most of these are small, befitting what is primarily a hatchery-supported fishery. Some rainbows of larger size are caught, but the browns of all sizes are generally wary and more selective. Most of the biggest browns succumb to a bait offering. Bait is very popular here, and may include marshmallows, cheese or salmon eggs; especially popular are processed baits like Power Bait.

Worms and crickets are also favorites. Fishing with small spinners, jigs and flies is less popular but certainly productive. Light lines and tippets are necessary because of the clarity of the water.

Most people fish out of long jonboats, either drifting or at anchor. To traverse shallow riffles, these are equipped with small outboard motors on a raised transom. Some anglers wade, especially when fishing with flies and lures.

The best angling is usually found in the upper reaches, in the North Fork River below the dam to its confluence with the White River, and on the White River from the dam down to the town of Cotter. It is a year-round fishery, with lots of small fish caught in the warmer months.

Details

White River, Arkansas/Missouri, United States

Location/getting there: The White River is located in southwestern Missouri and northcentral Arkansas. Springfield, Missouri, is the closest major airport.

Info sources: For fishing information contact Lilley's Landing, 367 River Lane, Branson, MO 65616; call 1-888-545-5397; or visit www.branson.net/llresort or www.ozarkanglers.com. Also contact Gaston's White River Resort, 1777 River Rd., Lakeview, AR 72642; call 870-431-5202; or visit www.gastons.com.

Prime times: Winter is best for a chance at a trophy brown trout, in part because dead and injured shad are often abundant.

Gear needs: Light spinning and fly tackle is the rule, with an assortment of baits used, as well as flies, small spinners, and small hair and soft-bodied jigs.

Guide/tackle availability: Guides and tackle are widely available.

Accommodations/dining: A full gamut of lodging and dining options exist in the area.

Etcetera: The water level of the White is largely regulated by the amount of water being released from reservoirs, which varies according to the time of year, weather etc., so be aware that conditions can change. Note that one of North America's premier entertainment centers is nearby in Branson, Missouri. Also, the headquarters showroom of Bass Pros Shops in Springfield, Missouri, is well worth a visit.

Wollaston Lake

Saskatchewan, Canada

- Uranium City
Lake Athabasca • Stony Rapids

Saskatchewan

Wollaston Lake

Reindeer Lake

Although an unfamiliar name to most people outside of Saskatchewan, Wollaston Lake is one of North America's top northern pike waters and has the distinction of being the answer to a puzzling and tricky trivia question. Flowing *both* northerly into the Mackenzie River and easterly toward Hudson Bay, Wollaston is the largest lake in the world to drain naturally in two directions.

The third biggest lake in Saskatchewan, and the 15th-largest in Canada (excluding the Great Lakes), Wollaston spans about 800 square miles. There are 2,700 miles of shoreline, 370 islands and loads of angling opportunity spread over big water with only a few fishing lodges.

Thanks to old uranium mining operations, western Wollaston is accessible by auto, although it is a day-long

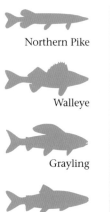

Northern Pike

Walleye

Grayling

Lake Trout

RIGHT
Shallow weedy bays are plentiful at Wollaston, and are good for pike action.

Details

Wollaston Lake, Saskatchewan, Canada

Location/getting there: Wollaston Lake is in northeast Saskatchewan about 100 miles below the Northwest Territories. It is accessed by vehicle on Gravel Highway 905. Most people fly directly to lodges by charter plane from Saskatoon.

Info sources: For fishing information, contact Minor Bay Lodge and Outposts, 204-1700 Corydon Avenue, Winnipeg, Manitoba, Canada, R3N 0K1; call 1-888-244-7453; or visit www.minorbay.sk.ca. For Saskatchewan information, contact Tourism Saskatchewan, 1922 Park St., Regina, Saskatchewan, Canada, S4P 3V7; call 877-237-2273; or visit www.sasktourism.com.

Prime times: The season is from early June through early September. The first weeks after ice-out are preferred by many pike anglers for shallow sight-fishing, but it is good all season long.

Gear needs: Varies depending on species and fishing method. See Selwyn Lake for gear details (see page 198).

Guide/tackle availability: Guides are part of the package cost, but not provided at outpost camps. Lodges usually have a modest supply of tackle, but you should bring what you will need.

Accommodations/dining: Accommodations at most lodges are in motel-like rooms or cabins equipped with heat and private showers. Dining is first-rate morning and evening. Shore lunches are a daily staple.

Etcetera: The cost for a main-lodge trip to Wollaston Lake ranges from $1,995 to $3,195 for three to seven days, all inclusive from Saskatoon. Outpost trips are less, and fly-outs are extra. An overnight stay in Saskatoon is necessary on the way in. Many visitors see moose, and there are occasional bear and timber wolf sightings, plus plenty of waterfowl.

BELOW
A trophy northern pike caught at Wollaston.

drive from Regina to reach pavement's end at Points North Landing. From here, floatplanes take anglers into various remote fly-in lakes. Road access brings in some anglers with their own boats, but because of the many barely submerged rock reefs in the lake, running it can be dangerous.

The main attraction is plentiful northern pike and walleye. Wollaston Lake has pike and walleye in the same way that Saskatchewan's southern prairies have wheat. It may be possible to fish here during the summer without catching one of either species, but it is hard to imagine what catastrophic circumstance, or degree of ineptitude, might make this happen.

Northern pike are simply everywhere in this lake, which averages 30 to 100 feet deep but has untold numbers of pike-holding bays. Many pike here grow big, as Wollaston is known for trophy pike (generally considered over 20 pounds); a few specimens in the 25- to 30-pound class are landed annually.

Walleyes are also abundant, although seldom caught in large weights. There are plenty of shallow, sandy areas that hold this species. Likewise there is a good number of lake trout in Wollaston, with some of fair size though few monsters. Grayling are caught in area rivers, usually via fly-outs, although the Geikie River, which is crossed by the highway where it flows into the south end of Wollaston Lake, produces grayling to anglers who fish behind rocks and in eddies.

Wollaston is serviced by only a handful of fishing lodges, and there is seldom any need to make a long run to get to a good fishing area. Some of the lodges have plenty of fly-out opportunities, as if you need to go elsewhere to catch fish. However, a change of scenery is sometimes worth a fly-out here, and the reward can be tons of action for walleye, pike and grayling. Lodges operate on a catch-and-release basis, other than small fish for shore lunch.

Practical advice for traveling anglers

There is a lot to consider and prepare for when traveling to fish. Here's a brief review of some important issues.

TROPHIES VS. ACTION
Large fish allure many anglers. But not everyone catches trophy specimens, even when visiting a place at the best time under the best conditions. While stupendous fishing does happen from time to time, be wary of grand claims. That said, it is good to be able to fish in places where there are big fish and where any moment might produce a leviathan.

Avoid being swayed by the promise of catching big fish and make a realistic assessment of what you really want out of your visit to any top fishing destination. The pursuit of trophy fish is an obsession for some travel-wise anglers, but a steady dose of action is usually what turns people on the most.

Many anglers do not have the patience to target big fish exclusively, and get bored by inaction when seeking big fish exclusively. So, when you are evaluating a place to visit, think seriously about what you want, and how dedicated you can be to achieving it.

TIMING: WHEN IS FISHING BEST?
There is always immense interest in fishing at prime time. In northern Canada, heavy outfitter bookings for the opening of the season confirm the most popular time. There, many anglers want to be first, or among the first, to visit a lake each season. These anglers feel that the fish are shallow and most accessible then, have had a long winter's respite from lures and boats and motors, and are more vulnerable to deception. For anglers of moderate ability or skill, this may be true. And no doubt some fish, especially pike, are abundant in the shallows early in the season and you stand the best chance then for continuous action.

But first is not always best, in Canada and elsewhere. Sometimes, early-season anglers outfox themselves because weather affects how the fishing (or personal comfort) will be when a camp or lodge first opens. And yet, a lot depends upon your skills no matter what time of the season you visit. When someone says, "The whole season is good," it may only be true if you are a skillful angler.

A good lodge owner/manager will be honest about season-long prospects. But it is a fact that some people will have terrific fishing on any given week, while others will have poor success at the same place at the same time. That is not necessarily attributable to luck, although it could be attributable to the guide, if one is used. The bottom line: do not assume the fish will jump into your boat, and practically assess your own skills and interests.

GUIDE MATTERS
When you use a guide, establish immediately what you want, and how you care to fish, but accept the guide's suggestions and recommendations, especially at the beginning of a trip. If you are a knowledgeable, experienced angler, so much the better. Not all guides are professional anglers and, if you have enough experience, you can make a valuable contribution to the effort of finding and catching fish. Do not be afraid to experiment with lures and places, or to make suggestions to the guide.

The more you communicate with each other, the better. Just do it without being obnoxious, and keep in mind that most guide customers are not experienced anglers, so guides are used to doing everything their way.

Communicating when there are language differences can be a struggle, and sometimes frustrating. This happens occasionally in Mexico. Some agents and lodge owners provide a translation list of useful terms to relay some basic fishing and personal interests to a guide in Spanish. Knowing how to tell a guide to get closer to or further from the bank, to put the boat in shallower or deeper water, to go to another place, etc., is very useful.

Guides should not fish unless they are asked or invited to. If you have a problem with a guide, talk to the head guide, camp manager/owner, or the guide to get things ironed out. Do not give a guide alcohol at any time, especially when running the boat, which could be dangerous, if not illegal.

BOATING MATTERS
At a remote camp, check out your boat prior to departing the dock every day, especially the first day when everyone is eager to get headed to the fishing grounds. Make sure that life preservers are available; that there is an adequate supply of beverages and ice (especially important in hot weather); the boat has a net or gaff as necessary; the seats are set up properly for your comfort; the lunch box is packed and onboard etc.

Before running off, make sure that your gear is properly stowed and secured so that it does not get damaged while running across the water. Do whatever you can to keep graphite rods from being banged about; rod covers may help with this.

WEATHER AND RAIN GEAR
No matter where you go or what species you pursue, weather can be a factor. There is nothing that you, a guide or an outfitter can do about it. Virtually all photos in advertisements, magazines, brochures, and tourism literature show moderately dressed anglers in idyllic lake settings on bluebird days. But it does not always happen like this. If you are not prepared, the fishing will have to be awfully good for you to forget your discomfort.

In cold climates, dress for cold weather, and use the layered approach. You can always remove clothing to get cooler. Bring rain gear that will meet the toughest tests for water repellency, comfort while fishing, and wind protection (warmth). Bib overalls are preferable to pants; overalls and jacket must fit comfortably over other clothes. Carry rain gear whenever you go fishing. Few lodges or guides supply rain gear, although in coastal British Columbia, most lodges provide their guests with suits and rubber footwear.

Finally, always wear polarized sunglasses and use sunblock lotion with an SPF factor of 30 or higher.